"Drs. Judith Sherven  a
beautiful and lucid ɓ   ɔr
those struggling in t   .s
are wonderful, their ... . right on target, and
their practical suggestions for coping with the challenge of
differences are invariably helpful."

—Nathaniel Branden, Ph.D.
author, *The Art of Living Consciously*

"An extraordinary book by an extraordinary couple who
know the meaning of true love and are willing to share their
secrets. If you long to bring more passion, romance and
ecstasy into your life, run—don't walk—to your nearest
bookstore and buy *The New Intimacy*. Judith and Jim offer
the most brilliant, powerful and honest advice about love
that I have ever read."

—Riki Robbins, Ph.D.
author, *Negotiating Love*

"Judith and Jim are the two people who I trust most to do
the difficult work in a difficult field. They have maturity,
wisdom, humor, kindness and love, and yes, I'd put myself
in their hands without hesitation or compunction. That is
why I urge you to read this book. It is a distillation of their
advice and observations, and I think it's terrific!"

—Asa Baber
MEN columnist, *Playboy Magazine*

"Judith and Jim's expertise goes beyond formal education
and years of expertise in the field of relationship counseling
and training. They have personally faced and surmounted
the pitfalls to intimacy that plague us all to create a happy,
fulfilling and enduring relationship. Sensitive, sensible and
entertaining, their book, *The New Intimacy,* tells you exactly
how to find the romantic satisfaction that has eluded you up
to now."

—Elizabeth Asunsolo, M.D.
psychiatrist, private practice

"In *The New Intimacy,* Judith Sherven and James Sniechowski take on one of the toughest problems in creation—How do you establish and maintain a loving relationship?—and come up with answers that are both pragmatic and profound. No book can cure everyone's relationship problems, but Sherven and Sniechowski have produced an invaluable guide to sanity in romance."

—Ellis Cose
author, *Color-Blind*

"Judith and Jim guided us in exploring the differences that had separated us. The result—a new relationship filled with the love, commitment and understanding we both had hoped for."

—Nicole Cerwin Nichols, entertainment publicist
—Ben Nichols, film executive

"Judith and Jim are doing for romance what industrial psychologists have been doing for the workplace—helping us to honor the differences. They do it with a wonderful blend of inspiration and confrontation, and vision and practicality. I recommend this for anyone who is single or already in a relationship."

—Warren Farrell, Ph.D.
author, *Why Men Are The Way They Are*

"Judith and Jim's training gave us a new awareness that the real beauty of love is in exploring our differences. We were afraid that we had too many differences and we kept looking for our similarities. Now we see that the curiosity, the interest and long-lasting love lies in our differences."

—Jill Leuders, travel agent
—Bob Leuders, executive

"They show that gender reconciliation is possible, that men and women can share power and enjoy their differences. Judith and Jim are brilliant examples of what is possible."

—Robert Ware
founder, NEW Leadership Network, Melbourne, Australia

THE NEW INTIMACY

Discovering the Magic
at the Heart of
Your Differences

JUDITH SHERVEN, PH.D.

JAMES SNIECHOWSKI, PH.D.

Health Communications, Inc.
Deerfield Beach, Florida

www.hci-online.com

We would like to acknowledge the following publishers for permission to reprint the material listed below.

Hold Me by Jules Feiffer, ©1977 Jules Feiffer. Reprinted by permission of author and The Lantz Office, Inc., 888 Seventh Avenue, New York, NY 10106.

"*Dracula Moon,*" by Eric Bazilian, Rob Hyman, Joan Osborne, Rick Chertoff ©1995 Human Boy Music (ASCAP), Dub Notes (ASCAP), Womanly Hips Music (BMI) and Monkey in the Middle Music (ASCAP). All rights o/b/o Human Boy Music (ASCAP) and Dub Notes (ASCAP) administered by WB Music Corp. (ASCAP). All rights reserved. Used by Permission of WARNER BROS. PUBLICATIONS U.S. INC., Miami, FL 33014.

"*Dracula Moon.*" Written by Joan Osborne, Rick Chertoff, Eric Bazilian and Rob Hyman ©1995 Songs of Polygram International, Inc., Womanly Hips Music and Monkey in the Middle Music (as designated by co-publishers). Used By Permission. All Rights Reserved.

(Continued on page 332)

Library of Congress Cataloging-in-Publication Data

Sherven, Judith
    The new intimacy: discovering the magic at the heart of your differences/Judith Sherven, James Sniechowski.
    p. cm.
    ISBN 1-55874-511-4 (trade paperback)
    1. Intimacy (Psychology) 2. Love. 3. Interpersonal relations.
  I. Sniechowski. II. Title.
HQ801.S5245 1997   97-27656
646.7'7—dc21   CIP

Publisher: Health Communications, Inc.
       3201 S.W. 15th Street
       Deerfield Beach, Florida 33442

Cover design by Lawna Patterson Oldfield
Cover photo by PhotoGear ©1997

Contents

Acknowledgments

⸎

*T*his book has been in development for several years. Over that time many people offered their priceless help and support. We are especially grateful to Asa Baber, Joy Blanco, Nathaniel Branden, Warren Farrell, Anita Goldstein, Corinne Balzac, Elizabeth Hickey, Akasa Levi, Stuart Miller, Susan Page, Riki Robbins, Michael Russo and Ron and Susan Scolastico for the many different ways they pointed us in new and useful directions, and encouraged us to go forward, often emphasizing how much both single and married people need our message.

Many people read drafts of this manuscript, giving us their valuable feedback:

Angie Brown, Curtis Burch, Cristin Cronin, Elizabeth Davis, Craig Geiger, Paula Ising, Katherine Johnson, Carolyn McCue, Karl Ohs, Debbie Panish, Joel Roberts, Richard Sherman, Helen and Ralph Sherven, Linda Sherwood, Helen and Ed Sniechowski, Lynn and Stephen Steinberg, R. J. Ward and Justin Weiner. We thank you all.

Elizabeth Asunsolo, Michael Hayne, Bill Sniechowski, Don Marrs and Paige Reynolds-Marrs deserve special praise and appreciation for their very cogent and creative input and help. And we're also indebted to Michael for boxes of movie scripts that we recycled as we printed out draft after draft.

Darla Isaakson gave us her passion for this project and a lot of personal input along the way. We are profoundly appreciative.

Art Klein, our dear e-mail buddy, was our number-one cheerleader, great editor, title rejector, you name it—he was there for us throughout this adventure. And Pat Feinman, his dear love, joined him as a strong booster, repeatedly telling us how meaningful an early draft of our book was to their relationship.

We are indebted to Bill Furlow for his caring, insightful and respectful editing which guided us to the final version of this book.

Melody Starr has blessed our lives with her love, wisdom and guidance, always reminding us to "write from our hearts."

We want to especially thank Jodee Blanco, our agent, publicist and friend for shepherding this book to its final home with Health Communications, Inc. Your vision and excitement have been terrific!

And finally, we want to say how pleased we are to be affiliated with Peter Vegso, Christine Belleris and Kim Weiss at Health Communications, Inc. Your integrity and vision are deeply appreciated. It has been very rewarding working with you throughout the many stages of development necessary to see this book in print. Thank you!

The Meaning of "We"

*P*lease note that "we" is sometimes used generally, referring to all people, and at other times it refers to the authors.

We trust the difference will be made clear by the context.

Introduction

*T*his is a book about love and intimacy. But, more importantly, this is a book about finding love and intimacy in what you may believe is a very unlikely place—in the differences between you and your partner, between you and your date. The fact is, differences can be a treasure chest of pleasure and wonder, discovery and growth, passion and spiritual fulfillment. When you both know how to open to that treasure, you'll each know what it's like to be loved for who you really are, and that is the heart of the new intimacy.

So this is also a book about being who you are and being loved for all that you are, imperfections, excellences, everything. Sadly, for too many of us, that thought sends chills down the spine. How about you? Do you live with the fear that if anyone really got to know you, they would ... what? What would they discover? We're betting they'd find a person who is eager to be loved and who is eager to give that love in return, someone who is human, with ups and downs, with heart and history.

Yet, it's also a fact that not many of us experience love that is truly satisfying. Many never feel that they are loved by the person they marry. Others don't believe that what is called "love" has much meaning. The idea of love and dating can be almost laughable. Looking for love can feel like wandering in a desert and there's no fun in that.

So as a society, we are hungering to understand how life and love and intimacy can be experienced more fully, more passionately, and with more spiritual depth. And since you're reading this book, you too must want to feel more love, to have your relationship contribute more significance to your life.

No Preparation

As important as love and intimacy are, did you ever receive any reliable preparation for dating, for a committed relationship or marriage? In our workshops, weekend trainings and on our web site, we've asked thousands of people that question and almost to the person they've said no. The few who have had some responsible guidance received it as adults through therapy or workshops and always at their own initiative. It's no wonder that most of us can only stumble around trying to make a passionate, meaningful and spiritually rich relationship somehow happen.

To complicate things, you now have complete freedom to date whoever you want and marry, or not, anyone you choose. Yet, you have to know what to do with freedom and personal responsibility because they always go hand-in-hand. And since intimacy is deeply personal and powerfully freeing, without down-to-earth preparation it can be overwhelming and even terrifying.

Where We've Come From

Judith: We've had to struggle with the same issues. I married for the first time at 44, to Jim. I was beginning to believe my life was going to be one long perpetual date. I'd received a number of proposals, but they were from men I knew would ultimately turn out to be future ex-husbands. So what was the point?

Jim: Before I met Judith, I had been in a number of serious relationships as well as twice divorced. Even though I'd grown up being taught that divorce was forbidden, I couldn't stay in a marriage or a relationship that wasn't working. So I left.

Judith: I always knew I would do well in a relationship if I could only get into one.

Jim: I could always get into a relationship, I just couldn't make one last. Judith and I have now been together for 10 years, married nine. This is the relationship of our lives.

Judith: Through our experience together, we have discovered a profound intimacy, the kind that is only available when two people approach love and relationship as an open, passionate and conscious dedication to creating the life they want together.

We began by accepting one another—our similarities and the differences between us—as the starting point of our being together. That didn't mean there were no changes we wanted. Of course there were and continue to be. But real change can't happen unless a relationship is built on a foundation of acceptance. We'll come back to this very important point later in the book.

Jim: We are each very strong-willed and in many ways very different from one another. If we don't continually honor and meet one another's different needs and support each other's different aspirations, our relationship would be doomed. So, in order to keep what we have passionate and growing, we've learned that we must recognize, value and cherish our differences. We hold them in trust, becoming more alive as we get to know one another more and more intimately. As a result we've both grown more confident, more self-aware and less encumbered by our personal histories.

Judith: If you decide to embrace and surrender to the full experience of loving—whether you are in a relationship now or are looking for one—the intimacy you create will be your teacher and healer, your sanctuary and playground, a challenge, a mystery and your closest experience of the greater reality that surrounds us all. That is the promise of the new intimacy and what we share with you in this book.

Why Another Relationship Book?

With so many relationship books already on the market, why did we write this one? We wrote it because personal differences are the heart and soul of a long-lasting, fulfilling relationship, and the way you understand and treat them determines whether your relationship will be heaven or hell. Yet opening to the differences between two people in relationship is something not many of us do well. You can adapt to and cope with your partner's differences, but those are surface adjustments, compromises and management techniques. You can take care of your own needs by going to friends and/or family and then talk yourself into believing that you're doing it in order not to "burden" your spouse. But that's just avoiding the issue.

Relying on either of these common tactics will leave the richness of what you have together unexplored, undiscovered and unappreciated. Eventually you both will end up disappointed and wanting because who you really are has been left out of the mix.

So, this is not a book about managing or coping or tolerating. It's a book about plumbing the depths and reaching the heights of intimacy that are available through your differences. When you love with this kind of awareness, you can release the spiritual fullness of your shared love, taking you beyond the merely personal, expanding your relationship with all of life.

Here's a short example.

Judith: I'd always imagined dinners with my husband lit by candlelight, the table set with beautiful linens and fine china. We would sit at dinner, talking, being together. But I was soon shocked to discover that Jim was a grazer.

Jim: I like to snack and munch throughout the day. There was nothing wrong with formal meals, particularly on special occasions. But I usually ate when I felt like it.

Judith: I was disappointed and hurt.

Jim: I knew Judith felt badly about what we called our "meal problem," and I was willing to accommodate her. But a future of sit-down dinners every day was too much, like being imprisoned.

Judith: We knew we had to work this out, with respect for each other's ways, and we also knew that this could drive a serious wedge into what we were creating together if we were not sensitive and open to new possibilities.

Jim: We also knew that if we both just gave in and agreed to some coping solution—like we'll munch on Monday, Wednesday and Friday and have formal meals on Tuesday, Thursday and Saturday—we'd both need Sunday just to rest from the obligation and tension that would build up during the week. No, we had to find a way that was mutually enriching so that neither one of us felt like we were losing, giving in just to get it over with.

Judith: What we needed to do was genuinely appreciate our different eating styles as valuable, seeing them as a chance to learn something new.

Jim: That way we would each be the source of discovery and growth for one another.

Judith: Jim's way taught me about freedom and flexibility and what fun grazing can be. But more importantly, I realized the dangerous power of my expectations and how I was caught up in my own unwillingness to see things differently. If I'd insisted on only my point of view, that would have ultimately driven us apart.

Jim: I had to face my resistance to what felt like being "tied down." The truth was, the imprisonment existed only in my own head. When I opened myself to Judith's way I could see how intimate and elegant a formal meal could be, and could enjoy the power and beauty in the protocol of preparing and sitting down to dinner.

Judith: So our "meal problem" became a path of discovery and change that reached far beyond the surface issue of how we were going to spend dinner time together.

By using stories from the media, our own relationship and those of clients and people who have attended our workshops (whose names, identities and relationship specifics have been disguised to protect their confidentiality) we walk you through the major challenges that love and relationship inevitably bring and then show you how you can turn them into the basis for the deepest intimacy and personal growth that real love has to offer. That is the key to the new intimacy.

Reading This Book

Most, if not all, difficulties in relationship stem from the differences two people encounter as they grow more and more intimate. That can happen during the first few dates and, of course, throughout the life of a long-term marriage. Very few people have either the vision or the emotional skills to respond to their partner's differences with curiosity and respect. So many perfectly good relationships crash on the rocks. But they don't have to.

The Promise of Relationship

Chapters 1 and 2 describe what is possible.

When you and your partner can recognize and value the differences between you, you will be set free for an intimacy far richer than anything you've previously imagined. That is the essence of chapter 1. But in order to make a relationship work you have to open your heart to that real, day-to-day love. We are humans, not aliens, and we have to learn how to love one another right here on Earth. That's the point of chapter 2.

The Problems of Relationship

Chapters 3 through 5 focus on the difficulties of being in a relationship.

In chapter 3 we show why modern relationships are so difficult compared to what's come before, and why so many of us are longing for a rebirth of spiritual meaning in our love lives. In chapter 4 we explain why romantic fantasies are so dangerous and, in order to have real love, what you have to do to recover from them. Chapter 5 is about the patterns of relationship failure that many people are caught in, and how you can break out of them.

The Process of Relationship

Chapters 6 through 9 provide important tools to help you create and keep the relationship you want.

Chapter 6 offers a transformational process we call Conscious Creativity. It can help you negotiate your differences and turn conflict and disappointment into opportunities for learning and growth rather than self-destruction and despair. Since no relationship can thrive without the development of trust, the point of chapter 7 is the difference between positive and negative trust. In chapter 8 we take you behind the self-protective masks we've all learned to wear so that you can discover the heart of intimacy and the self-love that waits for you there. Chapter 9 describes the principles and rules of fair fighting, because there isn't a real relationship on this Earth in which two different people don't occasionally clash. Also, fighting can be a spiritual workout leading you to deeper and more compassionate intimacy, when you know how to fight fairly.

The Payoff of Relationship

Chapters 10 and 11 celebrate the wisdom and the wonder at the heart of a relationship built upon respect and regard for differences.

Chapter 10 shows you why your choice of partner is a wise one, provided both of you are willing to do the lovework your relationship requires. And chapter 11 expands your vision of the spiritual possibilities at the heart of the new intimacy.

People who've attended our trainings, which are based on the concepts and processes discussed in this book, have developed ongoing, trustworthy and passionate relationships if they were single. Or, if they were in relationships, they deepened and expanded the love and intimacy they already had together. They've left with new ways to imagine relating, new perceptions of one another and new attitudes and behaviors they immediately applied in their daily lives. They now understand that risk is necessary in order to find love; that courage is necessary to create a meaningful relationship. Most importantly, they see the spiritual value of learning to open their hearts more fully to themselves and to others.

This book is a strong, yet compassionate, invitation to leave romantic dissatisfaction and heartbreak behind. Once you do, you can be loved for who you really are, for all that you are and you can love someone in just the same way.

Blessed are the man and the woman
   who have grown beyond their greed
   and have put an end to their hatred
   and no longer nourish illusions.

But they delight in the way things are
   and keep their hearts open, day and night.

They are like trees planted near flowing rivers,
   which bear fruit when they are ready.

Their leaves will not fall or wither.
   Everything they do will succeed.

Book of Psalms, Psalm 1, Verses 1-3
Translation by Stephen Mitchell
The Enlightened Heart

Chapter 1

THE NEW INTIMACY: THE PROMISE OF DIFFERENCES

Everything that happens to you
is your teacher. The secret is to learn
to sit at the feet of your own life
and be taught by it.

—Polly Berrien Berends

As we learn to truly respect one
another's differences, the much sought-after
ideal—loving partnership that fosters
emotional and spiritual growth
—is becoming a reality.

—Art Klein

*D*id your relationship start out with great promise, filled with excitement, throbbing with life? Were you certain the two of you would create a vital and passionate future together? Did you see in your lover all the qualities you wanted, so that just the thought of being together was enough to fire your desire and make your skin tingle? Did you imagine your family with beautiful, loving children and two caring and protective parents all together in a warm and comfortable home? And as you imagined growing old together, did you see yourself sitting back, content and confident, knowing, "We lived and loved and we did well!"

Perhaps your relationship is only months old, perhaps years or even decades. Do you still have those feelings? Is your relationship still filled with promise and fulfillment? Does your partner still catch your eye and cause you to sigh, to murmur with contentment and desire?

In the more than 50 percent of marriages that end in divorce the answer is definitely, "No!" But, what about the other 50 percent? Sadly, many of them have settled into predictable routines with only occasional spurts of passion, wringing out whatever pleasure is left by reminiscing about "how things used to be."

Being single isn't easy either. For most singles, dating is a drag, unfulfilling and sometimes even dangerous. To make it even more difficult, traditional gender roles are deteriorating and daters are left adrift, not knowing how to act. Who makes the first call? Who pays for what? How is she supposed to act? What is he supposed to do? Men and women stumble through, date after date, trying to figure it all out. Some do. Most don't. Yet, being at home without a date can be even worse—the shame, humiliation, loneliness . . . the indignity of it all.

Does this sound all too familiar? Are you struggling in confusion? Are you trying to overcome your disillusionment? After all, weren't you told that being in a loving relationship is one of the deepest and richest experiences you can have in life? And yet it all seems so difficult, so maddening. When you lie down at night, does your heart whisper, "Is this all there is?"

"Real Life Love"

What if things could be different? Not just fantasy. Not mere hope. But the real thing. What if:

- You could be loved for all that you are?
- Your relationship could be open and free to change, and continually change for the better?
- Your conflicts, even the fighting, could be catalysts for further self-definition and spiritual discovery?
- Your relationship could be the doorway to a more expansive future than you've ever imagined?
- You could have that miracle of love in your everyday life?

Would such a relationship be worth working for? "Yes," you say. But then, no more than a heartbeat later, your silent and scared voice pulls back, saying, "Is all that really possible? Isn't that just pie in the sky?"

We assure you that no matter how difficult love may have been for you, no matter how many "paths of love" you've stumbled down, even if you haven't "come close," if you are willing, truly willing to commit yourself to building the relationship you want, you can have it! You can have a passionate and spiritually rewarding intimacy that is more of an adventure than any fantasy of romance can ever be. We call it *real life love*,[1] and it is the promise of this book.

> *It had done me good to be*
> *somewhat parched by the heat and*
> *drenched by the rain of life.*
>
> —Henry Wadsworth Longfellow

From Carbon to Diamond

"Okay," you say, "so that's the promise of this book. But how do I do it? How do I get from where I am now to a relationship that will support and nourish me and my partner—physically, emotionally, psychologically and spiritually?"

---

1 Our term "real life love," which we specifically use without a hyphen, emphasizes the real aspects of love versus the fantasy of love. Our term means being loved for all that you really are, excellence and imperfections included, embracing and valuing the very real differences two people inevitably bring to their intimacy.

To make any kind of change happen you must first have a vision of where you want to go and some idea of what it will take to get there. And, as much as we would all like change to happen in an instant, it doesn't. Real change is a gradual process marked by moments of transcendence. Understanding this is essential for the growth and development of a solid, supportive and treasured relationship. Diamonds are a perfect example of the way real, worthwhile change takes place.

Diamonds are prized among the world's most precious treasures. It's said that the ancients believed diamonds were drops of divine essence embedded in rocks when the world was created. In India, diamonds were cherished as a protection against evil. The Chinese used diamonds as engraving tools. Giving diamonds to symbolize the sacred promise of marriage is a tradition that dates back to 15th-century Europe. The market value of diamonds today far exceeds that of even gold and the emotional value of diamonds can sometimes be priceless.

But did you know that diamonds don't start out sparkling and beautiful? In the beginning they are just chunks of dull carbon, like lumps of coal. Then, under the power of heat and pressure they transform, they change into something they were not before—they become diamonds.

But even then, raw diamonds aren't very attractive. They are found in irregular shapes and are cloudy and almost opaque. To become beautiful, brilliant diamonds they must be carefully cut and shaped and defined. It's the same thing with people.

We all start out as infants, largely unformed, but with great potential. We need time and loving support if we are to grow fully into what we are. *Under the right circumstances, any one of us can develop the brilliance that's within, whatever it is, and we can be recognized for the value we bring to the world.* You have great potential for love and a committed relationship. To transform that potential into actual radiant intimacy you must be willing to:

- Open yourself to the unavoidable pressures and passions of a relationship created by the differences between you and your partner;

- Search out a deeper understanding of yourself and your partner when the challenges of being together cut into and disrupt what you believe and expect;

- Grow into someone you were not before love entered your heart.

Opening, searching, growing—these are the fundamental elements of what we call "lovework," the effort that's always required to create the reality of genuine, long-lasting love.

Yet, today the reverse is more often the case. Relationships start out high, blindingly brilliant, everything seemingly perfect. The lovers feel no need to be conscious or aware of what's going on with them, because they believe the love they have fallen into is all that's necessary. They've been swept away. Happiness seems to be theirs for life. This is very strange though, because nothing else in the world begins fully formed. Everything begins as possibility. Everything must be cultivated and nourished in order to grow into its full and mature potential.

Nevertheless, we're sure you've known people who cling to the belief that "When I meet the *right one,* he or she will beam high voltage love on me and make me feel complete." They are waiting for love to "happen" to them, with the silent hope that when it does they will be "rescued" from their lives and carried away into happily-ever-after.

During the early days of a relationship or in the honeymoon phase of a marriage, it can feel like the hope of being rescued has actually come true. Everything is perfect. Magical. Effortless. "We're so close, we even end our sentences for one another. I've never been so in love!" But, because the honeymoon phase is just a beginning, exciting but largely unformed, all real relationships must inevitably grow beyond it. When two people are unaware of this necessary and unavoidable change and the initial enchantment fades, they can become confused, frightened and eventually embittered. Sentences that were playfully endearing disintegrate into barbed misunderstandings. Touch that was tender and sweet becomes irritating and invasive. Two potential diamonds are left to wonder, "What happened?" Disillusionment sets in. They grow to mistrust not only themselves and each other but love itself. Some break up. Others stay in passive resignation. In either case, the vitality and promise of the relationship ends.

This doesn't have to happen!

Beyond Fantasy

Real life love is not made from fantasies of effortless, swept-away, happily-ever-after bliss. It doesn't promise to rescue you from the ordinary problems of everyday life.

In fact, the true spiritual journey of real life love can only begin when the fantasies end, when you and your partner are willing to be exactly who you are—no masks, no games. When both of you choose not to back away from the lovework it takes to become exciting and fulfilled friends, lovers and mates, your relationship becomes a spiritual vessel supporting each of you in your growth toward the beauty and richness of the diamonds you can become.

To do that it's crucial to understand that love will beam into all areas of your soul. It will shine its light on those parts of you that you cherish. And, as you open yourself more and more to receiving love, it will also bring to the surface those parts of you that you believe are unlovable and undeserving, those parts you have hidden and denied—because *love loves everything and everything wants to be loved.*

At first, you may be frightened. That's not unusual. To protect yourself and conceal what you fear or dislike about yourself, you may put on a mask, a false front. Or you may resist love's penetration into your soul by consciously or unconsciously creating conflicts and distractions to avoid feeling embarrassed or ashamed. You may even decide that "this relationship's not right for me. I better just break it off." Or you may blame the whole thing on your partner, crying out that "love is just too hard," and "this isn't what love is supposed to feel like." We understand. We've been there. We've both done that. Ultimately it doesn't work. *In real life, you can run but you can't hide. Sooner or later the real you shows up. Then what?*

*Life shrinks or expands according
to one's courage.*

—Anaïs Nin

Kim and Jake

Kim and Jake were both fun, bright and successful professionals in their late 30s. They met, fell in love and were deliriously happy. After five weeks they decided to get married.

When Kim's best girlfriend asked her, "What's the rush?" Kim assured her that "Jake and I are so sure of what we have together, what's the point in waiting?"

For the first six months, Kim and Jake seemed to have everything anyone could want. They spent all their available time together. Sex was great. The future seemed bright. Jake delighted in telling her, "You know, Kim, we're so much alike, it's almost like we're the same person."

"I know, Jake. None of my relationships before have ever been so easy."

But little by little, they became aware of petty annoyances, subtle barbs and hurtful criticism. After a year and a half they found themselves fighting and miserable much of the time. They were shocked to discover how easily everyday differences could plunge them into verbal abuse, splattered with name-calling, leaving them feeling trapped, suspicious and on guard. "It's so ugly and painful," Jake sighed. "I don't know what's going on."

For example, returning home from a party one evening, Kim commented that the hostess had been "sickeningly sweet."

"That's ridiculous," Jake immediately fired back, "she was friendly and warm."

"It's not ridiculous," Kim shot back, suddenly furious. "Did you see how she was catering to everybody?"

"She was the hostess, Kim. What was she supposed to do? And besides, I've seen you do exactly the same thing."

"Never. I was never like her."

They were locked into a bitter struggle, each convinced the other was not only wrong but stubborn and purposely mean.

On the surface, Kim and Jake appeared to have it all together. But down deep, they each wrestled with self-doubt and insecurity. They had unconsciously longed for an effortless romance. What they got was a journey into the unknown, an experience of real love and real intimacy, and they didn't know what to do.

Confused and scared, they came to us hoping to find a way to "fix this mess—if possible." We assured them it was not only possible, but that their difficulty was a blessing in disguise. But in order to reap the rewards, they both had to learn that *real love exposes and burns away what is false, challenges all of us to face and accept who we truly and fully are, and, in the process, sets us free for a new kind of intimacy far richer than anything we previously imagined.*

*In the future, the "fittest"
relationships will be the ones that can
adapt to a new reality—the higher
expectations of good communication,
not mere survival.*

—Warren Farrell

The Transformative Process of Love

If you've ever been in a relationship, you know how threatened and defensive you can become in response to the ways your partner is different—differences in sexual styles, spending habits, views on how to raise children, career commitments, friends, personal idiosyncrasies, and even the right way to slice tomatoes. Sadly, most people interpret their confusion and disillusionment as a signal to physically leave or emotionally withdraw. However, more often the struggle is a signal that love is actually taking effect—going deep below the surface, beginning to weed out the stuff that prevents bright, diamond-like brilliance from shining through. When you avoid the struggle, you keep yourself and your relationship stuck in the carbon stage.

As we worked with Kim and Jake, they came to realize that the ways they were different from each other, though sometimes difficult, were actually the means for learning to love one another more fully. They grew to respect and accept each other's differences and began to see the powerful and deeply fulfilling spiritual adventure they could have together. Soon, their conflict over the party hostess became a spark for discovery and deeper awareness.

"When the hostess was around," Kim admitted, "I felt uncertain. I kept thinking, 'I could never do what she's doing as well as she does.' I tried to stop, to get rid of those thoughts but couldn't."

She also realized she felt the same way with other outgoing and self-assured women. "Who I really am seems to just disappear."

Although she had developed a good cover, inside she was cringing under the weight of a life-long sense of inadequacy, leaving her feeling humiliated, unworthy and silently enraged.

"So you take your rage out on me," Jake protested.

"Probably." Kim couldn't look him in the eye. "I'm sorry."

But Jake was not innocent. He had to acknowledge that he'd felt protective of the hostess. He described feeling sympathy for her because "she seemed to be doing the best she could." After a moment he added, "Besides, on the way home, Kim attacked her and then attacked me."

"I didn't attack you," Kim snapped.

Jake was ready to fight back when we stopped him. We asked him what would happen if it were true that Kim hadn't attacked him. What other possibilities were there?

After a moment, Jake confessed that he often felt like the underdog. "Especially with Kim. You know? Truth is, I'm afraid of Kim."

"Afraid?" Kim was stunned.

"Yeah," Jake whispered. "I feel like I have to protect

myself from you. It's crazy, but I feel like I have to be on guard or you'll look down on me. I feel like I'm going to lose."

"Lose! Lose what?"

"I don't know. Maybe me." That was something he hadn't really wanted to face. "I always give other people the benefit of the doubt," he conceded, "most of the time before I even know I'm doing it. I think it's what I want . . . what I want from you, Kim. The benefit of the doubt."

Once the depth and meaning of their feelings began to emerge, Kim and Jake could see how different, yet how alike, they were. Kim's insecurity led her to criticize the hostess. Jake's insecurity led him to protect her. Seeing behind each other's polished veneer, they could learn to feel respect and compassion for each other's vulnerability. They realized that neither of them really knew what the hostess was feeling because they'd never asked her. They'd both been unconsciously caught up in their own discomfort, convinced that how they perceived the situation was absolutely correct. Acknowledging this, they began to laugh, not surprisingly feeling closer and more trusting, and a new intimacy opened up for them.

By successfully facing this difficulty, they began to see a way of handling future conflicts. Realizing that it was only through their love for one another that they could feel safe enough to allow their respective insecurities to surface, they both felt the rich pleasure of being understood and accepted. They admitted they'd expected love to be easier, certainly not to be found at the heart of conflicting differences, and they were amazed by the hope and excitement that opened between them. By taking the risk to be honest with themselves and each other, they learned that differences and difficulties are part of every relationship and they can be the source of the deepest, richest and most spiritually fulfilling intimacy that being together has to offer.

> *Only love heals, makes whole,*
> *takes us beyond ourselves. Love—not*
> *necessarily mushy sentiment or docile*
> *passivity—is both right motive and*
> *right result. Love gets us there....*
>
> —Marsha Sinetar

Defining Spirituality

Many people are searching for spiritual meaning in their lives today, and there are many points of view about just what spirituality is. By "spirituality" we mean the deep sense of connection you become aware of and can feel when you face into and grow from the inevitable challenges of daily loving. When you no longer have to hide parts of yourself—when you realize you can be loved for who you actually are and love your partner in the same way—then you both can have the experience of being comfortable with who you are while expanding beyond what you already know, beyond who you already know yourself to be. Like a diamond cut from a rough stone, you become something more: a rich, sparkling and multi-faceted jewel. You become richer and more conscious.

Instead of withdrawing and shrinking, you live with a sense of freedom and openness to life—to the relationship you and your partner are creating. As you and your partner develop the skills and commit to dealing with whatever may happen, the differences and difficulties that are sure to arise become catalysts for transformation rather than harbingers of contempt and catastrophe.

We also want to be clear that what we mean by "spirituality" in no way conflicts with or contradicts anyone's religious beliefs. For example, communication and conflict resolution skills, recognition and respect for differences, expanding the ability to give and receive love are necessary relationship skills for everyone. When your love is real and down-to-earth, you can progress toward a greater and ever-changing understanding and acceptance of yourself and your partner. As you become more and more conscious, you continually move beyond your self-centered limitations toward a more inclusive frame of mind, a more open way of being. Then the mundane becomes sacred, illuminating richer purpose and meaning in everyday life. You come to know there is magic in the ordinary, while simultaneously appreciating the greater, universal forces that influence who and what you are.

This first chapter is a promise of what the new intimacy holds for you. To have that intimacy as part of your life, you must start where you are right now. So, with that in mind, each of the following chapters looks at a different aspect of relationship with the intent of helping you open yourself, to become more conscious of the pivotal role your beliefs and attitudes play in the success or failure of your love life. Through your willingness to be changed by reading this book, you have already taken a powerful step toward creating the kind of love you want. Congratulations!

Chapter 2

OPENING YOUR HEART: LOVING THE DIFFERENCES

Intimacy begins with the
willingness to hear who the other person
really is, to open your heart and be willing to
completely hear without expectation,
yet be filled with expectancy.

—Patricia Sun

What counts in making a
happy marriage is not so much how
compatible you are, but how you deal
with incompatibility.

—George Levinger

*O*pening your heart to love is a choice. *As power-ful as love is, it can enter your heart only if you let it.* You can resist love if you choose, and you've probably had the experience of doing just that. So you know that letting love in is not automatic. Even if it seems as though love is happening to you, you must still choose to open to it, you must choose to let it change you, and that choice can only be a conscious one.

What Women and Men Want

What do you want from a relationship? A simple enough question. We've asked thousands of people what they want from love, intimacy and relationship. They had no shortage of answers. Here's a summary of what they told us.

Most people want:

- Their relationship to be long-lasting, built upon a sense of commitment and emotional security;
- To know they are being loved for who they really are, so they can drop their masks and not have to play games;
- Their sex life to continue and get better and richer;

- Romance, fun and passion;
- To be respected for their values and ambitions and receive compassion for their fears and hesitations;
- To know how to resolve conflicts in ways that are beneficial and supportive of both partners;
- To have a partner who is both a lover and a best friend;
- To feel connected, consciously creating their relationship together;
- A spiritual purpose and meaning to their relationship and their life.

Our relationships succeed when we create them out of mutual recognition and respect for one another's individuality and differences. We sustain them through our conscious commitment in an atmosphere of mutual participation and regard. That enables us to live in an expanding sphere of ongoing discovery, willing to learn more and more about who our partner truly is—and who we really are.

When we've asked people, "What gets in the way of the relationship you want?" they said:

- Fear of commitment coupled with a fear of being the one who is left behind;
- Having to live up to their partner's expectations, never able to relax and be who they are;
- Fear that sex will taper off and become mechanical;
- Boredom;
- Poor communication that leads to confusion, frustration and a sense of hopelessness;

- Fear of conflict that leaves them at a loss for what to do;
- Being taken for granted;
- The lack of emotional intimacy, a sense of distance that's not worth living with;
- The absence of meaning or purpose in their relationship.

Relationships fail when we are unable to recognize and respect how different we are from one another, when we insist on only one way of doing things—our way. That leaves no room for the differences that are an inescapable part of every relationship. Without a respect for individuality and uniqueness, we become trapped in a never-ending power struggle, repeating over and over again the same patterns, the same words, the same feelings, until we get so tired of each other that we either split up or sink into an orbit of mutual repulsion.

Many people use their differences to trash their relationships. They use them as excuses to avoid or abuse each other. They have never learned that there are powerful emotional, psychological, sexual and spiritual treasures waiting in their differences—if only they knew how to open to them.

Selfish is not living as one
wishes to live; it is asking others to
live as one wishes to live.

—Ruth Rendell

Molly and Ted

Molly approached us after attending a workshop we gave in Washington, D.C. Her story is typical of so many relationships—two people refusing to open their hearts to change, stuck in repeated and unsuccessful patterns.

Molly and Ted met through a mutual friend. Ted was 30, tall, good-looking, an art collector/entrepreneur who loved to sail. Molly, 27, was an attractive, ambitious designer of housewares and textiles. They were very attracted to each other almost immediately.

Ted insisted that they avoid "the typical date." So they walked on the beach at dawn, took long drives through the mountains stopping to listen to the wind, went antique hunting for folk art and Native American handcrafts and danced on the rooftop of her condo complex. He also loved to take her to his favorite out-of-the-way restaurants and she loved his attention.

After Molly cooked her first meal for him, she was quietly impressed. "Ted washed the dishes without being asked," she told us. "And the next day I got flowers at work. He signed the card, 'To many more romantic evenings together.' "

This was love, she knew it. He was perfect.

Ted used the anniversary of their first month together to take her sailing for the first time. In honor of the celebration, Molly wanted to get just the right outfit. She ended up wearing her best sea-blue warm-up over her favorite black bikini. When Ted arrived she was shocked. He had on baggy old trunks and a dirty visor, with white zinc oxide smeared across his nose. "He looks ridiculous," she thought.

Ted was surprised by her surprise and awkwardly suggested that she "might be more comfortable in less precious clothes." He knew immediately that she didn't get what he'd meant by "precious" and, when she didn't want to change, he backed off.

The morning was overcast and cool as they made their way out on the ocean. Ted was quiet, different than she'd ever seen him. When she spoke he answered, but seemed remote. Finally, after she persisted, he told her, "I'm not ignoring you, I always get thoughtful when I'm out here," which was true.

Molly was hurt, confused and angry. The day was turning out not like anything she'd imagined. "It's not that he looks so tacky," she thought, "I can live with that. But where's he coming from?"

As midday approached, Ted suggested she go below and fix lunch. Molly shot back, "You said you'd take care of lunch."

"I did. I bought it . . . and the champagne." It was Ted's turn to be shocked.

"I thought you'd make this romantic. Today was supposed to be so special."

"It is, isn't it? What do you mean?"

Molly tried to speak but her voice cracked so she went below.

Now Ted was confused and angry. "What the hell was that all about?" he muttered.

While making sandwiches, Molly tried to assure herself. *This is no big deal. He's just a casual guy. So what if he's quiet?* Then she snapped aloud, "But nobody tells me to go make lunch."

On deck Ted tried to piece it together. *We've never been sailing before. Maybe she's just nervous and needs to chatter.* He could accept that. *But why is she so uptight?*

Neither knew what to do. They made small talk over lunch, doing their best to hide their disappointment and the emotional distance between them.

During the next few weeks they continued to see one another, but Molly's image of Ted had been punctured. She struggled with feelings of loss and betrayal. Unable to prevent the emotional withdrawal she had experienced with other men, her attraction and affection for Ted began drying up.

Ted felt as if he had become invisible to her. No matter what he did, it wasn't enough. He became increasingly irritated with her—discovering more and more "evidence" that she was "the wrong one."

Not much later they broke up, feeling sad and betrayed—feelings that were all too familiar to both of them.

Whether you are married or single, the kind of disappointment, confusion, anger and hurt Molly and Ted experienced can happen at any time, especially if you don't know how to welcome and handle the unavoidable differences that arise in all intimate relationships. They can occur on the first date, shortly after marriage, with the arrival of a baby or even when that "baby" moves out of the house.

All of us are susceptible to having the reality of our relationships collide with our expectations of "how it's supposed to be." Tragically, we're liable to side with our illusions rather than give reality a chance.

Life is not the way it's
supposed to be. It's the way it is.
The way you deal with it is what
makes the difference.

—Virginia Satir

A Missed Opportunity

It's a shame Molly and Ted were so unprepared to face one another's differences. After their disastrous day on the ocean, they each took to silently blaming the other, progressively retreating, closing down into their beliefs about "the way things should be." *If they had understood that their discomfort was really an opportunity to explore further intimacy, to do the lovework every relationship requires, they would have had a real chance together.*

The truth is, Molly had been frightened by Ted's silence. More important than feeling rejected, she was afraid that if she expressed her fear Ted might be scared away. Instead of discussing it with him directly, she held back, choosing to remain obedient to her fear. In response, Ted became guarded and aloof, leaving Molly feeling vindicated and so she withdrew even further.

Ted's sense of inadequacy grew. Like Molly, he defended himself, unwilling to reveal what he was feeling. "Not after the way she acted," he assured himself. He blamed Molly for becoming cold and unapproachable and he was right too. Molly had grown colder. But rather than deal with her directly, he withdrew.

Have you ever behaved like Molly or Ted? What could they have done differently?

Had they understood that the differences between two people are the life blood of every long-lasting, fulfilling relationship, they might have been willing to open up and make themselves available to one another. They could have expressed their actual feelings and concerns, learned about each other's particularities and, more importantly, understood the impact each was having in the other's life.

Molly might have explained that she felt left out and lonely in the face of Ted's silence. Ted might have told Molly he felt powerless and resentful when she attacked him about his request that she make lunch. Being forthright with their feelings would have been a sign of respect for themselves and each other and opened an opportunity to reach an understanding and a resolution. *As it was, they cut themselves off from the truth of their own feelings and began to spin fantasy explanations that ultimately overwhelmed them.*

Had they opened themselves to the issues separating them, they would have realized that they both loved sailing and the sea but for different reasons. Through the sea, Ted connected with the power and mystery of the universe. He loved being comforted by the roll and rhythm of the waves and was awed by their majesty. "That must be what God is like." For Molly it was all about freedom. Sailing was a chance to get away from it all, "to be anybody and do anything I want."

Ted was no stranger to freedom. His entrepreneurial lifestyle was a testament to going his own way. Had he understood that for Molly being on the water was her way of breaking loose, freeing the energy and vitality she felt, she would have seemed less strange. He could have seen that her attraction to the sea, though different, was just as meaningful as his. He could have appreciated the freedom she felt, a feeling he knew quite well and valued deeply. That way he could've opened himself to a deeper connection with her.

Had Molly understood that Ted's reverence was his way of getting away from it all, he would have seemed less strange. She could have seen that they were having the same experience, just differently, and opened herself to a deeper connection with him. They could have touched the wisdom hidden in their choice of one another, and being together could have become an adventure of discovery—intimate and exciting. Sadly for Molly and Ted, rather than fostering a deeper intimacy, their responses only served to tear them apart.

What do you know about such painful disappointment? How many times have you thought you were in love? Everything was going along fine. Then, without warning, your "beloved" lost interest, for no apparent reason, at least no reason that made any sense to you. Or have you suddenly felt yourself falling out of love, and couldn't stop it? Perhaps something set you off because your partner was different than you had thought, and in some way you just couldn't tolerate.

A real-life relationship, one that is fluid and open to change, can reveal the mystery that is always present when two different people join to make a life together. In such a relationship Molly and Ted could have learned:

- To trust each other with their real feelings, the only basis for being loved for who they truly are;
- To feel safe facing the inevitable conflicts that all couples experience;
- To relax their resistance to the lessons of love;
- To enjoy and treasure the esteem and mutual regard that comes from true respect and interest rather than fantasy;
- To acknowledge and accept each other's differences, while still reserving the right to want some things to change;
- To feel less need for romantic illusion and more desire for real romance and intimacy.

It is critical to understanding the new intimacy and experiencing the deep power of love to remember that, when differences seem to get in the way, two people are simply at the threshold of an opportunity to get to know one another more fully. If they do not withdraw, if they do not use techniques to merely cope, they can learn to open themselves and move toward each other to become more deeply and securely intimate—just one of the profound blessings found in the magic of differences.

Instead, for Molly and Ted, theirs is another story of disappointed love. But why?

*There is only one happiness in life,
to love and be loved.*

—George Sand

Our Preoccupation with Romance

So many of us believe that love is real only when we're flooded with feelings that wash away our capacity to be conscious, to think and make choices. Love seems to exist out beyond us and, under the right conditions, it swoops in and sweeps us away. We call it "romance," and it comes packaged with intense emotions and high drama. Our insatiable preoccupation with romance is one of the most remarkable characteristics of modern life.

Our hunger for romance is both driven and supported by movies and television that tantalize us with stories of "happily ever after." The advertising industry continues to instill in us the idea that if we just empty our pockets and run up our charge cards we'll find hot sexual attraction and long nights of passion and play. Magazine racks overflow with advice on how to catch a man, how to be the best lover she ever had or how to marry rich. Most major newspapers devote entire sections to lifestyle issues such as dating, remarriage, gifts for your sweetheart or the struggles of being single. Dear Abby and Ann Landers are famous for dispensing advice to the lovelorn and romantically needy. Clearly, the longing for love is worth billions.

But think about it. If we were all receiving love, the kind of love that makes us feel whole and valued and satisfied, the "love makers" would be out of business. We couldn't be lured by erotic fantasies of torrid passion and unquenchable desire, because we wouldn't be desperate to find "the perfect moment," that "ultimate embrace." We wouldn't be consumed by our fevered yearning for that "certain something" we can't even define but are convinced will transform our lives from bewildered frustration to transcendent happiness. More often than not, the opposite is true. So we press on, hoping our marriages will improve or that the next relationship will be "the one."

What's the truth for you? Perhaps you have become convinced that love is a mystery beyond your reach, something that happens only to other people. Or perhaps you've found love, over and over, only to awaken at the end of each relationship or marriage heartbroken yet again. Take this moment and listen to yourself. Do you feel a longing for love?

Our need for love never dies. It is as fundamental to us as air and water. Our desire for love inspires much of what we do, what we think and believe, what we value and cherish. Love is the nourishment most treasured by the soul.

It is not enough to want to succeed.
You must make it your conscious
purpose to succeed.

—Nathaniel Branden

Desire Is Not Enough

Although desire for love is essential, desire is not enough. You have to be prepared for what commitment and monogamy require. You have to be prepared for the creation of an enduring yet ever-changing love. That's the paradox of real life love and the new intimacy. You can trust it to remain constant over time while it continually grows and changes to express who you and your partner become together. Unfortunately, most of us know of too many relationships that were mostly about desire. They flashed like fireworks in the beginning only to quickly flame out.

The most compelling evidence of our inability to create loving, intimate relationships is the staggering divorce rate. It echoes the false and futile expectations women and men hold of one another. It reveals our unresolved confusion, anger and frustration about how to create and keep real love alive. It tells the story of the deep and painful inability of women and men to connect with meaning, trust and maturity. *The divorce rate represents a cry from the depths of our collective consciousness that we have come unmoored and are adrift in our own bewilderment.*

Even so, many, many men and women hunger for intimacy and a relationship they can trust and count on. They want a mate with whom to live their lives, to share their joys and sorrows and gracefully grow old together.

Even the God of Calvin never
judged anyone as harshly as married
couples judge each other.

—Wilfrid Sheed

Loved for Who You Really Are

Isn't it true that, more than anything else, you want to be loved for who you really are? Not just for money or beauty or something extraordinary you may have done.

Certainly not because of some mask you hide behind. But, to be loved for all that you are, just as you are.

Imagine it—someone knows you, all of you, your talents and eccentricities, your generosity and dark moods, what you look like at your best and at your worst. Imagine that you've opened all of yourself, no masks, no gimmicks, no affectations and someone says, "Yes. I see you, all of you, and I love you for the person you are. I value you and want to be with you for the rest of our lives." That's what makes love so precious. That's what real romance and intimacy is all about.

But, would you believe it? Would you be able to take in such a real, full acceptance of who you are? Or would you feel unworthy? Would such love conflict with what you believe about yourself?

And the trouble is, if you don't risk anything, you risk even more.

—Erica Jong

Love Is Not Without Fear

Have you ever whispered to yourself, "If someone ever really got to know me, they would . . ."? The end of that sentence has countless variations, but they all mean essentially the same thing. "If I open myself and let you in, you'll see my flaws and find me wanting. It's better that I avoid the rejection by avoiding you."

Some of us struggle to become "perfect" in an attempt to overcome our self-belittling judgments. Some try to quiet the critical voices inside by working to be even more pleasing. Others avoid conflict, anger or bad moods. But these strategies are only distractions that serve to erode our willingness to become intimate.

In any real relationship, the masks you use to keep what you believe are your faults and flaws from being exposed will inevitably wear thin as the daily challenges of being with someone constantly push more and more facets of your personality to the surface. Given that fact, if you want to continue to hide parts of yourself, you'll have to grow increasingly resistant and remote. Then protecting yourself from discovery becomes more important than anything else.

The truth is that opening your heart to love can be a frightening, sometimes even painful experience. It's crucial to understand that as you move closer to your partner, emotionally, physically and spiritually, you will necessarily discover new areas of yourself, of your partner and of your being together. *The fear that arises in response to such deepening intimacy is a natural part of the journey.* If you choose to respect it and live through it, the process of revealing yourself will bring you to an even closer, safer and more caring connection, a deeper more exciting intimacy.

---

*There are no perfect beings and
there never will be.*

—Henry Miller

You Don't Have to Be Perfect

The beauty of real life love is that you don't have to be perfect. You can start opening to real intimacy right where you are now, today. In truth, if you want to find a satisfying relationship, you have no other choice. You are who you are. That's all you can be. When you try to impose predetermined roles, expectations or "shoulds" on your relationship, you will be trapped in loving only what you think should be. You will not be able to love what is. You will destroy the opportunity to be loved as a unique individual and to love your partner in the same way. *However, if you don't have to be perfect, if you don't have to try and force yourself into some image of how you "should" be, then who you are is always enough.*

Angie was shocked when Carlos took her in-line skating and announced as they started out, "I'm just learning. So I'll probably struggle at first." She would never let a date see her awkward, stumbling around, being a learner. Yet, Carlos let himself be seen as real and imperfect, able to enjoy the day and laugh at himself when he fell. Angie felt a challenge to her perfectionistic ideas about what it meant to be appropriate and "have it all together." Because of his willingness to be simply and honestly who he was, she had to admit she liked him more, not less, although she felt some embarrassment around her own need to appear flawless.

Chas enjoyed teasing Lucinda about her "brown thumb" in the garden. Yet he took offense when she razzed him about the condition of his truck. She suggested he was cheating himself by becoming defensive when the shoe was on the other foot. He would be better off if he realized that she was teasing him lovingly. The criticism and fear he felt were coming from inside himself, not from her. He was carrying his own brand of self-disapproval that was far more critical than anything she'd said.

When you can recognize and appreciate one another as two distinct and different persons, an atmosphere of acceptance emerges. As you learn to trust yourselves, you will experience the safety to open even further. Your connection will reach beneath the surface, beyond the transitory blush of first love, into the rich, fertile intimacy that is available as you become more and more present, more and more comfortable, more and more real. Then the magic of your relationship unfolds as you both feel deeply understood, emotionally respected and personally valued. Out of your acceptance and appreciation of the differences between you, a feeling of wholeness grows, a sense of being right with the world, right with life. That is real romance and the depth of the new intimacy.

My obligation is this; to be transparent.

—Pablo Neruda

Recall a Time: An Exercise

This is the first of several exercises in the book. We recommend you do them as a way to pay attention to your conscious thoughts and summon up your unconscious feelings about who you are and how you relate to others. Doing them will help you open to change more readily because you will have experienced something rather than just thought about it. You can do the exercises alone or with your partner, whichever works best.

So now bring to mind a time when you were afraid, perhaps even terrified, to reveal something about yourself but you did it anyway. For example, you may have said something behind someone's back that hurt them. You may have had sexual experiences that you feared were unacceptable and so you kept them a closely guarded secret. You may be ashamed of your family background and vowed never to let anyone know. And what you bring to mind need not only be negative. For instance, you may have won awards for your talents and skills but worried that other people might envy you or call you a braggart if you talked about your accomplishments.

Whatever it is you recall, be sure it was an instance when you were rewarded for your decision to open yourself up and become vulnerable. It should be a time when you received compassion, respect or some other form of acceptance and validation, not the reprisals you feared. Can you remember your initial response? No doubt some of it was relief. Perhaps you wept, or laughed or sat silently. Perhaps you were shocked, having believed that only by being perfect—certainly not by revealing your dark secret—could you gain respect and concern from others.

Now, remember how, after you revealed your "dark, horrible secret," you not only felt better, but your terrible secret no longer seemed as bad as it did before. *Your willingness to open up was a sign of your self-love. Being accepted by another was a sign of your being lovable.* By allowing love in, you were relieved of the burden of your secret and were healed, able to accept and express more of who you truly were.

From Our Own Life Together

Opening to love is not something that only applies to those in new and budding relationships. Not at all. Since opening to love and intimacy is not automatic, it doesn't matter how old you may be or even if your relationship is really solid and quite wonderful. There is always more to you, your partner and your relationship than you are presently aware of. That's what makes a relationship so exciting, so enlivening and ultimately so rich. And, of course, that is what can prevent your relationship from going stale.

The following is one of a number of stories from our own relationship we share to help make certain points. We include this one to illustrate how something new and fresh can arise if you let it, no matter how old you are.

Judith: For us, it wasn't "love at first sight." We met on a blind date. I was 43-years-old and never married. Jim was 45 and twice divorced. He grew up Polish and Catholic in Detroit and I was raised as a WASP in Los Angeles. We found we were different in many ways as we spent three hours over dinner discovering and enjoying each other's high energy and easy openness. We talked about our fears and disappointments as well as our strengths and ambitions. Although we enjoyed each other's company, it wasn't "chemistry."

Jim: After that first evening I thought, "She's nice enough. But we'll probably just be friends." Judith felt the same. We had a good time though, and so we continued dating—getting to know one another.

It wasn't until our fourth date that we even held hands.

But when we did, an intense energy passed through us, leaving us both surprised and shy.

"I've never felt this before," I told her.

"Neither have I," she assured me and herself. "It's wonderful and it scares me."

Judith: We spent that evening talking about how we were not each other's "type." I told Jim he was unlike anyone I'd ever been with and he said the same about me. We confessed that we had never experienced this kind of dating, and that neither of us was at all sure of what to do or how to proceed. It wasn't until several dates later, in my living room, that we kissed for the first time. We were both awed by a wondrous but totally unexpected response.

Jim: I was seated on the floor. Judith was on the couch. We were tentative, respectful of the growing bond between us. We took nothing for granted. When I rose to my knees to move toward the kiss, we were both very aware that what was happening was far more than sexual attraction and desire. We were acknowledging our willingness to come closer, to discover who we were together.

Judith: The kiss was gentle, more an invitation than a demand. Suddenly I was weeping involuntarily. Jim saw that I was okay, so he wasn't concerned. However, tears were the last thing I expected. Jim sat next to me, very still and respectful. Both of us had always taken pride in being sophisticated and experienced. Yet, there we were, two innocents, in awe of something we'd never known before.

The kiss was a sacrament, an expression of our sacred joining, of our willingness to meet in, and commit to, spiritual, emotional and physical discovery. Something extraordinary had entered our lives. It was real romance and a love that has never stopped growing.

*The most beautiful thing we can
experience is the mystery.*

—Albert Einstein

Opening to Love

*At the heart of the new intimacy is the capacity to
consciously open yourself and take in more and more of
who your partner truly is.* That's much easier when what
you want to take in is familiar, something you already
know and like. But when it comes to differences, ranging
from those that are mildly dissimilar, to those that are foreign, or those you've been forbidden to even consider,
then love may no longer be so easy or even so attractive.

Simply put, loving someone who is like you is love, but
it's elementary and will remain relatively superficial.
Loving someone who is different is a love that requires
commitment and consciousness and care. It can take you
into profound realms of personal growth and remain a lifelong adventure.

The more you are willing to learn, to extend yourself
beyond what you've known, beyond what you are accustomed to, you will be opening yourself to the vast
panorama of life and love. That is the magic. To open fully,
it is essential you become more and more aware of yourself, of those around you, of the psychological and cultural
setting in which you were born and live. As you do, you
will become more inclusive and your whole idea and
experience of differences will change.

That kind of openness was very rare as recently as 100 years ago. People hardly moved away from home. They married someone from the same community, whose lifestyle and values were like their own. Their roles were clear and set by tradition. They didn't need to concern themselves with creating their own relationship and the married life that followed. They knew it would be very much the same as their parents', their relatives' and virtually everyone else's in their community.

Today many of us move away from where we were born and raised. We meet people who are very different from those we knew growing up. We change, opening to meet the invitations and demands of our new communities. What we want and expect from intimacy and relationship is far less determined by rigid social guidelines and more the result of our personal desires. That means we now have to rely on our own knowledge, experience and consciousness to discover what we want and how we will conduct our lives.

We also face a dizzying array of possibilities in the selection of a mate as well as in the lifestyle and role definitions we choose. Even if we do not move away from home, it is vitally important today to bring a strong sense of identity to our relationships, because increasingly we are free to make personal choices and are responsible for managing the consequences. A strong, healthy identity will allow you to stop experiencing differences as tiresome, even threatening, so you can come to respect and cherish them as the exciting blessings they are. *You can embrace more and more of the world around you, letting go of fear and mistrust and prejudice, viewing life and all things*

*alive within it as the setting for an adventure, an oppor-
tunity for you to give and receive love.*

In addition, we live during a time of heightened psychological and spiritual awareness. Personal development,
individual expression, the need to heal childhood wounds
and the hunger to discover new ways for women and men
to relate to one another adds very new pressures to what
we expect from our intimate relationships.

Creating and sustaining a fulfilling love relationship is
one of the most important things we do in life. Yet almost
no one receives any preparation. Would you send your
child to a school with unprepared teachers? Would you
take your car to an untrained mechanic? Would you trust
your surgery to someone whose only credential is an
intense longing to be a doctor? Yet, with $25 for the
license and a willing minister or judge, anybody can leap
into a trial by fire—get married and have kids, all on the
dream of "happily ever after."

We live in very challenging times, so we need to have
compassion for ourselves. But there is much we can learn
to make loving and being loved more rewarding and
deeply fulfilling.

---

*For one human being to love another:
that is the work for which all other
work is but preparation.*

—Rainer Maria Rilke

Very good

What Do You Believe? An Exercise

Answering the following questions will give you an opportunity to take stock of your present beliefs about relationship and about differences. Your answers will shed light on what you imagine a relationship to be.

1. What is your most cherished fantasy about how your relationship should be?

2. What do you expect to receive from your partner in a relationship?

3. What do you expect to give to that person?

4. Can you or your partner or any future partner live up to what you imagine? In other words, are your expectations realistic? If you're female, are you expecting Prince Charming to make a life for you? If you're male, do you want to marry Lady Perfect?

5. How comfortable are you with the fact that your partner will never exactly match your hopes and dreams?

6. Are you prepared to give up your fantasy expectations in honor of the real person you are with?

7. How tolerant are you of other people's differences?

8. How prepared are you to learn from and be changed by the ways your partner is different from you?

9. Are you truly available for a relationship?

10. Are you comfortable with emotional vulnerability?

11. What is the purpose of intimate relationship?

12. What do you imagine your relationship will teach you?

13. List those things which are nonnegotiable for you, those which your partner *must* meet.

14. Describe, for each of your nonnegotiable issues, why difference in these areas is out of the question.
15. Do you feel a yearning for spiritual connection in your relationship?
16. How would the growth and expansion of your relationship affect those around you?

What You Need for a Conscious Partnership

You've no doubt heard relationships described as two halves coming together to make one whole. What about a partnership of equals—whole person to whole person—cocreated and coresponsible? This is a new vision of relationship, one of <u>practical spirituality</u>.

By "practical spirituality" we mean an adventure of deep love. A sacred adventure that leads to self-acceptance and acceptance of others. It leads to embracing life rather than struggling against it. It reduces the fear and pain of potential rejection while increasing the pleasure of just being yourself with other people. Practical spirituality is a conscious, daily exercise of freedom and personal responsibility.

To fully open your capacity to the practical spirituality of loving and being loved, you have to:

- Respect the differences between you and your partner and cherish them as the source of discovery in your relationship;
- Welcome and grow from the challenges that arise because of those differences;
- Accept that you both are responsible for your relationship;

- Realize that the relationship you desire is cocreated out of your committed and ongoing passionate intention and awareness;
- Understand that creating a life with another person is a soul-expanding, lifelong process, not a goal to be met and finished with.

When you understand and accept what love is, instead of what you imagine and insist it should be, your committed relationship evolves into a conscious practice, a daily meditation on loving. It will lead you to value the beauty and specialness inherent in the one you love, and you get to discover the same in yourself. You get to see who you are together and what promise you hold for each other.

As your awareness opens and matures and you consciously move toward your beloved to accept and enjoy more and more of who you both are, you will come to see your once-dear illusions fall away in favor of the wisdom that real love brings. You will come to know that in real life love there is something greater, something drawing you closer to the connected, creative energy of all that is.

Chapter 3

A NEW REALITY:
THE FREEDOM OF
DIFFERENCES

Freedom breeds freedom.
Nothing else does.

—Anne Roe

Now, for the first time in history,
every couple is on their own—to discover how
to build a healthy relationship, and to
forge their own vision of how
and why to be together.

—John Wellwood

I mages and ideas of love and courtship, marriage and intimacy have changed over the centuries, but only very slowly. Before the 20th century, the primary responsibility of couples who were marrying was to repeat the patterns and lifestyles of their ancestors. In short, they were to do as they were told.

In the United States, however, over the last 100 years, radical changes have erupted in what we believe about courtship and romance. And those changes are happening faster than ever before in history. *So, when it comes to who and how we love, we now live with expectations of individual freedom and personal responsibility that men and women have never had to face.*

In order to manage today's complex relationship issues, it's important to have an overview or context so you can understand the powerful shifts happening in our culture and in your own life. By knowing what's going on you can develop more compassion and appreciation for yourself and anyone else who is trying to navigate dating and relationships in the turbulent, often confusing times we live in.

So, that's the story of this chapter—how all of us have to deal with the dramatic increase in personal freedom—which sometimes is fun, sometimes overwhelming—that allows us to choose our mates and create our own unique relationships. At the same time we have to accept the personal responsibility that comes with our expanded freedom of choice.

> *To love anything is to act*
> *freely, without compulsion or coercion.*
> *To be free means to do what one loves to do.*
> *Freedom is love and love is freedom.*
>
> —P. A. Sorokin

Increasing Freedom and Responsibility

When it comes to love and intimacy, during the last 100 years there's been an extraordinary and steady increase in our personal freedom. But there's also been a growing need to become more and more conscious, more and more personally responsible for what we believe and do. The modern birth control pill, which became commercially available in 1960, is just one example of how we all must grapple with an extraordinary increase in personal freedom and the responsibility that automatically follows.

Historically, birth control methods were, at best, extremely unreliable. The idea was to stop the sperm from reaching the egg. But sperm are very clever. All too often they managed to get around the guards at the gate. No one could really trust that pregnancy would be prevented. As a result, couples, single or married, were always threatened by the risks of marginally protected sex.

The modern birth control pill is radically different. It manipulates a woman's body chemistry to create a state of false pregnancy. That almost always prevents her from actually becoming pregnant. And, because of its reliability, women and men can now assert their sexual liberty while trusting they are safe from pregnancy. Never before in human history have we had the opportunity to be so sexually free. But freedom is never really free.

Freedom is more than simply a matter of unrestricted choice. Freedom is always coupled with responsibility, in other words, with the impact our choices have on us and those around us. The pill may have freed men and women from their concern with pregnancy, but that doesn't mean engaging in sex is free of consequences. Setting the obvious health risks aside, we are still responsible for the intimacy of sex and for the value we give to one another before, during and after sex. If you believe anything else, you are likely to abuse the emotional and spiritual power of sex, to cheapen the connection made possible through sex and to trash the beauty inherent in every act of love.

In the 1990s, there is widespread uncertainty about love and commitment, marriage and divorce, sexuality and self-esteem. Traditional ideas of what it means to be a woman or a man are dissolving. The stigma of divorce is just a strange and distant echo. Living together before marriage is common. We have unprecedented freedom to create the relationships we find most satisfying. Yet we seem more bewildered and frustrated, on the one hand, and increasingly caught up in fantasy and impossible dreams, on the other.

This wasn't true just 100 years ago. Rigid sex roles were in place with regard to courtship and marriage, and women and men knew exactly what was expected of them. Yet, in one brief century, the relationship landscape has undergone seismic transformations. We are now personally responsible for creating and defining the meaning and purpose of intimacy and relationship, and personal differences, as they express individuality, are a prime consideration. This is far more perplexing than most people have imagined. So many people feel abandoned, left on their own. A new vision of relationship that is both physically and spiritually fulfilling is needed.

To help you put today's beliefs and expectations about love and intimacy in perspective, we will briefly tell the story of how courtship evolved in America. This chapter will help you get your feet solidly on the ground by understanding the current forces that shape your beliefs and behaviors. More importantly, it will help you recognize and address many misunderstandings and false expectations that stand in the way of your happiness.

The Search for Intimacy in America

Arranged Marriages

Most likely you take for granted that emotional attachment and personal growth should be part of any good, loving relationship. But did you know that the idea that a relationship should foster both passionate intimacy and self-realization is a very recent addition to the meaning and purpose of two people making their lives together?

Throughout most of history, the principal purpose of marriage was procreation. Having many babies ensured that the customs and beliefs of the clan, family or community would be preserved. So couples had to follow the dictates and traditions of their community. Personal differences that make up an individual's identity and serve as the basis for attraction and affection, as we understand them today, were all but invisible. What we now think of as an individual sense of self, to our ancestors, was more like a community self, shaped and sustained through strict conformity with what they were told rather than personal desire and expression. What two people may have wanted for themselves, if they were even capable of imagining such personal desire, was completely irrelevant.

Relationships were more like business deals. Couples were brought together by community elders, religious leaders or professional matchmakers, and marriages were negotiated between families. The bride's family usually offered a dowry, either money or personal property, to make her more attractive on the spousal market. We hear an echo of this tradition in current marriage ceremonies when the minister asks, "Who gives this woman to this man?" It's usually her father who answers, "Her mother and I do."

Because their daughter's marital future was accounted for, the bride's parents could breathe a sigh of relief. For the groom's family, it was often about profiting from the exchange. The new couple had to repeat the same rituals their families had performed for centuries. Change would have been blasphemous were it not unimaginable.

As we were writing this chapter, we heard a news brief that 33-year-old Hakeem Olajuwon, the star center for the

Houston Rockets basketball team, had agreed to a marriage arranged by his family. Following the precepts of his Muslim faith, he married an 18-year-old girl he had never met. "There's no dating, no boyfriends or girlfriends in Islam," Olajuwon said. Although rare in the United States, arranged marriages are still common in many societies today.

The custom of arranged marriage does not permit any freedom of choice for the bride or groom. Love and attraction mean absolutely nothing. Maybe the couple will learn to love one another, maybe not. That's neither necessary nor important. Obedience is the key. Through the practice of arranged marriage, it's the job of the bride and groom to support the cultural and religious survival of a community, first and foremost. Personal responsibility is not an issue, because there is very little sense of the "personal."

Early America

The hardships of life in early America dictated how men and women lived together. The practice of arranged marriage was not unknown to them, but colonial Americans, who fought to win their independence, preferred individual choice as the method for both genders to select their mates.

The fact that a woman had community approval to choose her husband was revolutionary. Previously, only men had known such freedom. But this new independence didn't mean that a wife was an equal with her husband. Hardly.

The family was the center of their personal and social

life. There was no doubt that the husband/father was the unquestioned patriarch. He was God's representative on Earth. His wife's primary duty was to obey him. What a husband and wife felt as love, they expressed, first and foremost, as a submission to God. Next came the survival of the community and its traditions. Only then would their need for personal intimacy come into play.

Because of the constant challenge of survival, it was customary for several families to live together in close quarters, so that most couples had almost no physical privacy. They had little chance to develop tender, intimate emotional bonds. Also, many marriages were formed when two families wanted to pull together and expand their land and other properties. Under those circumstances, courtship was often little more than a formality. Although colonial Americans did love, what we call "love" and what they knew as "love" are very different experiences.

Does the idea of marriage to increase property holdings seem foreign to you? No surprise. However, such arrangements were still part of everyday life for many Americans long after the colonial period. For example, Judith's grandparents on her father's side, immigrated from Norway and Sweden to Minnesota in the early part of this century. When the government opened Indian lands to homesteaders, her grandparents each staked out a claim. As it happened, their farms were next to one another. Because the work was hard and the winters were severe, they decided it would be easier if they merged their land and lives through marriage. They raised a family primarily as a source of labor in their struggle to stay alive. Love, personal attraction or affection were not even thought of as part of the bargain.

Necessity brought many couples, such as Judith's grand-parents, together. Yes, they had more freedom to choose than in strictly arranged marriages, but their first responsibility had to be to survival. If their personal differences or personal desires didn't support survival, those differences were suppressed. Individual expression was hardly the point.

The Victorian Ritual of "Calling"

During the last half of the 19th century and the first part of the 20th, the Victorian practice of "calling" was quite common, bringing eligible young women and men together. As an expression of the aristocratic world of flowing gowns and side sabers, afternoon tea and cigars on the veranda, "calling," was a social custom based on the medieval practice of "courtly love." Everyone obeyed rules of conduct creating a totally predictable world of sweet charm and proper elegance. Knowing your place and following protocol were the highest values. As a code of manners, calling shaped the way love and marriage were managed.

Calling generally took place in the home, recognized to be the woman's sphere. It was the young lady's privilege to initiate these meetings, even though first contact most often occurred through her mother or aunts. Sometimes, social connections might be made at public balls under the ever-watchful gaze of the mothers and other female chaperons. Calling served as a way of testing the prospective suitor's background and his intentions. It had less to do with money than with proper form and grace, etiquette and breeding. If a man made the first move he was considered boorish, an invader of "woman's society."

Fashion magazines considered calling to be the height of personal and social refinement. They advised young women and men on how to look, how to behave and what to expect. These magazines were so popular that everyone—from the southern plantations, to the northern factories, to the farms out West—knew the "proper" behaviors. Anyone who wanted to be respectable followed these rules to the letter. The movie *Gone with the Wind* embodied the courtship etiquette of that period.

Although the details of calling varied, depending upon the social class and financial standing of a young woman's family, the basic process remained the same. When a young girl came of age, she was allowed to socialize with prospective husbands. But she had to behave in a way that protected her feminine virtue. She could spend time with potential suitors but *only by appointment.* A typical afternoon entertaining her gentleman caller would have followed very specific guidelines.

Her mother or another female guardian would invite an eligible man to "pay a call." When he arrived, he presented his calling card at the front door. Then he would be escorted into the parlor where he waited. After the proper waiting period, the young lady would be presented to him. Once they exchanged greetings, she might serve refreshments, sing for him or play the piano. But none of this happened without a female chaperon to watch over them. Privacy was forbidden. They were permitted to engage in polite conversation which was limited to appropriate topics focusing on his interests, not hers, and they were never to become too personal. At the end of their scheduled time, the young woman was strictly forbidden to accompany her caller to the door, much less linger, talking with him before he left. If she did and word got around, her reputation could be damaged.

Calling placed the needs and intentions of the society and community above those of the men and women involved. Personal love and individual expression were valued, but only after marriage and only if they conformed to the manners of proper etiquette and decorum.

Although personal freedom was increased somewhat, individual choice and responsibility still took a back seat to obedience. Young people were expected to duplicate what had come before. Any choice to be different could threaten their social standing and hopes for a good marriage and family. The rules of calling kept the social order and its refined customs intact by choreographing measured steps for these formal dances of attraction and acceptance.

The strict guidelines of calling are now outmoded, but some of its effects still linger. If you're male, do you remember dating in your teens? How nervous you were as you walked up the sidewalk to your date's house, knowing you would have to meet her parents, and hopefully meet with their approval? If you're female, did Mom and Dad forbid you to see certain types of boys—making it clear they weren't good enough for you? Your own experiences can give you a sense of what those who came before us went through on their way to holy matrimony and, by comparison, how much more freedom of choice and personal responsibility you have today.

The Intimate Self

It's essential, at this point, to introduce the idea of the "intimate self" because it is the foundation on which women and men have evolved the courtship patterns that are characteristic of the 20th century. The intimate self is based on our belief in the primacy of the individual. The individual's freedom of choice and the importance of each person's particular differences—what makes a person who she or he is—is at the heart of our modern idea of romantic love. Without the idea of the intimate self, the way men and women have related to each other romantically over the last 75 years or so would be unimaginable.

Do you believe every person is unique? Do you experience yourself as an individual, with qualities and character traits that only you possess? Do you imagine when you love and are loved, both you and your partner will share the innermost part of your unique selves with each other—and only with each other? Most of us would answer "Yes!"

The intimate self is your unique, personal self, shaped by your own desires, thoughts and feelings, distinct from those of your family or community. That means that you have developed your own point of view, and you are not interchangeable with anyone else. Your romantic life is your choice, not arranged or managed by family, community or anyone else. You are your own person.

Because you are your own person, the intimate self is an expression of your innermost feelings and beliefs, the richest treasures you have to give—often separate and different from what you show the world. It's what makes you one of a kind and is the basis for your making a unique connection with someone else. *It allows for the possibility of real romantic love, because you and your partner are free to be attracted to each other as individuals, based on what you each think and feel and your desire to be together, and you are responsible for the life you build together even if your choices go against what your family or community expects of you.*

Your commitment to share your intimate self is what makes deep emotional involvement possible because what you are sharing belongs to you and no one else. Revealing your innermost self is what makes your relationship truly passionate, intense and intimate.

Although the idea of the intimate self has been around for some time, historically for most people it was unthinkable, because they were compelled to be whatever their God and community demanded. Not until this century have women and men, at large, experienced the need to be uniquely different as a real-life expression of self, and it was dating, a singularly American innovation, that first provided the opportunity for such individual freedom and personal expression.

Dating

One day a young man from the country asked a girl from the city if he might call on her. She accepted. But when she greeted him at her door, she had her hat on. This very short story perfectly illustrates a profound shift in courtship expectations. He expected to pay a call. She expected to be taken out.

By the mid 1920s the new custom of "dating" completely replaced the system of calling. Young men and women went "out on the town," without chaperons and without any intentions of marriage, just to have a good time.

Unheard of! What did having a good time have to do with maintaining social values? What did it have to do with preserving tradition? Quite the opposite, "having a good time" was self-centered. Young people did nothing but think about themselves and their own pleasures. At least that's what the critics of dating said.

Within this new idea of courtship, couples moved out of the realm of the mother, the woman's world, and into the man's world—out into the public world of money and competition. The man made all the arrangements. He asked, she waited. He planned, she accepted. He drove (if possible), she was driven. He paid. She smiled in gracious appreciation.

Roles had reversed. A man's value was determined, not by manners and protocol, but by the entertainment he planned and the amount of money he spent. He was in control of the entire event. A woman's value was measured by her ability to attract "free spenders." Who he was didn't matter as much as what he spent.

Dating best expressed the new freedom of the new age. Old-fashioned, turn-of-the-century obedience and propriety were replaced with self-direction and personal choice. The '20s roared with new possibilities, free for the taking. But was it all really free? Compared to the past, sure. But everything has its price.

Safety and certainty, which had been the goal of the formal rules of etiquette, vanished, as if overnight. Neither the

young woman nor the young man could expect the protection of a nearby chaperon. So, they both had to deal
with a new pressure—the opportunity and personal
responsibility for sex.

Women were no longer on the pedestal their gentlemen
callers had been required to place them. Many men felt
entitled to an exchange for their lavish attentions. He paid.
She owed. In fact, the word "date" comes from the world
of prostitution, echoing the "dates" women booked with
their johns.

Sexual urges have always been part of the attraction of
courtship. But privacy, which is necessary to follow
through, had not been readily available before. That all
changed when the newly invented automobile was added
to the mix. A couple could travel away from their homes
and neighborhoods into isolated areas where they were
free to do as they pleased. The idea of the "back seat" with
the lure of its possible pleasures, but also its horrors,
entered the cultural consciousness. Anxiety and doubt
became part of the new dating scene. The innocence of
former times was fast receding.

Another social change made the anxiety of dating even
worse. By the 1920s, America's economy was driven by
the rules of consumerism and the marketplace. Value and
worth, advertising and merchandise, supply and demand,
win or lose permeated the entire culture. With regard to
romance, not only was money a key to successful dating,
but magazine columns and personal-advice books told
daters that popularity was everything.

For example, one popular magazine column advised a
young woman that just before she left for her freshman

year at college, she should tell all of her friends and relatives to write letters to her at her college address. That way, word would spread around campus that a very popular girl was about to arrive.

Popularity had very little to do with a person's good qualities or character and everything to do with how she or he was perceived in the competition. Men and women had to invent ways to convert their "personality assets" into dates—which had to be both visible and with as many different people as possible.

Another technique for gaining popularity was the practice of "cutting in" on the dance floor. Before a dance, a young man would instruct his friends to cut in on him and dance with his date. That way she would be known as a "once arounder," never dancing with the same partner more than one turn around the floor. A man's competitive status depended, in part, on the reputation and popularity of his dates.

The goal of dating was to be seen. Image was critical. Winning, looking good, impressing people—these were the cornerstones of popularity. In the courtship marketplace women and men became commodities. A woman looked for "the right man" to support her and the children. In trade she offered sex and beauty. A man looked for sex and beauty as the symbol of his power. In trade he offered ambition and hard work.

In this highly competitive climate, dating became a contest of adversaries, a matter of competition and display. Men went out "on the prowl." Women looked for a good "catch." In contrast to the tradition of duplicating their parents' ways, men and women opted for personal creativity, elevating individual expression to the pinnacle of attractiveness and social value. Individual style and flare could launch someone to the top of the popularity charts.

Increased personal freedom allowed for very new and different possibilities. However, personally managing the responsibilities that were part of the bargain was another story. Free choice had its consequences and young people had no history to guide them.

Think about the pressures you have experienced wanting to appear popular—trying to get in with the right crowd, wearing trendy clothes and looking cool, never letting it be known you're alone on a Saturday night—pressures that only make you feel anxious and inadequate if you don't do it just right.

Going Steady

World War II had a serious impact on courtship. Men returning from war were no longer impressed with the glamour and games of popularity and dating. They had seen the ravages of combat and wanted more from women and relationships. Women were faced with a serious shortage of eligible men. Getting one and keeping him wasn't all that easy. In the post-war climate of scarcity and tension, random dating lost its power and "going steady" became fashionable.

The popular media celebrated going steady as a way of preparing for marriage, and the acceptable age for marriage dropped. Girls were terrified of becoming old maids if they weren't married by the time they were 20. Many 20-year-old men married 18-year-old "women," all with society's approval.

In 1949, according to the *Ladies Home Journal*, social status for a high-school student was largely dependent upon whether or not she or he was going steady. Eleven years later, *Cosmopolitan* magazine told its readers that anyone who wasn't going steady was "square." Although particularly prominent among teenagers, in the late 1940s and throughout the 1950s, the idea of going steady reached all the way down to pre-adolescents. It was not uncommon for 10-year-old fifth-graders to be going steady.

Steadies rejected the competition of popularity and dating. They preferred safety and security over freedom and fun as the new values. Being someone's steady took some of the pressure off having to always make a good impression. Girls didn't have to spend so much time worrying about their wardrobe or become hysterical about the latest pimple. Boys didn't have to plan special entertainments and spend their money on girl after girl after girl. Being with your steady all night bobbing back and forth on the dance floor was in. Cutting in was out.

Going steady had its own rules and protocol. A boy was required to give his girl something to let the world know they were steadies. It could be his class ring, either worn on a chain around her neck or sized smaller with gobs of tape or yarn, which she wore on the third finger of her left hand. It might be his letter sweater, an ID bracelet or matching corduroy "steady jackets."

The boy was expected to telephone and/or take out his steady between two and seven times a week. They always knew where each other was and whom they were with. And if a special event came up that would be expensive, such as a prom or class outing, they worked together to save the money required—even if that meant staying at home in the meantime.

The old form of dating many different people became known as "promiscuous dating." A boy who dated around was called a "playboy," and a girl who played the field was known as "fast and loose."

One of the major concerns voiced about going steady was the sexual pressure it placed on both boys and girls. It was easier to say "no" to someone you'd been out with just once or twice. But steadies were exclusive. The simple fact of being alone increased temptation, and persistent desire had a way of wearing down defenses.

Going steady was very different from what was once known as "keeping steady company." Two people kept steady company when they were serious about marriage. They were adults who were preparing for a life together. In contrast, most steadies were adolescents engaged in a sort of play marriage—with all the responsibilities of being exclusive and *no preparation for how to handle it*. It wasn't long before the lid blew off.

Social and Sexual Liberation

SEX, DRUGS AND ROCK AND ROLL!
QUESTION AUTHORITY!
MAKE LOVE NOT WAR!
DO YOUR OWN THING!

The idea of having the freedom to be yourself had been growing more powerful throughout the 20th century. The increasing desire for personal freedom further weakened the strength of authority and community to dictate behavior. In the 1960s that desire exploded, and revolution burst onto the American scene. Personal choice and idiosyncratic expression was the standard of the times. Free sex and free spirits led the way toward exploration and enlightenment. The sexually liberated flower children denounced the past and proclaimed a psychedelic new future for mankind. Love was free and so were they. "If it feels good, do it" became the mantra of the new world.

In the midst of all that change, going steady grew up. Couples started living together, rejecting the notions of what it meant to be respectable, arguing that "a marriage license doesn't make us any more or less in love." Parents were befuddled. Grandparents were shocked. What had become of the world?

The women's liberation movement announced the independence of women, as activists took to the streets declaring, "The personal is the political." They claimed the right of women to be equal with men in all spheres of life and they expected to be treated accordingly. Nothing less would do. Their analysis of and protests against the second-class status of women further undermined traditional authority and the roles men and women were expected to assume.

The civil rights struggle and the Vietnam War stormed into everyone's living room. Blood on the streets and on the battlefields shattered the fantasies of a clean and pure America. The credibility that public officials at all levels of government once enjoyed was quickly replaced by cynicism and contempt, and the cry rang out, "Don't trust anyone over 30!"

Hippies blatantly refused to live conventional lifestyles. They embraced marijuana and LSD, "turned on, tuned in and dropped out." Men and women joined communes and practiced "free love"—sex with any and all. The Psychedelic '60s shot way past what the Roaring '20s ever imagined.

Even middle-class America wasn't immune. Those who were most adventurous experimented with "open marriages" that allowed for more than one sexual partner, "swinging" in which married couples traded partners, and the occasional *menage à trois*.

Closets opened and gay men and lesbians demanded to be treated with dignity and respect. Senior citizens, who were believed to be beyond sex, suddenly were telling the world of their pleasures and desires. Even priests and nuns renounced their vows to find and marry one another. Customs and conventions were disintegrating.

While there was wide-open freedom to redefine sexuality and relationships, there was also a feeling of chaos. People began to discover the price for the freedom they so insistently demanded—consciousness and personal responsibility. Without that, freedom could easily be a bad trip, or "just another word for nothin' left to lose."

Wide-open freedom without preparation and personal responsibility could not last. Too many lives were lost to mindless drug use. The "freedom" of aimless wandering turned into a prison of disenchantment and alienation that lasted throughout the '70s. By the 1980s society had made a serious correction.

Radical '60s parents were embarrassed by their "yuppie" children who didn't care about social issues and the freedom of being "outside the mainstream." These young men and women of what was called the "me generation" were more interested in their careers. They wanted money, status and security, and they could get it through law and business. They married later in life and limited the size of their families. Carving out a "piece of the pie" had become much more compelling than marching in the streets or living in a Volkswagen van.

The feminist voice grew louder and more strident. The radical feminist leadership insisted that women be treated like a protected class with special laws and safeguards while they relentlessly condemned the patriarchy—the "white macho establishment." They applauded single mothers for being bold and courageous and encouraged more women to make it on their own. The need for men was publicly questioned with slogans like, "A woman without a man is like a fish without a bicycle," and the most radical voices even equated heterosexual sex with rape.

Ironically, while some women demanded respect and equality, profits from the sales of Harlequin Romance novels, read almost exclusively by women, were astronomical. According to researcher John Market and *Forbes* magazine, in 1991 approximately 25 million women read romance novels at an average of 20 novels per month. Men tried to please women by becoming "sensitive," but in comparison to bold and daring romance novel heroes, they didn't stand much of a chance. In the wake of increased confusion and pain between males and females, gender bashing became a national sport.

Not surprisingly, courtship became more difficult than ever. As a result, dating services became big business. They promised to help people meet the "right one" or to find that "special intimate connection"—for a hefty fee, of course.

Meanwhile dark clouds were appearing over the social sky. One seemed completely mysterious and very deadly— AIDS. Another was the epidemic of out-of-wedlock births.

Now in the '90s, after nearly 100 years of profound and accelerating change, love and intimacy are in disarray. Many people simply don't know who to be or how to behave with the other gender. Confusion, mistrust, heartache and yearning enclose the hopes of both women and men. What do we do?

Just about everyone I know hates dating. People are confused about what to bring—an accountant, a lawyer, an interpreter or a résumé. Sadly, we often forget to bring ourselves.

—Greg Potter

Where We Are Now

Today, we have almost limitless personal freedom to choose our mate and our lifestyle. What we lack is the training to live with the personal responsibility it takes to mine the riches available within such freedom. As a result, many people feel the need for a new vision of intimate partnership, a new purpose to make dating and commitment spiritually meaningful and fulfilling. Do you? Do you want a new perspective, a new orientation to take you beyond popularity and peer pressure, beyond mere physical attraction or the lure of materialism, beyond the conventions of family and church and even beyond solely personal desire? If so, you are one of millions searching to find the deeper fulfillment that is available in the contemporary challenges of intimacy. You are among those looking for ways to understand and value the differences between two people living intimately and building a life together.

A spiritually rewarding relationship is built upon differences: the differences between you and your partner; between who you have been and who you are becoming; between what you believe and what's going on in society. Unlike relationship styles of the past, your willingness to embrace change is central to your ability to create a robust and lasting love.

Your relationship will wither if it is not fed from within by intimacy, love, openness and your mutual intention to make a fulfilling life together. It will also wither if you both become isolated from outside sources of stimulation, challenge and achievement—if you lose perspective on your connection with the world around you.

Your relationship is a living, breathing reality that grows—if you let it. Your commitment to learning about and developing a respect for differences and change is the key to the deepest, richest and most meaningful relationship you can imagine. *To succeed, you both have to be willing to be changed by love.*

Making a life with someone, as you both recognize and appreciate how different you are from one another, reveals the magic in the mundane while also allowing for moments of exquisite transcendence. As you learn to give more of yourself and receive more of your partner in the process, you are made larger in your heart and soul, more capable of loving what is and more open to being loved for all that you are. Ultimately, that's all anyone really wants.

Chapter 4

FANTASY AND ROMANCE: DANGEROUS DIFFERENCES

I had unrealistic expectations
about how being married would make me feel.
I thought it would fix a lot of things. . . .
I just thought being married would complete
me somehow, or make me feel safe.

—Cindy Crawford

Is not this the true romantic feeling
—not to desire to escape life, but to prevent
life from escaping you.

—Thomas Wolfe

*C*hances are you never thought you needed to be rescued from romance. In fact, you probably feel you need more romance in your life, not less. The truth is that most hearts are broken in the painful difference between the possibility of real romance and the insistence on the fantasy of romance—with the real thing taking the loss.

*R*omantic Fantasy Versus Real Romance

Do you remember as a child closing your eyes and making a wish when you blew out your birthday candles? Remember how you hoped with all your heart your wish would come true. In all likelihood, those that did come true were made to happen by your parents or another relative, someone who had the power to bring your wish to reality. Didn't it seem like a miracle when you got what you dreamed of? All you had to do was wish and there it was!

If you can see a rabbit in a cloud or a face in the bark of a tree; if your heart can be opened by the giant chords of a powerful symphony or you can discover something where nobody ever looked before, you might be praised for the wonder of your imaginings. You might even be called a genius. Do you have to give up imagining? Not at all. The price of giving up imagining is the death of the soul.

But we need to make a critical distinction at this point, a distinction that's so important it carries the weight of whether you will have a successful relationship or not. *You cannot prefer your imaginings over reality and you cannot allow reality to squash your dreams. You have to weave them together to make a whole and fulfilling life.* Unfortunately, for too many, this distinction is not made, and they consciously or unconsciously choose what they imagine over what actually exists in and around them and are reduced to living in heartbreaking fantasy.

To experience real love and true intimacy, we have to understand that, because we are all confronted with differences, we cannot have everything we want just the way we want it. Have you ever been in a relationship with someone who turned out to be different than what you imagined? Perhaps the reality of this person was even pretty terrific, but he or she was different from your expectations and you had to adjust. Even when that works out well, there's still a feeling of loss when you have to let your fantasy expectations go.

For far too many, however, the loss is intolerable. Rather than having to "settle" for a person they can't help but see as ordinary and unexceptional when compared to their fantasy, they choose their own world of romantic make-believe. They prefer the stories they've made up rather than having to live in the truth of who they really are and what it's like to be with a real person who is different. And nothing is more effective at destroying real intimacy than opting for the images and emotions of romantic make-believe.

These make-believe fantasies take many forms. They can be very subtle and hardly noticeable, or they can be outrageous and unbelievable. The key to spotting such fantasies is that they always compensate for a sense of loss, hopelessness or any feeling of inadequacy. For example:

- Niki can't stop her date's unwanted sexual advances because "I'm afraid if I say 'No,' he'll lose interest in me." So she ignores her own response and creates a fantasy about him—that he's so much more open and honest about his sexual needs than she is—and she lives inside that story rather than the truth that she doesn't want to go to bed with him and doesn't have enough self-esteem to make her feelings known.

- Kareem looked forward to surprising Keesha by taking her to a new restaurant. After they arrived, she said she'd been there the week before with her networking group. He was crushed because he wanted to be the first one to take her there. Rather than adjust to the truth of reality and enjoy the time with Keesha, he spent the evening sulking, caught up in feeling betrayed mixed with not feeling special.

- Anthony wanted his marriage annulled when his wife told him of her previous sexual encounters. He wanted to believe she'd been a virgin even though he hadn't been. Rather than working out a reality-based relationship with his wife who he claimed to love, he preferred the fantasy that a wife should always be a virgin for her man. Anything else would be degrading for him. "It breaks my heart to have to leave her," he sighed, "but I have no choice."

Not one of these people has their feet on the ground. Each displays a dangerous preference for their idealized notion of "how it's supposed to be." *They reject the differences between reality and their own fantasy and then have no way to intimately connect with the people they're with because they are unconsciously loyal to the stories they have contrived.* For Niki, Kareem and Anthony to ever feel really loved, they will have to rescue themselves from their allegiance to fantasy. Here's an example of just such a rescue.

Yvonne and Sam

We read about a young couple, Yvonne and Sam, in the *Los Angeles Times.* They married after the birth of their first child. She was 16. He was 21. They both were gang members and said they fully expected that marriage would mean "instant happiness."

"Why not?" Yvonne insisted, "That's what our culture teaches us."

Instead of effortless happiness, their marriage quickly plummeted into despair. Sam couldn't pull away from his homeboys and he lost his job. Yvonne had another child, cried all the time and was beaten for her tears. This is a vivid illustration of the dangerous differences between the fantasy of instant happiness and the demands of intimate relationship in the real world. But their story has a happy ending. Together they changed their lives.

In desperation, Yvonne found her way to a very supportive continuation high school with an on-site day care and parenting program for teen mothers. While she worked to earn her diploma, the teachers helped her believe in herself and increase her determination to take responsibility and change her life. She gave Sam a choice: Leave Los Angeles and the environment they were trapped in, or she would leave him.

They moved to a new town, started couple's counseling, and the violence stopped. Rising up out of the quicksand of unconscious fantasy and the pull of their allegiance to their families' and neighborhood's way of life, they renounced their self-sabotaging habits and made conscious choices to change their lives even more. Yvonne now attends college with plans to go on to law school. Sam works full time and is pursuing his high school diploma.

They began as children mired in hopeless romantic fantasies of effortless happiness, but they are doing the necessary lovework, committed to developing themselves as proud, positive, increasingly successful individuals. They are learning to identify and value their differences, becoming more intimate and loving with one another and good role models for their children. They're making their way, hand in hand, through the challenging adventure of leaving their past behind, interrupting the unconscious duplication of what came before, in order to find their own lives and be true to themselves and their children. After such a difficult start, they're learning to rely on their love to achieve the excitement and power of real romance and a new intimacy.

> *Psychological sin does not*
> *consist in sex nor in being physical nor in*
> *"immorality" but rather in calling a thing*
> *other than what it really is, treating it as*
> *something other than what it is.*
>
> —Robert Johnson

Only in Your Everyday Life

A full and vital relationship can only happen right here on Earth with another flesh-and-blood human being. If you deny or resist this fact in any way, you lose the power to create your life and the love you want.

Jim: We've certainly had our own romantic illusions to deal with, and, on occasion, still do. But we assure you that the richness of real, day-to-day loving outstrips, outshines, and out-entices anything you can concoct in fantasy. If you want wonderful, real life romance, you'll never find it in the play-acting of fantasy.

Remember the story we told about our first kiss? There was no dramatic mood. The stereo was silent. No wine. No candles. It didn't happen on a beach in Tahiti. We were in Judith's living room in Santa Monica. And yet, we crossed a threshold that night. Simply and beautifully. We entered into a new intimacy that neither of us had ever experienced before.

There is magic in real life, and it's available to you, but not unless you decide to recover from romantic fantasy, not unless you accept yourself and your partner as the different persons you are and rely on that truth to build your life together. Do you recoil at that thought? Perhaps love has been so disappointing that romantic fantasy seems necessary just to make life tolerable.

Real Love Doesn't Stand a Chance

If you expect to be with Prince Charming or his female counterpart, Lady Perfect, you are totally undermining your chances for real life love and intimacy. That may seem obvious. Yet far too many people deny or merely tolerate the real-life differences between them and their flesh and blood partners, preferring images and hopes of perfection. Compared to the perfection of fantasy, real men and women can't possibly be good enough.

One female client, who was wrestling with trading what she called "cheap thrills" for what she hoped would be the real thing, admitted, "I've always been attracted to bad boys. Even though I know they're not good for me, I don't want to give them up. They're so hot in bed!" Because of what she dreamed love would be like, she was unable to find emotional and sexual satisfaction with any man who didn't provide an edge of danger.

Or as a man challenged us during one of our seminars, "Why would I want intimacy when that's what destroys the romance?" He proudly announced that it was "a man's job to keep romance alive." But when we questioned him further, he admitted he'd been unable to sustain a long-term relationship and he was the one who always broke it off. Is it any wonder he balked against intimacy? He didn't know how to be involved except on his own terms.

Real life can be eclipsed by the longing for the power

and control of fantasy. But, eventually, real life catches up. It must ... and then?

When I was not liking myself I'd
make him into a project.

—Elizabeth Davis

Lydia and Bryan

Lydia was very proud of her marriage to Bryan. She'd never had to work, and she traveled the world with him on his business trips. She loved telling people that her husband was the president and CEO of a large advertising agency.

After they'd been together almost 20 years, Bryan's company was bought out, and he was without a job. Since he was financially independent, at 52 he decided to retire. Lydia was horrified. She threatened divorce. It wasn't about money. Bryan tried to reassure her they could travel even more extensively. Nothing he said consoled her. She felt humiliated and exposed by the image of being married to a man who was "unemployed."

Born into an upper-class family but neglected by parents who were more interested in social climbing, Lydia had never really been sure of herself. In her secret heart she harbored the shameful conviction that "I'm not much on my own."

No one ever guessed. In high school she was a cheerleader, in college an active sorority member. As a wife she was always ready to devote herself to some project or cause. When she could no longer be the wife of a CEO, however, she came face-to-face with "feeling like nothing"—a feeling she'd successfully contained her entire life. When Bryan decided to retire, Lydia had nothing inside to help her adjust. Her false identity collapsed and she panicked. Faced with the need to change, she became emotionally paralyzed, obsessing over the idea of convincing Bryan to go back to work, believing it would be "for his own good." She thought of leaving Bryan but loathed the humiliation of trying to find someone else. In her darker moments, she flirted with the possibility of suicide.

Married couples do not escape the dangers of unconscious fantasies. *In fact, marriage often acts as a catalyst bringing to the surface fears, wishes and insecurities that remained dormant while the person was single.* When that happens, both people are caught off guard, most of all the person in whom the fantasy has been exposed, and they are unprepared to deal with what's going on.

This fantasy of a man in a gray flannel suit is one that independent, strong-minded women of the '90s are distinctly not supposed to have, but I find myself having it all the same. And many of the women I know are having it also."

—Katie Roiphe

Anyone Is Vulnerable to Romantic Fantasy

You may not think Lydia's predicament speaks to you. However, the fact is that preoccupation with romantic fantasy, whether subtle or outrageous, is rampant in our society. We're all susceptible to its temptations. The best education, the largest stock portfolio or the most fervent religious beliefs can be overtaken by the seductive fantasy of an effortless, perfect love.

For many, romantic fantasy is far more than merely temptation. It can be an addiction. According to *Forbes* magazine, 49 percent of all mass-market paperback books sold are romance novels. An astonishing statistic. *When you confuse your fantasies with actual life, you flounder between what is real and available and what is an impossible illusion.* That's very dangerous. You're stuck yearning and pining for something that was never attainable in the first place—in other words, you are chasing *ghostly lovers.*

In 1990, the editors of *Savvy Magazine* conducted a survey in the July/August issue asking their predominantly female readership for their favorite sexual fantasies. Their report, "Sex and the Savvy Woman," represented working women whose average age was 35 and whose average annual income was $35,000. The magazine published the following fantasy as the outstanding example of what *"80 percent of the women who answered the survey say they are not getting enough of in their lives."*

> .... *a very distinguished artist or writer takes me to his loft. Bach is on the stereo. Slowly we get closer. We make love all night long, all over the loft—in the shower, by the fireplace, on the roof. When I wake up he is gone, but there is a note and a package for me. The note says, "You are a beautiful, strong, vital woman—revel in your life." In the package is a sketch of me he made that morning.*

Then my silver-haired blue-eyed artist walks back through the loft door and says, "Never leave."

Are you captivated by the dreamy sentiment of this fantasy? If you are, that's no surprise. Remember, 80 percent of the women who responded said they wanted their men to supply this kind of romance in their actual, everyday lives. They really believed men should act like this, and they wanted more.

Okay. So it's just a fantasy. It's fun and even delicious. The problem arises when the fantasy is preferred over reality. When it's expected to be a model for real men and women, we'd better take a closer look.

He tells her she is strong and vital, yet she hasn't initiated a thing. He's completely in charge. He takes her to his loft. He makes love to her. He is the artist. And he's perfect. Is she?

Her sense of value is completely dependent on what he says and does. What would she have felt like if there hadn't been a sketch of her, or if, when he came back, he asked her to leave? Who would she be then?

She gives her autonomy and sense of authority over to him. In real life that would ensure she'll never be free to be who she is. She will have to be what he wants and behave in ways he expects. How long before she begins to think that he's a self-involved, insensitive, overbearing jerk? But will she assume responsibility for having given herself away?

The man in the fantasy also leaves much to be desired. First of all, he's attracted to someone who doesn't have much of a sense of herself. He likes to be in control—the very thing many women rage about in men—"He always wants to be in charge!"

He also lacks good judgment. She hasn't demonstrated anything to lead him to believe that she's strong and vital. Yet, he sees her as extraordinary. Why? One conclusion we can draw is that he's only interested in sex and is telling her what he knows she wants to hear. Or he's caught up in his own romantic fantasies about her.

Can you imagine this fabulous, erotic, seductive artist fumbling with her bra clasp? What if he pins her hair with his elbow so she not only can't move, but she's in pain. Imagine her moving in to kiss him, her mouth wet and full, her passion intense, and she is suddenly overcome by a coughing fit? Or, as they are approaching the heights of ecstasy she stops to get the hair out of her eyes? What happens to the romance then?

In your fantasy, everything goes just as it should, just as you want it to. No mistakes. No awkwardness. Certainly no confusion or doubt. And certainly nothing different from what you expect. Each moment flows easily into the next, all building toward perfection—a flawless, exhilarating climax—and usually a wedding ring.

> **Judith:** I was caught up in the same kind of fantasy. I expected to be seduced and rescued, not by any ordinary man, but someone very distinguished, very powerful and very sensitive. I passively waited for "it" to happen. In an article, published by the *Los Angeles Times,* I wrote:
>
> > *Like most women, I grew up believing in the romantic myth of Prince Charming—the perfect Knight in Shining Armor who would sweep me off my feet, carry me to his bed, make passionate love and propose marriage. He would be tall, dark and blindingly handsome.*

> *His elegant sophistication would be offset by the dangerous glint in his eye. We would live in wealth and happiness forever and ever.*

Wouldn't life be a breeze if that's how it worked?

Love, relationships, sex and intimacy can be beautiful, inspiring, even awesome. But not if you deny the fact that they are also complex and challenging. That's why it's critical to realize that all escape routes lead to nothing but illusion and inevitable heartbreak.

The Dangerous Price of Preferring Fantasy

Romantic fantasies, like drugs and alcohol, offer the hope of getting what you believe you can't get on your own. Also like drugs they are temporary and never ultimately satisfying. When the spell dissolves, you're lost in the pit of heartbreak, shortchanged by life yet again.

On the other hand, when fantasy is not a substitute for reality, it can be a playful source of pleasure. You can slip beyond the limits of daily life and play in a make-believe world. You get to go anywhere, be anyone and experience anything you like. However, enjoying romantic fantasies is one thing. Preferring them over reality is quite another. That's a crucial distinction.

When you expect your fantasy to come true in reality, bitterness and recrimination will routinely be part of the package. Remember, reality can be overwhelmed when it has to compete with the perfection of fantasy. When reality fails, disappointed love often turns vicious.

Have you ever physically or emotionally hurt someone just because she or he failed to match your dream of the perfect lover? Have you ever suffered the failure of not living up to someone else's dream image of the perfect love? We ask these questions during our trainings, and, without exception, the majority of men and women confess they have experienced both sides of this problem. Chances are, you have, too. Then, when a real-life relationship makes its inevitable demands, you shrink from a feeling of personal inadequacy, afraid you won't be enough, afraid you will come up short. *The trance of romance is deadly. When we're caught, we reject what is, preferring what "should be."*

Who You Are Has to Be Sacrificed

The major problem with a commitment to fantasy is that whoever you are for real has to be sacrificed. If you're feeling scared, awkward, confused, angry or whatever, you can't show it. That would burst the fantasy. You have to create a substitute self. You have to pretend to be secure, comfortable, clear, composed, whatever it takes. However, your false self contains a huge trap, one that's not immediately apparent. *A false self can never be enough, because its whole purpose is to compensate for your initial decision that who you are, as you really are, is unacceptable.* A false self never removes the feeling of being unacceptable, that's not its job. It merely hides it, so that you become more and more afraid that if you relax you will be revealed ... and rejected.

When you condemn yourself as unacceptable you are unavoidably lost. Without a credible sense of your own self, you're left to depend upon other people's values, ideas and beliefs as the basis for your identity—your family, community or church; fads or trends; media deceptions; a life based on "how I'm supposed to act." You're like a child living in somebody else's world. You can't trust yourself. In fact, you can't really trust anyone else, because you don't have a reliable sense of self to make such decisions. Is it any wonder you might fear being rejected by others? You can't feel any safer with them than you do with yourself.

Too many people spend their lives more faithful to an imagined lover than to the people they could be with (or actually are with). They prefer to be special in the eyes of their ghostly lover rather than ordinary in the embrace of a real person. Beware your wish for the Prince or Lady Perfect. They always begin as images of hope and promise. In the end, they turn out to be demanding and unforgiving tyrants, permitting no real person to ever be enough— especially you!

When a person abandons himself,
he is no longer anything, and when two people
both give themselves up in order to come
close to each other, there is no longer any
ground beneath them and their being
together is a continual falling.

—Rainer Maria Rilke

Awakening from the Dream

Judith: One morning, after years of endless searching for the "right man," I was stunned by a vivid breakthrough. Even though I had developed a successful private practice as a psychologist, I was chronically mystified by the difficulty I had finding someone I could commit to marry.

Standing in my kitchen that morning, I suddenly realized that the only man I considered worthy of marriage was Jonas Salk, a giant in his field, compassionate, a humanitarian and internationally celebrated. If we married, my status in the world would be secure. What I'd accomplished on my own didn't matter. I secretly felt unacceptably ordinary. It would take an extraordinary man to make my life right.

There in front of my refrigerator, I knew, in a flash, why I'd been single all those years. I had never really been available for a real marriage to a down-to-earth man. No man had ever been acceptable. Just like Lydia, a real, flesh-and-blood man would have diminished me. And yet, I had to admit that even Jonas Salk was mostly just an ordinary man.

That morning I was released. I was free to see myself as the substantial woman I was. I saw how my loyalty to my unconscious fantasy had actually sentenced me to a life of perpetual romantic failure.

Every illusion carries pain
and suffering in the dark folds of the
heavy garments in which it hides
its nothingness.

—A Course in Miracles

Learn to Avoid the Fantasy Trap

You can learn to recognize when you're falling into the fantasy trap or when your date or partner is more captivated by his or her fantasy of you than with who you really are. You can learn to stop sabotaging real life love. Here are some common beliefs and expectations that can cripple your availability for real intimacy, followed by practical suggestions to overcome them.

The Desire for a Discomfort-Free Life

The story of the Garden of Eden rumbles deeply within the Western psyche. It tells how Adam and Eve led a trouble-free life in which everything was provided without effort. They were carefree and innocent. But Adam and Eve were thrown out of the garden because they disobeyed. They dared to have minds of their own, to be different than they were told. A dark angel was placed at the gate forbidding them to ever re-enter. The story tells us that it is here on Earth, not in Eden, where we must make our lives. We cannot remain innocent, guileless children. *We have become conscious and we are responsible to ourselves and others for who we are and what we do.* But the continuing power of the story's attraction echoes a deep longing in us to be released from the burden of consciousness, from the unavoidable need to make decisions and especially from the weight of being held accountable for our actions.

To be fair, we've all sometimes wished that life weren't so hard. Haven't you said something like, "Wouldn't it be nice if . . . ?" or "If only she would've . . ." or "He should have known that . . . "? Hidden within such wishes, aren't you really saying, "I want what I want without having to make the effort to get it"? But that's not what the Eden story teaches. Quite the opposite. It tells you to beware the desire for a discomfort-free life, because that's not how it is here on Earth. It cautions against wishing to be taken care of, because that will keep you a child. And it advises you to pay attention when you want your life to be somebody else's responsibility, because that will lead to certain disappointment and a painful loss of self. When you want someone to be different than they are, remember that "should" is wishful thinking, not reality. These are all sure signs of being possessed by fantasy, and nothing but trouble.

We aren't advocating discomfort as a high ideal. Nor are we suggesting that you seek it out. You won't have to. It's part of life. Unfortunately, many people try to deny discomfort. They manipulate themselves and those around them to maintain the pretense that everything's just fantastic. The more they strive to keep the difficulty and demands of life at a distance, the more arduous and disappointing their lives become.

Suggestion: When you or your partner shy away from the challenges of your relationship, you may be crying out for a return to Eden. You may be expressing a desire to be taken care of, absolved of responsibility for your life. You think it should be easy and simple, but that isn't real. In truth, wishing for a discomfort-free life is deeply disempowering. It will make you emotionally, psychologically and spiritually impotent—and it will play havoc with any relationship you're in.

Certainly there are times when you'll need caretaking, times when you don't know something, are ill, or your resources have been depleted. We're not talking about that. We're talking about a deep-seated, chronic wish for life to be easy, to have it your own way without effort. Remember, the dark angel will never let you back into Eden.

Taking action:

- Make a conscious decision to stop using the word "should." Neither you nor your partner can ever live up to "should." The demand of "should" must reject anything different from itself in order to stay intact. *To create real intimacy, you have to deal with what is.*

- Don't let yourself avoid important but uncomfortable conversations. For example, if you're single, don't have sex until you've discussed birth control and AIDS testing. If you're married, don't allow just one of you to dominate financial or child-rearing decisions. Make yourself known.

- Determine what's really going on when you complain that your relationship takes too much work. This usually indicates that growth and learning are at hand because the differences between you are demanding to be recognized and included. In order to have the miracle of the new intimacy, we all have to do the lovework of joining two different lives together.

- Beware when you're tempted to cheat on your relationship. You can do that in a variety of ways, some of which don't even look like you're cheating. You can cheat sexually. You can stay longer at work than necessary. You can become overly involved with your children, or pay more attention to your parents' needs than your spouse's, etc. Rather than struggle to make the changes necessary to build a fulfilling life with your partner, you're looking for familiar and easy satisfaction somewhere else.

Depending on Destiny

Does destiny play a role in the events of our lives or not? Who knows, really? *But, if you depend on destiny or fate as the governor of your life, you abandon your own creative power, a power that is only available through self-responsibility, self-reliance and personal initiative.* By surrendering to what you believe are the whims or forces of fate, you blind yourself to the need to remain aware and alert about who you are, what you want and what you're doing with your life.

In the *Savvy* fantasy, the woman's blue-eyed, silver-haired artist was far more than any ordinary lover. He seemed to have been ushered in on the wings of fate. How could she possibly have resisted? Love at first sight has this same quality. An attraction so powerful, it cannot be questioned. A moment so effortless, it raises no need for concern. Cupid strikes out of the blue and we're compelled to follow.

Cupid holds an exalted place in our psychic history and he's still very much alive. The successful movies *Pretty Woman* and *Sleepless in Seattle* are examples of being struck by love—and in the movies it always works. Isn't it interesting, though, that we have Cupid to represent "falling in love," but no mythical character to illustrate the painful stab of love's arrow when it's been left behind in a broken heart?

Jim: We're not saying that love and relationship are exclusively about conscious choices. Sometimes Kismet does seem to be involved. That was true in our relationship. We met on a blind date. We were introduced by a woman both of us barely knew. She didn't even come to our wedding. She brought us together and then went on her way. Is that destiny? Perhaps, to a certain extent. But we didn't rely on destiny to make our relationship happen. That was our responsibility, and it continues to be.

You must use your wisdom, your intelligence and your heart to inform you if a relationship is right. All too often the heat of unfettered lust, the excitement of conquest, the thrill of a little danger or the urgency of clinging dependency are confused with love. "If I feel this way, it must be fate." *But feelings are not, by themselves, trustworthy.*

Suggestion: Reading more (or less) into a situation than it deserves is very dangerous. That can lead to reinterpreting or overlooking your partner's behaviors in order to make them palatable, or to protect you from a conflict you fear might erupt if you complain. You seduce yourself into a relationship that's not really viable. On the other hand, misreading a situation can create a pattern of falling in love, only to have the relationship disappoint you. For example, have you held destiny responsible for breaking up your relationship, rationalizing your decision to leave with the assumption "something better" is waiting in the wings—the "grass is greener" syndrome?

Check what you and your partner are feeling and believing against the facts of what you are actually doing. If it's Kismet, fine. You have a good start. But that's all. You must take it from there.

Taking action:

- Never assume that just because of some particular coincidence, you're meant for each other. You may be caught up in your own fairy tale. Find out.

- Don't interpret events between you as predetermined. If you do that, you deny your own individuality, your own power to choose and you make yourself a pawn in someone else's game.

- Be aware that what feels like predetermined fate may just be your inflexible, unconscious loyalty to an idea of how it's supposed to be. Fate may be nothing more than your intolerance of differences.

- Work against inflating your relationship beyond what it is by deciding it has mystical meaning. Even if there are greater forces involved, you must still create your own magic.

The Fear of Intimacy

Intimacy becomes real and tangible when you bring more and more of yourself to your relationship. That means the good along with the bad. *If you want to show only your best parts, you're in hiding and not available for real love and intimacy.*

Yes, we know, most of us were raised to put our best foot forward. In order to make yourself acceptable, you too learned to suppress and deny those parts of yourself that you were told were unwanted. You judged some parts of yourself to be unworthy of love. Then you proceeded to hide them away—in other words, to not love them. So, by your own doing, you became what you believed about yourself. You became unlovable! All in the name of presenting only your best. The tragic paradox is, the more you succeed at this, the more you fail.

When you're afraid to be wholly who you are, you're also afraid to see the entire, complex personality of your partner, and that translates into a fear of intimacy. Of course, in romantic fantasy these concerns never arise.

Suggestion: Your feelings of being unacceptable, unlovable or unwanted are learned. You weren't born feeling that way. When did you make such fateful decisions? Did it happen when you exposed your neediness, your wild humor, your fear, your extraordinary intelligence, curiosity, brash opinions, anger or tears and you were then rejected, or ridiculed or in some other way squashed? Whatever it was, you don't have to stay bound in your own self-disapproval. You learned these beliefs and you can unlearn them.

Also, keep track of the ways you hide your intimate self from your partner. What don't you say? What don't you do? What don't you feel? *Whatever you're hiding is not nearly as dangerous as the unconscious message you are sending to yourself and your partner that you don't deserve to be loved for who you are.*

Taking action:

- Make a list of what you believe are your character "flaws" and another list of the skeletons in your family closet. Check off those you habitually hide from your partner.

- Play an intimacy game with your partner or a friend. Reveal a few of these hidden "flaws" and find out how she or he will react, having agreed that he or she will do the same in return.

- Check off those you hide from your parents or anyone else who is significant in your life.

- Identify what it was about those people that made them so unaccepting of you or threatened by you. *When you hide yourself, your primary loyalty is to their limitations and secrets.*

Fulfillment Should Be Automatic

Contrary to romantic fantasy, the Garden of Eden story tells us that fulfillment is not automatic. Deep connections take time. Even so, many women and men expect to meet the "right one" and immediately live happily ever after.

A relationship doesn't spring into existence full-blown. Furthermore, even if you've established your partnership with care and consciousness, you need to keep it alive and growing. You need to continually express your respect for your partner's similarities and differences to ensure that your relationship will flourish and withstand the unavoidable demands and stresses of life. It's important that you and your partner tell each other "I love you," both in big ways and in small moments. That reinforces your commitment, extends the intimacy between you, nourishes the heart of your love and provides the support that any long-term relationship has to have.

Suggestion: *Your relationship has its own pace, its own rhythms, different from any other. You can only know what those are by paying conscious attention to how you are together. If you force them, either willfully or through ignorance, you will distort your being together and suffer the consequences.*

How fast do you expect a relationship to deliver what you want? You may not be able to answer this in numbers, but surely you have a feel for it. Do you become irritated with your partner because things aren't moving fast enough? Or do you find yourself feeling not quite with it because you need to go slowly, because you want to develop intimacy in a manner that's meaningful and trust-worthy to you? Be respectful of your own timing. Know that anyone who's trying to rush you or make you feel bad about your pace doesn't have your best interest in mind. *Fast fulfillment is like fast food. It may taste good, but it can't ever be really satisfying.*

Taking action:

- Think about any long-term relationship you have, romantic or otherwise. How different was it when you first met compared to the security, depth and fulfillment you now share? What did it take to get to where you are now?

- Any time you need immediate gratification—food, sex, alcohol or whatever—take a moment before you indulge yourself. Look inside to see what emotional need your gratification is supposed to cover up. Stay conscious of what you really need and what stops you from taking the time necessary to create it. An important clue is—it's not anything external.

- When you're impatient with yourself or someone else, you're actually feeling out of control, not strong in your own identity. Instead, stop, take a moment and decide what you really need and what you can do to get it.

- Stay focused on developing your connection with who your partner or date really is rather than on some predetermined outcome. Manipulating to force a specific outcome never works. Remember the wisdom of Catherine of Siena—"All the way to heaven is heaven."

When I Find Her/Him, I'll Just Know

This is a common belief among those who are wrapped up in fantasy. They fully expect to experience that special moment when they'll find what they've been waiting for. No need for learning. No need to proceed slowly. No need to find out who the other person is. The match will be perfect. "That's how I'll know."

The woman in the *Savvy* fantasy has no fear of the artist, no concern with who he might be, no interest in what a life with him might be like, no curiosity about his past. Differences between them are irrelevant. By having him say, "Never leave," she tells us she's immediately ready to spend her life with him. He's the man she's been waiting for.

When a man is caught up in romantic fantasy, he usually creates a Lady Perfect who is utterly pliable in his hands. She adores his every word and validates his aggressiveness.

She loves his style, applauds his courage and always sees him as competent, smooth and worldly. Most importantly, she melts in the heat of his desire and sexual skill. All this happens inside his own imagination. If a real woman asserts herself and asks him for something different than what he, in his mind, is so magnificently delivering, he's likely to call her demanding, controlling and certainly ungrateful.

Suggestion: Romantic attraction is very powerful and very wonderful, but it's not the be-all and end-all. *If you don't consciously participate in establishing and sustaining your relationship, you may feel like it belongs to fate, chemistry, luck or the other person—anything and anyone but you!* Abdicating your responsibility to make conscious choices will, in the long run, act like a drag, slowly bringing down the vitality and future of what you have and want.

When you see someone new, do you find yourself wondering if he or she could be "the one"? Are you apt to reject someone because they don't "feel" right to you? How heavily do you rely on "chemistry" or "your type" as the best way of knowing if she's or he's the one? How will you know when you've found the person that inspires commitment? If you're in a relationship, are you still "looking," worried that "If only I'd held out, I'd never have to put up with . . ."?

Taking action:

- Make a list of qualities that are important in a partner, qualities you couldn't possibly know without spending time together—such as integrity, honesty, financial competence, the capacity to be a good parent, etc. Commit to finding out if the person you're interested in has these qualities. *Remember—there is no such thing as intimacy at first sight.*

- Pay attention to how sentimental you get over song lyrics, movie plots or anything that suggests an immediate connection is real. If your heart strings are quivering, you are susceptible to being blinded by your own expectations about effortless, swept-away love. Then when the challenge of differences brings you up short, you'll be shocked again at how difficult it is to find what you want.

- Date with curiosity. Keep in mind that your dates are not you. They are distinctly different, and you have to learn about them the way you want them to learn about you. The less curious you are, the more likely you are to use the other person as a projection screen for your fantasy life.

- Ask yourself, what, if anything, is so unattractive about doing the lovework necessary to develop intimacy with your partner? Why is real life love unappealing? So threatening? Your answers will help you break the hold your unconscious allegiances have on you so that you can build real-life intimacy.

Dissatisfaction with the Ordinary

We spend a great deal of time in the ordinary, routine, mundane events of everyday life. Bills need to be paid, cars washed, teeth brushed, diapers changed, garbage taken out. If you're dissatisfied with the ordinary, you are at serious risk for difficulty and disappointment. Why? Because you've judged the biggest chunk of your life to be unacceptable. Once you do that, where do you go? Into fantasy? Sure. But then you're living a substitute life, and you're necessarily alone in it.

Rather than accept the mundane, some people develop a fondness for bittersweet longing. They fill themselves with the sentimentality of heartache. They treasure the pleasure of love's afflictions. And every pang takes them that much further away from the love and affection they claim so desperately to desire. The magic that comes from the down-to-earth process of emotionally connecting with someone is beyond them.

Suggestion: Your expectations of an intimate, loving relationship can be unrealistic, making what happens in ordinary, everyday life—whether dating or married—seem inferior. Then the mundane will never be good enough. Real people will always fall short. The world will be confusing and maddening because you won't be able to find a way to connect.

During a talk-radio broadcast we hosted in Los Angeles, we asked the question, "What is love?" A 37-year-old woman called in and told us: "When I was young I thought love meant changing my husband into what I wanted. He didn't like that idea very much. When he tried to change me, I didn't like it either. Fifteen years together and three children later, I've realized that love is very simple. It's day-to-day. It's about diapers, lunches, quiet times with my husband." She then asked if she could say something to her husband who was listening in the next room. With curiosity, we agreed.

"Honey," she began quietly, "I love you very much and I appreciate your ways of letting me know you love me. I know I haven't liked you sometimes, but that's just part of it. I want you to know I wouldn't trade you for anything in the world."

That's real romance.

Taking action:

- Make a list of what scares you about having a long-term relationship with an ordinary person instead of the man or woman of your dreams. Watch how your fears block you from love and intimacy.

- Write down the ways you will have to change and grow as you surrender to the differences inherent in developing a real-life relationship.

- Make a conscious effort to see the romance in everyday events, whether it's choosing a paint color for your bathroom together or deciding what movie to see. Look for the care and connection that's already taking place if only you'll turn your attention to it.

- Make a conscious commitment to take as little as possible for granted, whether it's your wife washing your car, your husband making dinner or your date choosing a fun picnic spot. Consciously choose to feel gratitude and appreciation for such caring generosity.

The Need to Be Innocent

Underneath the preference for romantic fantasy is the hidden desire to be "innocent"—to feel you are without fault or limitation, without meanness or fear. The need to be innocent is the same as needing to live without the challenge of criticism or correction and without change and responsibility. *The need to be innocent is one of the most telling signs of a devotion to romantic fantasy.*

Innocence means more than just "not guilty." It's about trying to stay pure and unsullied. It's about choosing to deny your complex impact on someone else—someone who is, in many, many ways, not like you.

Another sign of innocence is a pattern of rage and accusation. It's always somebody else's fault. You're always the wronged party. The louder you rage, the deeper you commit to remaining innocent.

If you approach relationship expecting love to be simple, without risk and consequence, and certainly without any differences, difficulties and disturbances, you are trapped in the innocence of childhood.

When you were young, innocence was appropriate. But there is a season for everything. You must grow up. If you prefer perfection and the ease of fantasy, you are a child in an adult's body. You're living a distortion. If you persist, you have consigned yourself to a private hell of self-designed yearning and longing into which no other real person can enter.

A mature and meaningful relationship rests on the ability of two people to accept and grow from their differences. People who want to be innocent won't speak up when they're upset or in need. They adopt the posture of innocence by telling themselves, "I don't want to hurt anyone's feelings." This kind of "innocence" is a fraud, so the hurts, needs, irritations and disappointments happen anyway and cause more trouble and pain than the truth.

Conflicts are cocreated, too. No one is off the hook. Whenever a conflict arises, each one is responsible to some degree. Any claim to the contrary is a claim for innocence and is, at bottom, bogus.

Relationships are cocreated. We continually teach each other how we expect to be treated and what we will put up with. As a result, innocence is not possible.

Suggestion: Fraudulent innocence will lead you to be shocked by what's happening around you. It is the source of righteous indignation, rejecting and condemning anything that is different from the way it "should" be. Those who cling to innocence often end up inflicting pain on others in the struggle to stay pure and without fault.

When confronted with differences, have you ever blurted out something like, "I just can't believe it," or "I'd never, ever do that!" or "How could you possibly?!" You no doubt felt righteous, certain your point of view was correct. But was there any room inside your fiery judgment for the other person to be not like you?

Taking action:

- Pay attention to the times you have trouble saying, "I'm sorry." It doesn't matter whether you are wrong or your partner just got hurt by something you did or said. Say "I'm sorry," whenever it's appropriate and notice what goes on inside of you.

- Pay attention when you feel entitled. When you find yourself thinking, "I shouldn't have to struggle," or "Everything would be great if my partner would only change." What's so terrible about negotiating differences, about being responsible for who you are?

- Be suspicious any time you defend someone's unpleasant or harmful behavior. What do you lose if you see them as they are?
- Don't lie. Whenever you lie you are trying to appear innocent. And, more importantly, you're making a statement to yourself that who you are isn't good enough to be shown to the world.

Instead of being a fantasy image, your lover becomes a real person.

—Riki Robbins

Recovering from Romantic Fantasy

Recovery from romantic fantasy is based on your willingness to accept who you and your partner are—without deceit, without drama, without all of the false puffery so many of us put around our images of love, relationship and intimacy. *Recovering from romantic fantasy does not mean living without it. It means you will have, perhaps for the first time in your life, the chance to experience reality-based romance that is meaningful, fulfilling, passionate and can actually help you to create a relationship you can trust and delight in.* This kind of romance—real romance—can fill your soul with the feeling and knowledge that you are loved for who you are, just as you are, and it can inspire you to love deeply and fully in return.

What can you expect should you decide to recover from swept-away romantic fantasy? Here's an example.

Judith: One evening, we bought a special pie for a friend, to thank him for a favor he'd done for us. It was a strawberry-banana-cream pie with a collar of sculpted whipped cream around the top. Careful not to tip it, Jim set it on the floor of the car behind the driver's seat and we made our way home.

The day had been particularly difficult for Jim, and he was feeling raw and vulnerable. When we got home, he picked up the pie and the box caught on the edge of the seat, tumbled over and landed top down. It was that kind of day. He looked to me and timidly said, "Maybe it'll be okay." He opened the box and the pie, of course, was demolished, more like strawberry-banana-cream porridge. Jim slumped.

I was angry that the pie had fallen and shocked when Jim announced it might have survived intact. I knew better. How could he not have? But, more importantly, I knew Jim was suffering. I understood what he was going through. So, I put my arm around him and told him, "It's a mess, isn't it? I'm so sorry. . . . Let's get another one later."

It was a moment of real romance that left both of us feeling whole and human, compassionate and connected, loved and loving. In contrast to the grandiosity of romantic fantasy, we were just in our garage with a fallen pie, and yet we both experienced a sense of grace and beauty and a special bond of intimacy.

Can you picture yourself sitting around dreaming up a romantic fantasy where a dropped pie leads to heartfelt love? Most people, being honest, would have to say, no. That's just not how romance is thought of in our culture. Besides, romantic fantasy always ends up being punitive. It is contemptuous of "fallen pies." It's dismissive of human imperfection, derisive of anything that doesn't reach the lofty heights of romantic bliss.

Imagine how you would have responded to the fallen pie if you'd been in the clutches of a Prince Charming or Lady Perfect expectation? Would you be shocked? Would your disappointment turn to rage and ridicule? *When we're possessed by romantic fantasies, we use imperfection to crucify one another.*

And what if you were the one who dropped the pie? How would your need to be the Prince or the Lady have skewered you on a spike of self-hatred? Think about the times you've been contemptuous of someone, including yourself, for failing to live up to your expectations. Does the bloodletting feel justified?

When you open yourself up to real romance, you can use fallen pies to honor your humanity, to approach your partner with compassion and grace, to meet at the intersection of the heroic and the mundane.

Real romance comes from the unknown, from beyond what you already know. It's spontaneous, unrehearsed and open-hearted. It's about what's happening in the moment, about the attention and affection between two people.

When you're open to the heightened awareness of real romance, a vivid, even ecstatic experience can spring from any unexpected moment. Suddenly, there it is. Like a breath, it rises, crests, subsides and is gone, leaving a sense of wonder at the beauty of life. If you try to hold onto it, you cancel your invitation for life to catch you off guard and take you into the deepest places of your heart and soul.

Some people are still unaware
that reality contains unparalleled beauties.
The fantastic and unexpected, the
ever-changing and renewing is nowhere so
exemplified as in real life itself.

—Berenice Abbott

Tips for the Recovering Romantic Who Is Single

1. Beware the person who comes on too fast. Chances are she or he is "in love with love," not you. There is no such thing as intimacy at first sight.

2. Pay special attention to needing instant chemistry or limiting yourself to falling for "your type." You're probably caught up in the challenge of conquering someone who's not very available.

3. Avoid creating romantic scenarios during early dates. Don't play sexy music. Stay away from darkly lit, elegant restaurants. Wait awhile before giving gifts or flowers. Find out who you're with and whether you're really interested.

4. Hold off on sex, even kissing. If your relationship proves to be real, there'll come a time when love-play actually means something. Don't confuse heat with heart.

5. This one may be difficult, but it works in the long run. Abandon the Prince Charming-Helpless Damsel ritual of the man being the one to call, ask for the

date, plan and pay. Both women and men now have jobs and money, telephones and driver's licenses. One of the best ways to protect against the traps of false romance is to make dating an equal opportunity event. Share the asking, planning, paying and even driving. Then you're both on equal footing as competent, available adults—rather than a powerful man and the little lady who's waiting by her phone.

6. Avoid trying to entertain or impress your family, friends and acquaintances with stories about your dates. The drama of the story can confuse your perception of what really happened.

7. If you've just started dating someone, and you're fantasizing about what marriage with her or him would be like, stop. That's only make-believe and will keep you off balance in reality.

8. Go on nonromantic dates—walks in the park, sports events, charity fund-raisers, museums or bookstores. The point is to get to know what your date is like in his or her real life.

Tips for the Recovering Romantic Who Is Part of a Couple

1. Avoid comparing your spouse to some perfect ideal, especially when it's the "right" way to do things— your way. She or he will always flunk the unpassable test of your secret checklist.

2. When you feel critical of your mate, check yourself out. What's your intention? Do you want to be helpful

and caring? Or are you just trying to control the situation and get your partner to more closely match your fantasy?

3. *Don't confuse "having sex" with "making love."* There's nothing wrong with either one. But no amount of candles, wine and Quincy Jones will turn sex into real romance. Sex for the sake of sex can be frolicking fun. But making love only occurs when you are open and present, from the deepest reaches of who you really are.

   Whatever you do, if you're feeling unloved or not getting enough attention, don't look to sex to take care of your frustration. Sex is very powerful, but it's no substitute for the open expression of your needs and concerns.

4. Guard against the very dangerous belief that if you're having difficulty with your partner that means your relationship is in trouble. More than likely it means your relationship needs a tune-up and oil change. Only in romantic fantasy does everything go smoothly without attention, care and change.

   When there's difficulty, honestly air your feelings. Identify the problems. Work toward a mutually satisfactory resolution. We'll show you how in chapter 6.

5. Pay close attention to the ways in which you feel you're not full partners in your marriage—not sharing household responsibilities equally, planning and finances in particular. Bring to the table your feelings that your mate is not pulling his or her load or that you're being left out of certain aspects of your life

together. These power differences are often clues that one or both of you are living out some romantic fantasy that keeps you stuck in sex role stereotype(s) rather than building your relationship from the real life contributions you both have to offer.

6. Beware anytime you focus on your spouse's physical flaws as a reason to fall out of love. You're comparing her or him with your ghostly lover. If it's something you sincerely want to see changed, like weight or hairstyle, speak up. Explain why you want what you want.

7. Be suspicious if you compare your status and wealth to others'. That puts your partner in a very bad light. You also devalue who and what you are. Love and relationship are not based on commodities.

8. Beware when you criticize your partner for selecting "such a stupid gift," rather than acknowledging the thought and care that went into it. Appreciate what we call the "small kindnesses" you do for one another.

A small kindness is not merely a nice gesture. It's a gift of consciousness. For instance, say you and your partner both like pears. You like them refrigerated and he or she likes them room temperature. You go to the market and buy six pears. You then put three of them in the refrigerator and three on the counter. Doesn't sound like much. But, when you are aware of what you are doing, you are consciously respecting and cherishing your partner, yourself and your relationship. Consciously give each other one small kindness a day and watch your relationship thrive and grow.

Self-growth is tender; it's holy ground.

—Stephen R. Covey

The Alchemy of Real Romance

When you connect with and experience your own feelings while, at the same time, taking in the feelings of the one you love, you are walking straight into the open heartspace of the new intimacy, into the special connections you make with one another, whether small and subtle or grand and brilliant.

The following story from our own courtship reveals much about the fear we all have of being truly intimate and surrendering to love. It also tells of the real romance that's available whenever you open yourself and let someone in—even when limited by your own fears and resistance.

Jim: After we'd known each other little more than a month, we decided to spend Easter Day in Laguna Beach. Judith drove. During the hour-long drive, I turned to her and said, "I'd like to know how you feel about me."

Judith: I was taken aback. And excited. After all, I was the psychologist and the female, I was supposed to be the one who was more emotionally skilled. Yet it was Jim who was taking this dive into deeper emotional waters.

I wanted to give him an honest answer, but I wasn't ready to reveal too much. So I said, "Well, I think the best way to say it is that I'm starting to find fault with you." What I meant was that the intimacy between us had developed to a point I was uncomfortable with, and it frightened me. But instead of living with my fear, I slipped back into an old pattern of fault-finding as a way of keeping the intimacy at a comfortable distance.

Jim: After giving some thought to her remark I said, "If I hear you correctly, I should take that as a compliment." I knew what she was doing and felt it had nothing to do with faults and everything to do with intimacy.

She was impressed. "Yes," she replied, with a shy, embarrassed smile. "You should."

That's one of the most cherished moments of our early relationship. Yet it's not difficult to imagine what a disaster it could have been.

To fully receive the love you desire, don't act out some fiction of how you think it's "supposed to be." If you do you'll just be swept away by the fake drama of your imaginings, and you'll lose any possibility for real intimacy. The heart and soul of real romance is all about being honest in the moment. Express yourself as well as you possibly can, with respect and appreciation for your limitations and excellence and the imperfection and grace of being human.

Real romance is an example of practical spirituality. You don't have to leap beyond this life to get what you want. Quite the contrary. You can have it by standing squarely at the center of who and what you are, with respect and pride, power and humility, personal authority and the wisdom to know that you are a living daily testament to the complexity, fullness and sacredness of life.

When we value life on Earth and celebrate love on Earth, the full breadth of who we are becomes conscious, and we are able to lovingly connect with one another.

When you feel accepted for who you actually are—for who you know yourself to be—you feel at home. You are alive, not as an instrument or a prop to be manipulated for pleasure or pain, but as a sacred expression of life, unique only to you.

Chapter 5

RELATIONSHIP FAILURE: A SUCCESSFUL RESISTANCE TO DIFFERENCES

I've had some very bad relationships.
I chose terrible men. I had a thing for very
beautiful, unpleasant men. The unpleasantness
wasn't an essential—it just seemed
to end up that way.

—Kate Nelligan

If there is anything for which
human beings display inexhaustible
imagination, it is for devising ways
to sabotage happiness.

—Nathaniel Branden

Many people struggle with resistance to love. Regardless of what they say, they keep making the same choices, keep repeating the same mistakes that keep them stuck. They generally end up explaining their "bad luck" by enlisting fate, "I just haven't met the right one." Or they blame the other gender, "There just aren't any good men left." Or they replay the same complaint, "All the women I meet are only interested in my money." Frustrated, bewildered and thwarted, they feel locked up and impotent, swearing they are being victimized by forces they don't understand and can't get beyond. No matter how they grieve, no matter how they rage, no matter how they work to be different, they have an unconscious commitment to remaining unchanged and it is far more important than the love and intimacy they claim to want.

There's no doubt you have sometimes resisted love because it was "too much"—too intimate, too intense, at odds with what you expected or were used to. We all have. Why and how it was too much is what this chapter is about.

A String of Failures

During an interview with *Cosmopolitan* magazine, actress Kate Nelligan talked about men and relationships.

I tended to alternate between very good men and complete schmucks. I'd use the good men to recuperate, then get bored and go back to the schmucks. You always think you'll reenact the drama of making somebody love you who's incapable of loving you. You're going to force him to love you by being generous and good. You're going to make the sun come up and save his life. That's what was so compelling about those terrible relationships.

One after another after another. All failures. But oh so beguiling.

Relationship failure is most often the result of loyalty to unconscious beliefs about the way things should be. Because you are unaware of these beliefs, you are locked into an image of what a relationship must look like. Then, when something different disrupts that picture, even if that something is clearly pleasurable, hopeful or even uplifting, resistance automatically rises to keep change at bay.

Couples are no more protected against resistances than are single people. One of the most painful complaints we hear when we work with couples is the feeling of having been cut off by a partner who withdraws from passion, even affection. Yet, in moments when they feel the presence of love and intimacy, they're stunned to recognize how they themselves balk and resist. They retreat into what they know, what they're comfortable with, and don't even know why.

Resistance

Resistance is a strategy that blocks change. *Resistance generally arises when we are confronted with differences and feel endangered.* It's instinctual to resist danger. But, when it comes to love, it's more complicated than that.

Kate Nelligan had a preference for men who were not available. She inevitably rejected the good men and went back to "the complete schmucks." Her attraction to men who were "incapable of loving" kept her on familiar ground, kept her unwittingly loyal to an unconscious belief that she valued more than the successful relationship she claimed to want. She was more intent on making an unavailable man come to his senses by sacrificing herself to the project of saving him, than she was in making a relationship with an available man who wanted one. Had she accepted love from one of the good men, she would have had to change. She would have had to abandon her need to save the schmucks, and she was unwilling to do that. Instead, she lapsed into boredom and fell back into her habitual drama.

Understood more deeply, resistance is actually an unconscious commitment to something we must be faithful to. Rather than allow anything new to influence how we feel and think, rather than allow anything different to change us, we are compelled to repeat patterns we learned much earlier in our lives. And, because this is mostly an unconscious process, we fail to take responsibility for our choices and we end up feeling helpless.

Nelligan tells herself, "It just seemed to end up that way," as though her relationship failures were just happening to her. That's no doubt how she felt. But, in truth, her failures didn't "just happen." She was involved, though unconsciously, and she is responsible for her choices, even though she was unaware of her self-sabotaging pattern.

Resistances can take many forms:

Refusal: When you are totally unwilling to take any ownership of the problems in your relationship or marriage, while blaming them entirely on your partner.

Entitlement: When you assume that your partner should automatically know what you need without being told.

Confusion: When you are unable to rule out the other potential candidates and settle on one person as a life partner.

Repeated poor choices: When you repeatedly select inappropriate partners and blame the bad results on fate or the other gender.

You may be in resistance if you are constantly overtaken by sleepiness or, as was the case with Kate Nelligan, you are chronically bored. Making self-deprecating jokes or becoming easily irritated with your partner can also be signs of resistance. Any excuse to flee from moving to a deeper level of intimacy that could require you to change is likely a symptom of resistance.

It's critical to understand that resistances are not experienced as resistances. They are so ingrained they just seem like normal, appropriate responses to the situation. When Kate Nelligan was with one of the good men she never thought to herself, "Well, this is getting to be too much. It's now time for me to get bored." She no doubt just felt a sense of boredom arise, and went looking for a man who would not be boring. Until she became aware of her own pattern, the "nonboring" men were those she had to save, and that kind of relationship is certainly filled with intensity and drama.

When you allow love into your heart, you will be changed. When you express love from your heart you will be changed. That's the power and beauty of love. But if you don't have internal permission to change, if change is forbidden, any indication of love you express or especially, receive, must be resisted. In that sense, love can be threatening.

---

*In some areas of our personality
we live bewitched, so that we not only
disappear from real contact with
our own feelings and thoughts and fall away
from the persons around us, but at the
same time we feel pulled into another world,
held fast there, bound in the irons
of our alien convictions.*

—Ann and Barry Ulanov

Allegiances

If you're stuck in a pattern of relationship failure, you're being driven by an unconscious allegiance to self-sabotaging beliefs. *Your intense attachment to these beliefs prohibits you from behaving in any way that would disrupt your allegiance and change the way you respond to the situations of your life.* For example, Kate Nelligan was in allegiance to something that kept driving her back to trying to save the unavailable men. Before she recognized her allegiance pattern, her resistance to developing a relationship with a good man would kick in and she would fall back into the only kind of love she understood.

We are blind to our own allegiance patterns even though we can see them in our friends and they in us. Because we can't recognize our own patterns for what they actually are, we have all manner of explanations for our actions. Think about all the people you know who claim they want to succeed at love or anything else, for that matter, but they routinely get in their own way. They've all got "good reasons," don't they? To hear them say it, what they're doing makes sense. But their explanations always ring hollow. The fact is their allegiances and resistances are out of their conscious awareness and exert a far more powerful force on the outcome of their intentions and desires. Here's a simple example.

If you say you want to lose weight but all the while you're eating fried chicken and cinnamon buns, you're in allegiance to an unconscious belief that's far more compelling than losing weight. To prevent breaking your commitment to that belief, you resist change by eating foods that keep you overweight. It works like this.

You may unconsciously associate extra weight with mother's love—"I feel so good when I see you eating like that dear. It's healthy to have a little meat on your bones." You are in allegiance to the belief that you will feel loved if you keep the extra pounds, but that's not something you are aware of. So you explain your eating by saying, "Life is too short to miss out on the taste delights of good food," or, "My work is too demanding. I don't have time to plan my meals."

Or you may unconsciously associate extra weight with self-protection. Some men and women who were sexually abused as children unconsciously believe they are helpless and under threat from the other gender. They keep themselves heavy as a way of being physically unattractive and in that way protected against further trauma. Of course, they have no idea that is what's really going on, so they justify their weight by claiming that "It's just my metabolism. Even though I'd like to be thinner, everything I eat just shows up on the scale." Their allegiance/resistance keeps them locked in their own world, terrified of the very change they so desperately long for.

Whatever your allegiance, the fact is you don't have internal permission to be thin. Until you recognize that fact, any attempt at losing weight will just be an exercise in futility. Your allegiance pattern will win out every time as you enlist whatever form of resistance you need to keep you right where you are.

When you say you want a loving relationship, but repeatedly choose partners who are emotionally or legally unavailable, abusive, addicted or unwilling to commit, then it's fried chicken and cinnamon buns instead of love. You claim you want love, but you don't have internal permission to be loved. Instead, you are unconsciously committed to some kind of self-sabotaging beliefs. So you keep making choices that have no real future. You resist the changes that love necessarily brings and remain wanting.

Your task is not to seek for love,
but merely to seek and find all of the
barriers within yourself that you
have built against it.

—A Course in Miracles

Around and Around

Most patterns for relationship failure originate in either the absence of love, the distortion of love or in the disrespect and disregard for differences. These failure patterns are usually responses to childhood experiences.

For example, children who are ignored or abandoned come to unconsciously believe they are emotionally or spiritually invisible. They grow up lacking the sense that love is even possible. They hear about it, perhaps see it in others. But for them it's an alien experience. They tend to repeat their initial experience of an absence of love and intimacy by creating relationships in which they are invisible and unloved. And because they don't know that what they are doing is being driven by an unconscious belief, or beliefs, their relationships just seem to end up that way.

Children who are abused, belittled or used as pawns in their parents' arguments or fights, grow up with a distorted concept of love. They cannot escape the belief that something is wrong with them. They just don't know what. They feel unworthy and deserving of punishment. As adults, they unconsciously associate love and abuse, because that is what they know about getting attention.

Ironically, they can become either the abuser or the abused or both. And again, because they don't really know what's driving them, abuse can seem like just a part of the way things are.

During her interview, Kate Nelligan spoke of her family life. Her father worked long hours in a machine shop and was away a lot. Her mother was an alcoholic who spiraled down a drunken path to end up on the streets where she died. Although Kate made it out of her blue-collar, alcohol-laden beginnings to become an accomplished actress, it's certainly understandable that she would have a deep desire to save those she loved. Being unaware of her unconscious dedication, she would become bored with the good men who did not need to be saved and go back to those who did. Although her love was distorted, deep down it was the only love she knew and it came from the center of her heart.

At the crux of our desire for love is the need to be loved for who we are—especially those qualities that make us unique, particularly when they are different from our partner. At the same time, disregard or disrespect for individual differences is everywhere in our lives. Contempt, ridicule, scorn, scapegoating, you name it. We all do it and have it done to us. Without an awareness and appreciation for the value and richness of differences, the whole idea of who you are as an individual is meaningless.

When we disregard or disrespect what makes a child unique, what makes a child his or her own person, we teach the child that differences cannot be accepted. They must be eradicated and replaced with conformity. The child must become what's expected of her or him, must do as he or she is told, and deviation is met with punishment. *When we deny differences we foster intolerance.*

Nothing has a stronger influence psychologically ... on their children, than the unlived life of the parents.

—Carl Jung

The Impact of Our Upbringing

Although what we learn about love and intimacy can come from many sources, the truth is that our parents are our most profound role models. Their example gives us our first and deepest lessons at a time when we're too young to discriminate. We take in whatever they have to offer—for better or worse—and unconsciously build our future relationships with that as our blueprint.

A cautionary note: Even though this section deals with parental influence, the worst thing you could do is take what we're saying and use it to justify blaming your parents for the condition of your life. Whatever your parents were like, they passed on what they learned. What else could they have done? If you take a fair-minded look at their lives, you'll see their longings, confusions, disappointments and struggles caused by their own resistance to change. You'll probably see their neediness, sorrow and weariness when it came to intimacy and love. They, too, hungered for recognition, approval and emotional and spiritual well-being. Perhaps not as intensely as you do.

Perhaps even more. Like you, they were children who grew up absorbing their parents' marriage as a model. They too lived with blind allegiances to self-limiting, self-destructive beliefs.

Having said that, it's true that the inner lives of many, if not most, of our parents were underdeveloped. Many of them found purpose and meaning by having children. They expected that we would fulfill their lives in some way. Most of the time they never said anything. They didn't have to. We felt it. And we knew it. They couldn't help but teach it to us.

Probably more parents than our society chooses to admit are profoundly destructive to their children. It's not just the physical abuse. *Much more often it's psychological and spiritual humiliation that forces children to suppress themselves and surrender their zest, curiosity and love of life.* That's a shame and, in some cases, a crime. But the greatest danger, even under the worst of circumstances, is to stay fixated on "what they did to me." If you do you will keep yourself completely impotent, because what's done is done. The question becomes, what will you do now?

We're not suggesting a lack of sympathy for yourself or others whose family lives were spiritually damaging. What we are saying is that real care and concern for yourself will lead you toward truthfully seeing how it was for you. Then you can rely on your compassion to help you identify and overcome your allegiances and move forward into a life of your own. *If you remain stuck in blame, refusing to change, your feelings of compassion can only decay into self-pity because you have stripped those feelings of their power to inspire action.*

Further Allegiances

Some parents feel like they function best when their children are sick, troubled or in need of help. Their children learn to associate love and intimacy with being needy and powerless and, based on that, develop an allegiance to helplessness. As adults, they keep recreating the same kind of relationship because that's what they unconsciously understand love and intimacy to be.

Some parents require their children only to succeed. When their children are successful in any way, they are lavished with praise, recognition and applause. When they fail in any way, they are met with criticism and ridicule. As adults, they never dare to feel or show any vulnerability. They can't be needy, unsure or ever without an answer. They develop an allegiance to being tough, independent, outgoing, always on top of things. Yet, for all their successes, they are haunted by a sense of lack, an emptiness that can't be filled.

Children whose parents are absent can develop an allegiance to an imaginary but perfect parent—someone who would "take care of me." Then they are trapped, longing for a perfection that will never come.

Children whose parents keep telling them that no one "is ever good enough for my little angel," can spend their lives rejecting love because, in loyalty to their allegiance, no real person is ever allowed to measure up.

Narcissistic parents can be in competition with their children. The parents have to be the only ones who shine. Their children, caught in the allegiance of protecting their parents' supremacy, spend their lives desperate for recognition, but unable to push themselves out in any way that might upstage mom and/or dad.

It's critical to realize that many of us grow up believing to some degree that our parents' needs are more important than our own. We form allegiances based on our naive and loving desires to satisfy those needs. We spend our lives resisting change, striving to fulfill our heartfelt unconscious commitment—a commitment that was doomed from the start.

> *No man can cause more*
> *grief than one clinging blindly to*
> *the voices of his ancestors.*
>
> —William Faulkner

Leaving Home

"Leave thy mother and thy father and cleave one unto another" is biblical wisdom having to do with allegiances. It first appears in Genesis, the opening book of the Old Testament. It's repeated again in Matthew and Mark, the first two books of the New Testament. What was so important that it echoed across the entire span of the Bible? What did it direct a married couple to do?

Should they live in a different house from their parents? Hardly. In biblical times, the idea of having one's own home was far from the reach of most people. Should they have moved to another village or country? Again, unlikely. Travel was difficult and dangerous. Most people spent their entire lives within their own village. Yet, from the highest biblical authority, wives and husbands were instructed to leave their mothers and fathers and be faithful to one another. What was the purpose and power of the command to "leave and cleave"?

When we are children and too young to discriminate, we're like sponges, absorbing everything. We take in what we see, what we are told and, perhaps even more importantly, what we feel—the ever-present emotional and psychological family atmosphere that invisibly envelops us. We ingest and metabolize it. We learn what's expected of us and what we can expect from others and we form a sense of right and wrong, good and bad. Since this is the only environment available to help us define reality, we go into the world without any idea that it will be different than what we know and where we've come from.

If parents are conscious that their child has no choice but to absorb the family's relationship dynamics and emotional atmosphere, that awareness itself can help parents be more trustworthy guardians. They can learn to understand themselves and their own needs and the responsibility they have to raise their children with as little dysfunction as possible. However, because the study of infant and child psychology is less than 100 years old, most people still don't realize the powerful impact the early years have on a person's life. Consequently, few parents have had this awareness to guide them.

Furthermore, when parents' needs are more than a child can handle, more than a child can fulfill, the child is overwhelmed. His or her budding sense of self is invaded and overrun. The child's life is surrendered and held hostage by the needs of the parents. Not surprisingly, these children go to great lengths to protect the feelings and needs of their parents. They don't know how to do anything else. As long as their allegiance to their parents' ways remains hidden in the unconscious, they keep following its commands, and life just seems to turn out that way.

As adults, they haven't determined for themselves what is right for them to believe, and so they merely duplicate their parents' world. In that way, they've never left home. It doesn't matter where they live geographically. They've never left the psychological environment of their childhood. It doesn't even matter if their parents have passed away. The parents are kept alive and demanding in the adult's faithful psyche. Even if they marry and have families of their own, they are still dedicated to their unconscious allegiances, unable to emotionally leave home and cleave unto their mate. *These chronological adults are psychological children, possessed by their past, living in allegiance to the world of their parents.*

For example, if you feel you need your parents' approval for decisions about your relationship, you are in danger of being more "married" to mom and dad than you are to your spouse. If you feel you need to please them, take care of them even though they can do that for themselves, avoid challenging their opinions or hurting their feelings, give them grandchildren, or stay close by them, you haven't separated enough from their influence to follow your own mind and heart. This can create conflict within you over which family to be loyal to—your family of origin or the one you are making with your partner.

None of us escape the fact that who we are is to some degree the product of the unconscious programming we took in well before we even had the ability to know what we were doing. Your relationship success depends upon dissolving your allegiance to those beliefs that prevent you from growing into your own independence so that you can build a relationship that is unique to the joined needs and desires of you and your partner, one that expresses who you both are—together.

We can all be captured by the spell of our allegiances. It's important to have some frame of reference to help identify them and the resistances that flow from them. That way you can become more and more conscious so that who you are and the relationship you are creating can actually belong to *you*.

Six Patterns of Allegiance and Resistance

Understanding and identifying allegiance/resistance patterns is critical to the success of your relationship, so critical that we will describe, once again, what they are and how they work.

The pattern begins with an unconscious allegiance to a self-sabotaging belief that was learned, usually in childhood, and must still be upheld. Then we invent resistances to prevent our allegiance from being broken. We put up our most intense resistance when confronted by differences—anything that suggests change—because, in order to remain faithful to the unconscious, motivating belief, change must be forbidden.

Rarely does a person develop only one allegiance/resistance pattern. These patterns are usually a mix-and-match proposition. Pay attention to those you identify with because they can lead you to discover the unconscious beliefs you are in allegiance to and with that you can break your commitment and open yourself to actually getting what you want.

Moral indignation
is jealousy with a halo.

—H. G. Wells

Needing to Be Right/Power Struggle

The need to be right is responsible for many divorces. Your need to be right will generally overpower your need to love and be loved by attacking the differences that make up who your partner really is. To enforce your point of view and stay loyal to your allegiance, whatever that may be, you have to suppress, if not sacrifice, your capacity to be open and to learn. You cannot allow yourself to acknowledge anything that would make you wrong. Consequently, needing to be right is sure to suffocate intimacy and destroy any possibility of real partnership.

The power struggle is the active form of resistance to love that operates in tandem with the need to be right. You insist on having it your way and making your partner wrong. He or she may fight back, trying to make you wrong, or will cave in order to keep the peace. No matter how you rationalize it, a power struggle is nothing more than a battle for dominance and submission. One of you ends up in control and the other one gives in, or you both just keep battling. Either way, you keep love and intimacy at a safe distance.

Example: Mack and Robin came to us for divorce prevention. Both in their forties, married five years and each divorced once before, they argued about everything. Putting up the shelves was as much a contest as deciding where to go on their vacation. They each felt as though their identity was on the line. So, neither one of them could relent.

"If I give in," Mack objected, "I might as well become her." Robin felt the same fear. For them, giving in would be a catastrophic act of self-betrayal. When we asked why they stayed together, Robin shook her head. "It's crazy, isn't it. It's like we can't help ourselves."

Allegiance: Both Mack's and Robin's parents were spiteful, punishing and very domineering. As children they were terrified of them, and as adults they continued to kowtow to them. Mack and Robin both lived with an unconscious belief of being under assault and having to survive.

In their marriage, every difference of opinion was provocation for a fight over whose way was the right way. Even a simple request would be taken as a command and lead to defensiveness. Neither understood just how deeply they were being controlled by allegiances that were set in place long before they ever met.

Resistance: As long as Mack and Robin are unable to recognize that differences are an inevitable part of every relationship, as long as they are unconsciously committed to their power struggle, they can't help but re-create the same fear-driven "war zones" they grew up in. Like their parents, that's all they know. So it's a knee-jerk response for them to start accusing, which drives them further toward being vindictive, uncaring and self-righteous. And, of course, it's always the other person's fault.

Resolution: First of all, they had to realize just how deeply connected they were to one another and how distorted their connection was. They needed to know just how intimately they relied on one another to keep their allegiances in place. If either of them suddenly stopped being argumentative, the other would be bored or lost. They were like bookends, connected by their shared unconscious beliefs about being under assault and the power struggle relationship that follows.

Next, they had to admit that the most powerful threat resides, not in the other, but in themselves. They had to assume responsibility for their own habits of seeing everything as an attack. It was true that they both behaved badly. They were fully capable of insensitivity and bullying. But it was how they interpreted each other's behaviors that kept their allegiance/resistance patterns alive, always at each other, always their parents' loyal children.

What About You? Do you have to be right? Do you feel threatened by the differences between you and your partner? Do your childhood fears pressure you to be the one who attacks? Or are you the one who backs down? How can you and your partner trust yourselves enough to stand simply, yet solidly, in your own points of view without having to fight for dominance and control?

To become less quarrelsome and more loving, you and your partner must recognize and overcome your allegiance/resistance patterns. You will both have to do this because it's not a one-way street. If you both aren't committed to change, there's too much risk. But, if you want your lives to be different, you have to open up and talk about your fears and concerns. Let each other know how bad it is to feel like you always have to win to survive and how you sometimes can't stop what you're doing. Then you can set up ground rules for taking apart your power agendas and explore alternative ways to develop your relationship.

Here are a few points that can help. They may be difficult at first, but with practice they can be the basis for re-creating the way you live together.

- Understand that your need to be "right" stems from a lack of confidence and generosity. If you didn't feel under assault, if you were more secure, there would be less need to revert to the protection of being right. That kind of "being right" is very lonely because it has to wipe out all opposition.

- Agree that there will be no such a thing as a "wrong" feeling or point of view. There are only differences to be worked out—together. That's not to say that you abandon your desire for you or your partner to change in certain ways. That's part of being in a relationship. It means that you both remain aware of how the accusation of being wrong is a trigger and how it's to your mutual advantage to understand and appreciate your differences as the doorway to further intimacy and healing.

- When you disagree, keep in mind that all you're doing is expressing differences. It's in your disagreements that you're likely to feel assaulted and then want to slip back into needing to be right, needing to be the winner. *The bald truth about a power struggle is that the winner never wins, she or he just dominates—temporarily.*

If you will begin to identify and take apart your allegiance to being right, soon you will feel less and less like you might lose yourself when differences arise.

---

*The belief that there is only
one truth and that oneself is in possession
of it seems to me to be the deepest root
of all the evil that is in this world.*

—Max Born

Refusing to Change/Narrow-minded

If you consistently feel the need to control yourself and others, you are terrorized by differences and the changes they necessarily bring. Refusing to change is probably the second largest source of relationship failure and divorce.

Twenty-five-hundred years ago, Heraclitus, a Greek philosopher, said, "You cannot step twice into the same river; for fresh waters are ever flowing in upon you." *In other words, life is movement and change is its expression. Refuse change and you refuse life.* You cannot love and be loved fully without being open to the spontaneous, unpredictable ebb and flow that happens between two people. It's change that keeps a relationship fresh and alive.

We have all seen couples who sacrifice themselves to what they believe is the safety of never changing. The elderly couple having breakfast at the next table who have nothing to say to each other. Or the couple who've lived in the same house on the same block forever. The couples who are very proud of never fighting. Or those who insist on self-restraint as the highest virtue. The security they strive for destroys their differences and with that their individuality. In the end, what they have is nothing but numbing repetition.

Narrow-mindedness and rigidity are the resistances that generally follow from the need to refuse change. You have to toe the line and not look too far to the right or the left or else.

Example: Melinda and Don approached us after a seminar we gave on Renewing Passion. Both in their early 50s and both schoolteachers, they had long since lost interest in each other but didn't want a divorce for religious reasons. She never voiced her complaints about the relationship. "I was certain Don would be horrified if I did." He talked about only minor issues because, "A man keeps things to himself." The longer they were together, the more silent they became.

Allegiance: In 26 years of marriage, they had never challenged each other. Raised under the pressures of strict religious dogma, they were possessed by fear of rocking the boat. From their youngest days they had been warned about "the wages of sin" and "the fires of hell," so divorce was out of the question. The best thing they could do was to become invisible and endure.

Resistance: Melinda and Don sought refuge in rigidity. They lived very "correct" lives—dutiful and uncomplaining.

But to continue as a couple, they had to keep a pretty tight lid on what they felt and thought. They insisted on things being certain, so that they knew exactly where they were and how to be. Because their lives were so calculated, they couldn't ever color outside the lines. They were little more than artifacts of themselves, terrified that the seams might blow and "something horrible would happen." No wonder they lost interest in each other and their relationship.

Resolution: For all the couples we're using as examples, the first two steps of the resolution are the same. Melinda and Don had to realize how deeply connected they were and how their connection was distorted. In their case, that wasn't difficult. Once their children were grown and out of the house, Melinda and Don were forced to realize that they were tied to each other like two scared bunnies and they could deny it no longer. They had to admit that the most powerful fear arose from within. It wasn't Satan. It wasn't the fires of hell. It was their allegiance to the untested belief that something horrible would happen if they relaxed and opened up. Their fear crippled them.

Religious allegiances are generally the most powerful because they involve a belief in the Ultimate. But if Melinda and Don wanted to rekindle their interest and attraction, they had to risk confronting their fears. They had to risk revealing themselves to one another and take the chance of rocking the boat. As they did, they learned that what they thought was love was, in fact, obedience. In a sense they were still children unconsciously keeping to what they believed was the right and true path, yet never for a moment questioning the assumptions that motivated them. Once they realized how restricted they had been, they agreed to open up and explore new ways of being together including some boat rocking when necessary.

What About You? Are you afraid of change? Do you want things to stay the same? Do you need your partner to be exactly how you imagine she or he should be?

You won't get safety or security by forcing yourself or your partner into deliberately predetermined patterns. That kind of rigidity is like putting a mask on a skeleton. It's an appearance covering over something dead inside. Aliveness comes from the permission you give yourself to be who you are. And, *real security comes from being confident with the changes that your relationship brings you.*

If you want to overcome your refusal to change you'll have to consciously disrupt some of the patterns that are keeping your relationship frozen.

- Promise each other you'll do your best to admit to and point out those instances when fear of change is running your relationship. When you do you will have to confront your fears so be aware that you will also need patience, determination and, above all, compassion.

- Agree to take a risk together and do something that goes contrary to what you've always done. This need not be something big. Little changes are enough at first. You'll need to practice adjusting to change just to get used to it.

- As you disrupt your routine, pay attention to how you feel—about yourself and about your partner. You'll be getting acquainted with more of who you really are—a self who needs change to feel alive.

To fear change is to fear consciousness. To fear con-
sciousness is to fear knowing yourself. To fear knowing
yourself is to fear life.

You musn't force sex to do the work of
love or love to do the work of sex.

—Mary McCarthy

Skyrocket Sex/Denying the Mundane

Most of the sex we see and hear about has to do with
first time, wild-about-you kind of sex. It's about conquest—steamy, all-night-long, pursue-and-capture kind of
sex. It's lustful, sometimes dangerous and, when it works,
it's very, very hot. But conquest sex isn't about intimacy—
except for the nakedness. The two people usually haven't
known each other for very long, and they've given in to
what they call "chemistry." The truth is, for most people,
steamy, all-night-long sex is mostly based on avoiding intimacy rather than creating it.

The feeling of "chemistry" is real. What first attracts two
people can last their entire lives and be the source of how
they create their relationship. But, there is more to a relationship than just hormones. We all know too many people
who fooled themselves into believing that their love was
real solely on the basis of what they felt—the chemistry.

People who are caught up in the need for "sky-
rockets" usually find real life very boring. Devoted to
searching for the high, they live in resistance to real

emotional connections, dismissing them as too mundane. Generally, they're very dramatic, addicted to the intensity of the chase and proving themselves rather than what it takes to make a relationship last.

Example: Brooke, a 24-year-old model, and Aaron, 36 and a high-powered attorney, got together while he was still married to someone else. They were thrilled to have found each other. "We couldn't believe how good we were for each other," Aaron told us when they came for help. "Yes," Brooke followed enthusiastically, "It was almost like meeting yourself."

Before his divorce, they spent a lot of their time playing sex games and competing for who could be the most outrageously seductive. Brooke loved the idea of being available at any time and any place. Aaron prided himself on being wild, out of control and completely uninhibited. But once he divorced and they married, it wasn't but six months before sex became infrequent and routine. As Brooke put it, "We still like each other. A lot. It's just that we're wondering if we're as meant for each other as we thought."

Allegiance: Brooke and Aaron were both entangled in an allegiance to their oversexualized and emotionally self-protective approach to love. That was no problem in the beginning. But they wound up desperate to hang on to what they called their "virgin days." Trying to resurrect what they called "the thrill of being in love," they invented more intense sex games, "doing it in places where we could get caught." They included other partners, they bought sex toys, looking for anything that would give them better, longer and more orgasms. They were dedicated to playing and were desperate for the rush of excitement that made them feel alive.

Resistance: Brooke and Aaron unconsciously avoided emotional intimacy. They so dreaded the idea of being reduced to the mundane that they consciously refused to become vulnerable or feel anything that would make them emotionally dependent on each other. That's when the sex toys entered their repertoire and kept them distracted from their resistance to vulnerability.

Brooke was the only girl and the second oldest child in a family of eight brothers. She was expected to mother her younger siblings and was told repeatedly that it was a man's world. In her secret heart she was afraid of and resented men. Once she left home, however, she adopted the attitude that "I won't let them get the best of me." Wild, thrill-seeking sex with Aaron was a way for Brooke to feel "liberated."

As a child, Aaron's deepest identification was with his mother. Although he'd never been sexually attracted to men, as an adult he was haunted by the concern that he was homosexual. Skyrocket sex with Brooke made him feel powerful and eased his fears—for a time.

Resolution: Realizing they wanted to break through their obsession with competitive sex, they had to risk revealing their anxieties and self-doubt. Their marriage offered them the chance to open into the intimacy that was missing and grow with one another. When they began to reveal their insecurities they found an ease and depth of connection that allowed them to stop competing. In time they were able to create a powerful, rich and spiritually absorbing sexuality based on their willingness to stop game playing and risk being honest, open and truly intimate.

What About You? Is skyrocket sex all that interests you? Is having an orgasm the main reason you jump into bed with your partner? Does the idea of lying next to someone without making love sound stupid?

There are very few, if any, models for what sex is like once the chase is over. Once you know you have each other, then what? What's love-making like beyond conquest? Physically, emotionally, psychologically and spiritually fulfilling sex is built on mutual trust and the freedom to continually discover one another. Would you like to celebrate the wonder of being together with your partner, honoring the depth and breadth of your love? Here are a few suggestions you can apply immediately.

If you are single:

- Conquest sex is about proving something. That's what gives it a dramatic, driven edge. Make a decision that you will only accept sex that can add to, rather than detract from, intimacy. Decide that when you feel competitive, or feel your partner becoming sexually competitive, you will stop and, even if you don't know what to do next, you'll commit to at least not repeating what you've always done.

- Pay attention to what scares you when you refuse to have competitive sex. Could you be afraid that your only value is your hot, aggressive sexual availability? Are you afraid nobody will want you if you need to be slow and gentle and tender?

- Make a list of what you have to offer besides sex and read it before each date. That way, if someone is only interested in you sexually, you'll remember—"there's more to me than just sex."

If you are in a committed relationship:

• Stop having sex for two to six months. Learn to express your desire, care, interest and love for each other in as many other ways as you can. You will be surprised at the depths you can reach that are very romantic, even passionate and yet not sexual.

• Notice how you feel when you even think about being celibate, let alone actually doing it for a given period of time. How tied are you to sex as the major way you experience excitement together? What is it about sexual heat you need to keep your relationship intact?

• Share any feelings and thoughts you may have about shyness, awkwardness, shame and the like with each other so that when you begin making love again you will be more present and available to what might happen.

As long as you focus on skyrocket sex, your relationship can be only superficial. The threat of intimacy will be kept at a long and successful distance.

Having a boyfriend would make me whole, I thought. Hell, having a boyfriend would make me exist.

—Cynthia Heimel

The Other Person Will Make Me Whole/Seeking Perfection

Many people expect to be saved by the romantic idea of marriage as two halves joining together to make one whole. Well, that works in arithmetic. One-half cup of sugar plus one-half cup of sugar does, indeed, make one whole cup of sugar. But two people, particularly two insecure people, can't be blended together in the measuring cup of a relationship and expect to automatically come out one whole anything.

It doesn't matter how much they lose themselves sexually in one another, or how good they get at finishing each other's sentences. Even if they feel sure they're a part of one another's every breath, they're still separate, individual and unique. It takes two distinctly different people, not one mixed-up mush, to make a real relationship.

Seeking perfection is the resistance that flows from this commitment to being made whole by the other person. However, because perfection is impossible, nothing is ever quite right. No one is powerful enough. Life on this Earth leaves a lot to be desired.

Example: Alma and Marty attended one of our relationship trainings in Chicago. Both in their 20s, they'd been together a little less than a year and, they announced, "We're in a lot of trouble."

"I have to continually jump through Alma's hoops," Marty complained. "Otherwise, she's not happy." Alma shyly agreed.

When we asked Alma to describe the hoops, she hesitatingly said, "Well, it's about our lifestyle. I want him to make a certain amount of money . . . and, you know, he needs to pay attention to the way he dresses when we go out." She had a long list of what she called "proper behaviors that a man should just do."

Marty finished with, "And when I don't match up, she gets enraged and then sulks."

Allegiance: Although Alma never saw it this way, her demands were her way of expressing the need to be made whole. This particular pattern generally comes from a core belief that, "There's something missing. I'm somehow incomplete." Alma felt it as a vague sense of emptiness, a need to be filled up by someone or something from the outside. She always felt inadequate and inferior and wanted Marty to make everything okay.

Alma's mother had told her that, "Your being born wrecked my life. If you hadn't come along, things would be a hell of a lot better for me now. You're the one who did it." Alma was just a little girl and had nothing inside to stop her from believing what her mother said was true.

Resistance: Alma insisted that Marty provide the "right kind of life." She pushed him, coerced him and nagged at him. She rejected anything that was not in exact alignment with what she defined as appropriate. Alma couldn't see that she was not in relationship with Marty.

Rather, she was alone, wrapped in the shroud of her own terrors and the fantasies she invented to protect herself from them.

But Marty was not off the hook either. When we asked why he put up with Alma's demands, he told us he'd been a caretaker all his life. After a few questions, we found out his mother had been a hypochondriac who could never find "the right cure." Alma's inability to be satisfied was not only not unusual, it was unconsciously appealing. Maybe with her, he could finally succeed.

Resolution: They came to see that unless they changed, they were destined to fail each other. Marty had to stop trying to fulfill Alma's demands. They were impossible. The more he tried, the more he succeeded at failing, at never being enough.

Alma had to face the hole inside herself. She could not reach wholeness by denying the emptiness inside. By blaming Marty, she unknowingly rejected responsibility for her own dilemma and simply replaced one kind of pain with another—impotence with frustration.

In Alma's case, it was best that she went into therapy. By making the commitment to explore herself, she began to see that she was not to blame for her mother's unhappiness. In fact, there was nothing wrong with her. She had to break out of the prison of her allegiance and see the truth of who she was, both alone and with Marty.

What About You? Are you familiar with the need to be made whole? Do you expect or demand perfection?

No one else can ever compensate for the self-destructive ideas you hold. They are yours. But you are now overdue to set yourself free. You will have to face the negativity you grew up with. You will have to decide it's time to leave home. What you learned was false—no matter the pain it may cause you to betray your upbringing. When you are ready to take your life back, here are several suggestions.

- Challenge yourself to grow beyond your sense of emptiness. Even though that's what you learned as a child, you can change by taking responsibility for dissolving those old beliefs about yourself and, by taking step-by-step action, get what you want.

- Be suspicious of the fear that comes up when you imagine going out in the world to make a good life for yourself. *Remember, no one can give you what you are convinced you cannot have.* If you don't take charge of your own life, you're stuck in the desperate hope that someday something will just happen and the emptiness will be filled.

- Understand there is no such thing as a quick fix. You can't become whole waiting for some external miracle. But you can face your limitations and grow through the lessons inherent in real life love.

Your life is precious. Please don't sacrifice it waiting for someone else to make it better.

We cannot become saints
merely by trying to run away from
material things.

—Thomas Merton

Premature Spirituality/The Absence of Negativity

A lot of people are muddled in what we call "premature spirituality." They want to transcend this earthly plane before they ever get their feet on the ground. They believe that true love should be a state of never-ending ecstasy.

Some of them believe that when two people love one another, there is never any reason to get angry. They subscribe to the fantasy that "Love means never having to say you're sorry." If anger surfaces, that means love is gone. Others embrace the idea that love has to be felt every moment. If they can't feel love, that means love has ceased to exist. Still others will tell you that sexual desire is the barometer for love. If passion wanes, love is gone. The idea that love is only about nice or transcendent feelings is much more than just fantasy. It is denial and completely out of touch with reality. Premature spirituality seeks to bypass the very real daily demands and lessons of life and love on Earth.

The resistance that is part of this allegiance is the need to create distance from negativity or any feelings that would upset this self-styled, self-contained paradise.

Example: Liza attended one of our weekend trainings, after her break-up with Travis, wanting to learn "how to do it right." A likeable young woman, Liza told us her story.

Travis had taught meditation and yoga, fasted regularly and was a strict vegetarian. He dedicated his life to the search for blissful enlightenment. "Perfect love and transcendence are all that matter" was his daily mantra.

Liza had been his adoring and gifted student. She had been impressed by his "spiritual" lifestyle and his keen interest in her and how she lived. When they moved from teacher-student to live-in lovers, Travis soon grew upset and annoyed when she failed to follow his spiritual practices perfectly. He blamed her for "ruining their love" because she defended herself instead of apologizing when he accused her of being "too worldly" and "not in tune with the harmony and oneness of the universe." He told her he knew they could have "the greatest love ever" if only she would just practice his rules of perfect spirituality.

Allegiance: Travis was raised by parents who had "dropped out" in the '60s to live in a commune to protect themselves against being contaminated by modern culture. As a child he was exposed to philosophy, meditation, mysticism and stories about UFOs. As a teen-ager, he took part in rituals that used various drugs to achieve "transcendence." He was continually told that he was special, lucky to be raised in a spiritual manner, and that he should never forget it. When he was 18, he moved to the city to teach "right living."

Liza's father was a self-made multimillionaire. She had everything she wanted except for the attention of her parents. Her clothes, trips, servants and private schools all seemed silly to her. "I was constantly feeling starved for something more," she said, "but I didn't know what."

Resistance: Travis believed that, because he was special, he was completely entitled to expect "a perfect love" to come into his life. He thought he'd found that in Liza. When she failed his expectations, he felt no compunction about criticizing and even punishing her when she "defiled the laws of the universe." He believed he was right to impose his rules on Liza and then to berate her when she "brought negativity into the relationship." To hear him say it, he was just "trying to bring her to right thought and right action," so they could live in "perfect worship of God's radiance" together. He was utterly blind to his arrogance and his meanness and his unconscious denial of mundane humanity.

Liza had been entranced by his never-ending attention

and his desire for right living. "Some of it was negative, I know," she confessed. But it was attention nonetheless.

Resolution: Intense self-righteousness is almost impossible to penetrate, but Liza tried. Because she wanted to be loved by Travis, and he had taught her a lot, she tried to show him that his treatment of her undermined his own principles. He lacked compassion and was uncaring about her complaints, in opposition to the very qualities he espoused. She told him she was willing to work on their relationship if he was. When he refused to acknowledge any fault on his part, she knew she had to leave.

What About You? Does this passage strike home with you? Are you more bound to "spiritual perfection" than to your relationships here on Earth? Are you involved with someone like that?

What you are calling "spirituality" may be more of a refusal to acknowledge the dark, unpleasant side of life. Your mortality may be terrifying. Keeping life at a distance may allow you to feel above it all, but your "ascendence" is just a tightly constructed hiding place.

If you're wanting to change, you will first have to accept that you're alive in a flesh-and-blood body. *Love on Earth can only be for all that you are—imperfections, especially, included. Your pathway out of resistance is through the gateway marked Ordinary.*

- Examine your horror about being ordinary, especially in light of your spiritual beliefs. Does whatever you hold as sacred really condemn your life on Earth? Can a truly spiritual conviction disavow and disown what is all around you?

- If you embrace your full humanity, imperfections and all, you can develop an abiding empathy, a sense of connection with the vibrant experience of life. That will be your best teacher, guiding you on the journey from fear, distance and failure at love to compassion, communion and cocreated partnership.
- Pay attention and value the times you are wrong, mistaken or unkind. They must be accepted as an integral part of your humanity. Allow yourself to be humble and learn from life's difficult and sometimes dark side.

Your time here on Earth is an adventure through the challenges, joys and tragedies of life. To acknowledge only one half of all there is denies the fullness of life and love.

I have a big flaw in that I am
attracted to thin, tall, good-looking men
who must have one thing in common.
They must be lurking bastards.

—Edna O'Brien

Proving Men or Women Are No Damn Good/Vigilance and Revenge

This allegiance/resistance pattern is all about hurt and rage that's been squashed down and stuffed away. If you are spinning in this whirlwind, you probably have little awareness of the self-loathing and hatred of life that is at the source of your discontent.

One clear sign is the need to show how useless, pointless and horrible the other gender is. Men are condemned as liars and cheats. Women are lumped together as manipulative and clingy. Those committed to this point of view simmer with a fury that "the whole damned lot of them isn't worth squat." And in the middle of their fury, they're absolutely certain about their innocence and that they're the ones who've been victimized. What they are not being honest about is the origin and extent of their pain.

Constant vigilance followed by revenge is the resistance duo that covers an underlying sense of loss and insignificance. Even though they gloat when they "discover" some flaw or weakness in their partner, their pleasure is short-lived because their insignificance tells them, "It's the others who really have the power."

Example: Anita attended Judith's women's seminar in Michigan where Anita talked about her experience with Russ, a 38-year-old pharmaceutical salesman. She met Russ through a friend. He was late for their first date but had called to let her know. When they came back to her place, he asked to spend the night and she accepted.

The next morning she was on the phone telling a friend, "Even though sex was spectacular, this guy's a cretin. He never even apologized for being late." When her friend asked if she would go out with him again, Anita shot back, "Why not? Can you show me anybody better?"

Allegiance: Anita came from a military family that moved every couple of years. Her mother, an angry alcoholic, believed in strict discipline. Although her mother had achieved the rank of lieutenant-colonel, she ranted about the "hopeless sexism and incompetence" in the military. Anita's father didn't have the will to resist, so he just went along. From infancy on, Anita could never do anything to please her mother.

Russ had described his father as "uncontrollably aggressive." His father prided himself on not letting anything stand in his way. And he didn't. Not his wife. Not his only child. Not even himself. One afternoon he slumped over from a massive heart attack and was dead in minutes. Russ was 11.

Resistance: Anita's self-loathing and sense of failure was so painful she didn't dare admit it. Rather than try to heal the damage, she made everyone else feel it, especially men. She felt the need to avenge the wrongs she perceived had been done to women. Her world of illusion kept her safely away from the truth of how she had been abused by her mother.

Russ, on the other hand, seemed to welcome any challenge. He told Anita that her toughness was just a front, just another barrier to get through. In telling her story Anita realized that Russ behaved just like his father.

Resolution: They didn't last long together. Her fury and his unceasing competitiveness were too much. They resolved their entanglement by splitting up. Even so, they still confessed to being very attracted to one another. Anita described Russ as "just the kind of man I love to hate." Russ thrived on the challenge of "getting through to her." They savored the dangerous intimacy of adversaries.

What About You? Do you know these feelings? Are you committed to proving just how lousy the other gender is? Do you find yourself routinely putting down all women or all men?

Both genders are emotionally, psychologically and spiritually wounded. If you feel bitterness and contempt for the other gender it's more likely an expression of your own misplaced powerlessness, hurt and rage. What caused you to depend on blaming the other gender? Explore your past. You're sure to find the reason. If you identify with this pattern and want to change, consider the following.

- Understand that your condemning behavior is the way you have learned to protect yourself from the pain of growing up helpless. Rather than feel the impotence, you strive to make others feel it. If you truly want intimacy and connection, you'll have to find the compassion for yourself that you might give to a best friend who was in the same situation.

- Remember that your loyalty should be to developing yourself and not to the patterns you learned growing up. As we've said before, by staying loyal to your patterns, you remain a child. In this instance, that just reinforces your sense of helplessness.

- When you decide to change, understand that you're in for an intense and ultimately gratifying process. You will need compassion and respect for what you went through in your early life. That can lead you to the other side of your need for revenge, where you can discover the love and kindness that is now available.

The loss of self in childhood is a tragedy. Let yourself need and get support and care during your healing process. You may feel disloyal as you begin to change in ways that were forbidden, but this disloyalty is necessary to save your life.

We have delineated these six allegiance/resistance patterns to give you a feel for how such patterns work. There are numerous others:

- Needing to please parents/Self-denial
- My love will change her-him/Devotion to romance
- I need to be taken care of/Entitlement
- I'm responsible for everything/Avoidance of neediness
- I'm not responsible for anything/Aggressive fault-finding
- I have to prove my professional competence/Rejection of intimacy
- I'm nothing without a baby/Idealization of motherhood

Do you identify with any of these?

There are two ways, immediately available to you, of spotting unconscious allegiances.

Pay attention to any of your behaviors that are compulsive. For example, are you driven by sex? Do you overeat? Are you a workaholic? Must the dishes be washed immediately after they're used? Do you have to buy two of everything? Whatever it is you are compelled to do is the behavioral symptom of a deep-seated allegiance. You can use what you're doing to explore what you are forbidden to otherwise feel or have in your life. If you have sex on your mind all the time, you can't really be intimate. If the dishes must be washed, you may be forbidden to relax. If you must buy two of everything, you can't ever trust there will be enough for you.

Another way to identify allegiances is to notice your refusals. For example, if you are a man and you refuse to allow a woman to pay for a date. If you are a woman and you reject the idea of asking a man out. If you refuse to participate in housework. If you refuse to hire a babysitter so that you can have an intimate evening together. All these refusals are signals. If you listen to them, they can lead you right to a self-limiting belief you are terrified to acknowledge.

If we haven't listed something you are familiar with, what's the allegiance/resistance pattern that limits your life?

... and that night marked the
last time I ever romanticized women.
As much as I hated losing my fantasies of
shelter and refuge, I knew then that women
were simply human beings, open to all the
glory and cruelty that label implies.

—Asa Baber

Breaking Through Resistance

Once you decide to overcome your internal forbiddances, what can you expect from love, intimacy and relationship? The following guidelines will help you to recognize what it is like on the other side of resistance.

1. **Love takes place in reality.** Fantasy is a dead end. You both have to be willing to let go of your expectations of

"how it should be" so that you can relate to what's actually happening in your relationship.

2. **Your partner must be your primary love.** You have to root out as many of your unconscious allegiances as you can. As long as you are loyal to something compelling from your past, you are cheating on your relationship because part of you is devoted to feelings that take you away from it.

3. **Honesty and emotional openness are essential.** Indirect or deceptive behaviors such as game playing, one-upmanship, hiding your feelings, lying, ignoring your desires or manipulating are destructive to intimacy.

4. **You both must get your needs met.** Care and consideration for each other is the basis for real love. If you put up with or silently tolerate unwanted behaviors, you're choosing resentment instead of love. The spiritual reality of your relationship blossoms when you and your partner make both of your opinions, values, interests and desires important and valid.

5. **Your loving must be free to change.** As you open your heart to the ongoing, unpredictability of being together, you will feel the spirit of love pulsating through you, taking you into experiences you've never before imagined. No one changes overnight. But you can begin to open yourself to living and loving, moment by moment. There is no other way.

You have the creativity, imagination and energy to uproot false prophets. That's clear or you wouldn't be reading this book. You also have the strength to survive failure, loss and disappointment, and, in some cases, many times over. You have the courage to keep returning to the challenge and trying again. We can guarantee that when you redirect all your marvelous qualities toward the growth process required for real life love you will eventually succeed in breaking through your resistances.

The curious paradox is that
when I accept myself just as I am,
then I can change.

—Carl Rogers

Beyond Resistance

As you begin to make changes, you will experience unfamiliar, unpleasant and sometimes even painful feelings and thoughts. It's important for you to remember that when you developed your resistances, both to love and success, you were young and needed to protect yourself from fear and the unknown. At the time, those experiences would have been overwhelming. But now, as an adult, you have to muster the courage to open yourself more and more to your feelings and come more and more to life. Even though they may be painful, the recovery of your hidden feelings is essential to reclaiming your most intimate self and opening your heart to your truth.

If you deny the pain, you maintain a false and distorted connection with who it was that caused your pain in the first place. Your dedication to that relationship is at the heart of your resistance. Truthfully admitting how it was for you growing up will set you on the path of freedom and new life. When you understand and feel the many ways you've sacrificed yourself, you can lay your old life to rest and believe it when you say, "Never again."

Never again will you have to give yourself away and go without so that someone else will feel better. Never again will you have to put up with bad treatment because you feel you're not worth more. Never again will you have to believe that the feelings of resistance are the truth. They are not. They are the byproduct of allegiances you developed in order to cope with the unloving demands of your childhood.

Until now you may have been controlled by your allegiances and resistances. But that doesn't have to continue. While you may live with serious challenges to the love and intimacy you seek, we know from our own experience that your determination and desire can open you to a depth of body and soul that will make all of your efforts worth every moment. Life is for living and loving. It waits for you.

Chapter 6

CONSCIOUS CREATIVITY: TRANSFORMED BY THE DIFFERENCES

While I know myself as a
creation of God, I am also obliged to realize
and remember that everyone else and
everything else are also
God's creation.

—Maya Angelou

The more deeply you understand
other people, the more you will appreciate them,
the more reverent you will feel about them.
To touch the soul of another human
being is to walk on holy ground.

—Stephen R. Covey

Conscious Creativity is a step-by-step process to cultivate your emotional intelligence and spiritual vision so you can sustain and nurture a new and loving intimacy, especially at those times when the going gets tough. It's built upon one of the most extraordinary abilities you have, the power to change your mind.

- You *can* change how you think and perceive!
- You *can* change how you feel and respond!
- You *can* change how you experience your partner!
- You *can* change how you experience yourself!
  In fact, this power you have is so great that when you change your mind, you change who you are, and how you relate—forever.

We All Lack Relationship Training

So many people, perfectly decent people, trash their relationships, bruising and abusing one another in the process. Why? Because they don't know what else to do. Brought up on a diet of "happily ever after" and caught up in their allegiance/resistance patterns, they've never learned how to handle relationship difficulties with loving creativity.

- Did you receive training and preparation in school or anywhere to deal with the demands of an intimate partnership?
- What about communication training?
- Conflict resolution?
- Sexuality in a committed relationship?
- Were you helped to understand and respect the cultural and psychological pressures that are uniquely different for males and females?

We're certain that for all but a very few of you, the answer to these questions is no. Is it any wonder then that disappointment, accusation and distrust can be found in almost all intimate relationships? How could the divorce rate be anything but astronomical? Why wouldn't child custody battles be merciless? And all the while spousal and child abuse expose the darkest shadows of our inability to deal with one another's differences. Please cut yourself some slack. When it comes to love and intimacy, the street school of hard knocks is almost everyone's alma mater.

The Three C's

What are the key issues that can either make or break a relationship?

Our clients and workshop participants routinely identify the "Three C's" as the major obstacles that can handicap a relationship right from the start: Commitment, Communication and Conflict.

That's no surprise. In every kind of relationship—with intimates, friends, workplace colleagues, even neighbors—the Three C's are unavoidable. *Relationships are impossible without commitment. Intimacy can exist only through communication. Personal differences are sure to provoke conflict.*

Without preparation or training to deal with these very real, everyday issues, they too often lead to hurt feelings, frustration, rage and even violence. But there is good news. The Three C's can also inspire love's deepest and richest blessings.

---

*Man must evolve for all human
conflict a method which rejects revenge,
aggression and retaliation. The foundation
for such a method is love.*

—Martin Luther King Jr.

Conscious Creativity

Conscious Creativity is the key process for creating the new intimacy. It provides you the opportunity to significantly change your consciousness and enhance your capacity for relationship, especially in fundamental areas like the Three C's. Conscious Creativity can also prepare you to live in the growing global village where the challenge of personal and cultural differences confronts us all.

The Problem

You know how sometimes it seems almost impossible to understand or feel any connection to another person's experience? That's true for both joys and difficulties, isn't it? And it is even more of a problem when you're stuck in a conflict.

Rather than using conflict to learn about yourself and your partner, you suppress your own needs and wants in order to keep the peace. Or you overpower your partner in a desperate attempt to get your own way. Such maneuvers do little more than just further fuel the conflict.

Those are not your only choices. Through Conscious Creativity we'll show you how to change your mind and relate in a manner that supports your love, *especially during conflict.*

How Conscious Creativity Works

Conscious Creativity is a simple, deeply spiritual process that specifically helps you to expand your awareness so you can recognize and respect your partner's different point of view while *simultaneously* recognizing and respecting your own.

Most importantly, you and your partner will be able to understand and appreciate both sides of your conflicts so you can openly participate together in reaching mutually acceptable and beneficial resolutions that inspire growth and healing and in which neither of you suffers any loss.

What Are the Rewards?

Couples have told us time and again that when they use Conscious Creativity, they discover the magic inherent in their differences. They come to really know one another and learn to love each other for who they both actually are—even in relationships that were careening toward failure.

You are the architect of your personal experience.

—Shirley MacLaine

Your Point of View

Before we detail the process of Conscious Creativity, it's important for you to know and appreciate the impact of your point of view. The power of your point of view is awesome. Through it you define, interpret and "create" reality.

For example, you've probably known someone who always sees life through "rose-colored glasses." No matter the situation, Pollyanna only sees rainbows, never clouds. But, like it or not, there is a dark side to life. Imprisoned in naiveté or shadowed behind denial, Pollyanna is shocked and devastated by the demands and difficulties of real love.

On the other hand, there's no shortage of people who see only the dark side. These misanthropes are constantly on the lookout for evidence that life, love and people are never to be trusted. It's no surprise they blame their lack of joy and fulfillment on everyone but themselves.

In their respective relationships, Pollyanna wants nothing to do with the inevitable fights and disappointments, and the misanthrope despises and distrusts happiness. They are embedded in their polarized views of reality. Believing and behaving in the only ways they know, they have little choice but to unconsciously re-create the same experiences again and again. They typically refuse to believe that they themselves may be perpetuating at least some of what happens.

Pollyanna, innocent eyes wide open, protests, "I want the world to be nice, you know, friendly, and I try so hard. Then these bad things just happen. I don't understand."

The misanthrope rages, "Do you really think I want to live like this? Would anybody?" Yet, if you suggest that life can be different, she or he will lash back with, "Impossible. You're not dealing with reality."

Understanding the power of your point of view to frame and create your life is crucial. *When you open your perceptual lens to include differences—to include the fact that other people are not you and their point of view is just as important to them as yours is to you—your world changes radically. Then, and only then, can loving become an incredibly magical and intimate experience.*

Janet and Lyle

Janet and Lyle came to us for relationship training because they were painfully stuck. They loved each other and wanted the relationship to work, but they could not identify the problem in any way that made a difference. It was all the more puzzling because their first year together, after having met at a tennis tournament, had been so wonderful.

"Whenever I ask her to change," Lyle began, "to do something differently, she always becomes defensive. Or she cries and accuses me of not loving her. I don't know what to do."

"Is that true?" we asked.

Janet agreed it was. "But I can't help myself . . . and besides, it's not just my fault."

After reassuring her that, generally, both people are responsible for what happens between them, we asked her what she expected love to look like.

"Oh. I'm very clear about that!" She sat upright and spoke as though she were delivering a proclamation. "He'll adore me and think I'm the perfect woman for him."

"What happens if he doesn't?" we challenged cautiously. "What if that's not really what love is all about?"

Bewildered and a bit frustrated but sincere in her desire to solve the problem, she whispered, "Well . . . I don't know."

Janet then revealed that she had been raised by strict and physically abusive parents, and as an early teen she escaped into romance novels. Now she worked as a wedding videographer "still trying to capture the romance."

"It's not that I want Lyle to match the men in those stories. That would be silly. I know that's not real." She began to gently weep. "I guess I want him to make my world happy, to make a good family I can trust and be safe in. But when he's critical, it feels just like being back with my father."

At 35, Janet had been through a number of failed relationships and was willing to listen when we explained that her dream was unrealistic and that she would have to change her mind to succeed at love.

"To do so," we encouraged, "you have to consciously reshape your images of love and relationship so you can create the life you want from the real people you actually are. Some of it . . . not all . . . but some will probably even be the life you dreamed of."

We used Conscious Creativity to get to the heart of Janet and Lyle's difficulty. They were able to open their imaginations to re-vision their respective points of view and redefine themselves on the way to a mutually satisfying resolution—in which no one lost.

The test of a first-rate intelligence
is the ability to hold two opposed ideas in
the mind at the same time, and still
retain the ability to function.

—F. Scott Fitzgerald

The Nine Steps of Conscious Creativity

Step One: Define the Issue

Begin by truthfully expressing what is disturbing you in as much detail as possible. Sometimes you may not know anything more than simply, "I'm uncomfortable." If that's all you have available, then that's where you begin.

Often people try to present what's bothering them in a better light. They will couch it or try to be polite because they don't want to hurt anybody's feelings. Or they will employ any number of other strategies to avoid being direct about their feelings and needs. This just leads to confusion and more trouble and pain when the truth is finally revealed.

The key principle at the outset of this process is that you must begin where you are.

The overriding issue for Janet was that she felt certain Lyle was being critical of her. She was frightened of him and felt threatened. She accused him of not loving her. When he objected, saying it wasn't true, she shot back, "that's the way it feels to me." She took his protest as further criticism and became even more defensive.

The issue for Lyle, who was a 42-year-old, twice-divorced business manager, was that he had no frame of reference to truly appreciate Janet's fears because neither of his parents had been abusive. When she felt threatened, he would try to persuade her that her fears were unwarranted. As she resisted, his frustration grew and he would double his efforts.

They were both painfully stuck in feeling innocent. Each was certain of his or her own sincerity and sense of the truth. The result was that they unwittingly badgered and bulldozed one another in their attempts to deal with the tension between them.

To make this process more real for you, bring to mind a situation in your own relationship (or former relationship) that is similar to Janet and Lyle's conflict. Think about the details. The nuances. What frustrates you? What confuses or angers you? What have you tried to do that hasn't been successful? Picture your conflict as fully as you can. We'll be asking you to refer to your own situation as we develop each step of Conscious Creativity.

Step Two: Feel Your Feelings

Feeling your feelings is very important. Your feelings are a direct response to whatever's going on. They are part of the internal information you need to reliably express what's happening and to decide what to do about it. *If you deny or in some way distort your emotional responses, you strip away part of who you really are and fill the void with who you think you should be and what you believe is appropriate.* This response is regressive. Here's how.

In order to deny or distort what's actually going on with you, you must give up who you are to become who you think you should be. To do that, you not only have to make the judgment that who you really are is not good enough, not competent enough for the situation you are in. You must reject and abandon your authentic experience in the moment. Once you've shut the door to your authentic experience, you've shut the door to a new future because you've cut yourself off from discovering anything new. Then you are left only with your past experience to depend upon. So, you are compelled to repeat who and what you've already been because that's all you have available. Your attempts to resolve the conflict can only lead to more of the same.

There's yet another problem. If you opt for distortion, denial or any other form of regression, you can only create illusion, because you've abandoned who you actually are in preference for what can only then be fantasy. That cannot—we repeat—*cannot* lead to anything but disillusionment and, ultimately, depression and despair. Feelings must be felt and expressed as truthfully as possible in order to honor the truth of who you are. Otherwise they bottle up and become an emotional tumor standing in the way of resolution and intimacy.

Although as an adult Janet cried easily, as a child she vowed to hide her fears because they just incited her father to more abuse. Stuffing her fear and becoming silent had been the only effective way to protect herself from him. As a result, she was unaware of the deep terror that governed much of who she was and how she responded. But Lyle was not her father, so her survival strategy was not only no longer effective, it had become destructive to her and the relationship she wanted.

Lyle worried that Janet's inability to be open in their disagreements would, indeed, destroy their relationship. However, rather than admit the impotence he felt whenever he asked for change and was then accused of being unloving, he kept pressing for what he felt was right. In his own way, he was blind to the hurtful impact he was having on Janet.

Determined to give their relationship a fair chance, they made a commitment to courageously "speak the unspeakable," that is, to honestly express their feelings for the purpose of exploring and communicating what was actually going on.

The immediate result was a sense of relief, followed by a cautious freedom. They knew they had entered unfamiliar territory. To their great surprise, they learned that summoning up the courage to be honest paid off in both self- and mutual respect.

What about your own situation? When you allow yourself to feel your feelings, just how upset do you become? For the purpose of getting the most out of this chapter as you can, don't inhibit yourself. You need to acknowledge whatever you feel, your judgments, frustrations, contempt, anger, sense of futility, in order to have a clear view of the scope and depth of your response.

Remember, feelings can't be wrong. They are a direct response to what you perceive a situation to be. However, your perceptions can be wrong, and so feelings are never the whole story.

Step Three: Remember That You Care

For most of us it is difficult to hold two different emotions or ideas at one time. For example, while you are feeling intense anger for your partner, the affection you usually feel can get lost, even forgotten. If someone could call a time out in the middle of your argument and ask you about your wide range of feelings for your partner, you probably would be reminded of the love you feel.

The key here is to keep in mind that ongoing relationships are a mosaic, made up of many facets. There is more to your partner and your relationship than any one issue. Granted, you may be very upset, and in the moment flooded with your own response. But whatever the problem is, it does not encompass your entire relationship. If you lose sight of this, you will unconsciously isolate whatever issue you're in conflict over, give it undue weight and react as though it is the entirety of your being together. That's both false and dangerously confusing. Until the confusion is recognized and clarified, the conflict will be impossible to resolve.

In her heart, Janet knew Lyle was on her side. He'd given her more than enough proof that he was her friend and ally. So, even though she felt criticized, and her feelings were intense, she consciously worked to recall the truth of his love and commitment to her. "He's a good man," she admitted. "He's usually very good to me . . . and I have to remember that he's not my father."

In the midst of his frustration and sense of impotence, Lyle had to realize that Janet was a strong woman. She was a friend and ally he could ordinarily rely on. "When she's not up in arms and accusing me of not loving her, she's intelligent, mature, competent and open to me. I've got to trust that."

It's important to understand that neither one of them was ready to give up what they were feeling. Janet's resistance and Lyle's frustration remained strong. But they began to see a way out of being stuck, a way that expanded their awareness and opened their hearts to one another's differences.

Review your own experience. Are you able to remember how you care for your partner while you're feeling upset? Can you see that whatever the trouble, it doesn't define the whole of who you are together?

Step Four: Beware of Self-Sabotage

During the Conscious Creativity segment of our weekend trainings there are usually a couple of courageous people who admit that during a conflict they are not able to focus on anything but what they are feeling in the moment. To then expect themselves to remember how they ordinarily care for their partner not only seems impossible, but, if they could do it, it would diffuse the intensity of what they feel and they fear that they would then end up losing. Also, their hurts and resentments are so powerful they just can't imagine anything positive in their partner at that moment, even if they could bring themselves to remember it. Invariably, others will acknowledge they have had the same experience. Given the absence of relationship training and the expectation that women and men are supposed to somehow just know how to make relationships work, that's no surprise. But it leaves the couple stranded in their own distress and helplessness.

When your distress overrides your awareness of caring, you are unconsciously sabotaging yourself and your relationship.

If you can't remember that you care, you are dedicated to your certainty that your position is the only valid one. *If you insist that your way is the only right way, you have no choice but to see your partner as wrong and he or she must be brought into line.* If this applies to you, you're deeply caught in self-righteousness and a power struggle that can only be won or lost, and you must win. That's not resolution. That's dominance and control.

Your inability to remember is an indication that you're disconnected from your partner as well as your own creative potential for resolving this issue. You have closed yourself off into a self-centered, defensive isolation rather than staying open to cocreatively and coresponsibly arrive at a mutual resolution. This isolation is usually the result of feeling something like, "If I give in I'll die." So, you can't and you won't.

Unfortunately, from this frightened point of view:

1. You must lock out the one you love, not by merely being critical but by withdrawing into self-righteous condemnation;

2. You undermine your own self-respect, because to win you must behave in a way that is controlling and insensitive, the very behavior that upsets you when others do it;

3. You must stay rigid and fixed on your own point of view, denying cooperation and change, closing yourself off from any state of mind that is more alive and expansive;

4. You endanger your relationship by reducing your partner to this one behavior or event. Your indignation blinds you to his or her fullness as well as your own. In short, you're stuck within the walls of your own rigid self-centeredness.

Ironically, the more you choose to disconnect from your partner the weaker and more vulnerable you truly are. That's because you've made yourself unavailable to the process of exploration, responsibility and resolution. Your self-righteousness is the root of your undoing because it prevents you from finding creative ways to get what you want.

So, now, ask yourself, "Does it really benefit me to continue as I have? Do I really want to destroy this relationship?"

If you don't know or your answer is yes, pay attention. Either the issue in question is so seriously offensive that it's wise for you to leave, or your primary allegiance is to winning and not to your relationship.

If your answer is no, and you can open yourself even just a little to the prospect of negotiating new terms, you are ready to change your mind.

Step Five: Change Your Mind

Feelings are only part of the process. Relying strictly on feelings to guide you, as many people do, will usually just intensify the conflict, because it is not the job of feelings to consider alternatives. *Feelings are a response to what is happening now. Alternatives must be imagined. Feelings can't do that.*

The point in step 5 is to open yourself to the fact that any issue can be understood and interpreted in a variety of ways. As a result, your take on reality cannot be the only one. That's not to say that yours is wrong or should be abandoned. Quite the contrary. It is essential that you respect your response or you are in danger of giving yourself away. That benefits no one. However, because *freedom and creativity are about imagining and choosing alternatives,* it's critical to simultaneously open your conscious awareness to allow for other possibilities. Otherwise, you'll continue to stay in a rut and progressively dig the hole deeper and deeper with every conflict.

Janet and Lyle were stuck because they couldn't see any other options. She was convinced that he was being critical and treating her like a child. He was sure that her fears were unwarranted and destructive.

To change her mind, Janet focused on the possibility that Lyle's behavior might not be as critical as she thought. She had to consciously adopt this alternative approach, because, left to her feelings, she was convinced otherwise. It was necessary for her to think, to bring her reason to bear. When she was able to stop relying exclusively on her feelings as evidence of what he was doing, she was surprised that "Lyle began to sound different . . . not as condemning . . . not nearly as threatening." She was more able to hear him as voicing his own desires and needs for her to interact with him differently.

At first Janet was suspicious of her new response. It seemed so far from what she had been sure was an accurate understanding of Lyle's behavior. But rather than just slip back into old reactions, she decided to consciously test what was happening for her. Even though she sincerely wanted change, she didn't want to get fooled. So, before revealing to Lyle that she was experiencing him differently, more in line with how he described himself, she asked him if he felt like he had changed. "Sure, I've been angry and frustrated, no doubt. But I've always only intended to be supportive. I really care for you, for how you are."

"If you're truly not any different now from how you were when I felt you were just being critical, then I guess it has to be me who is seeing things differently," she concluded.

On the other hand, Lyle had to move off his conviction that Janet was unnecessarily frightened in order to allow the possibility that her fears were not only real but that he could be harsh and overwhelming. "But I feel so caring," he argued initially. "All I want is what's best for us."

Both of them had blind spots that limited their options. *And they both had to learn that what was best for their relationship was different from what each of them thought separately.*

Janet realized she was not threatened when her friends asked for her to change in their relationships. "That's when it struck me. . . . It just happens with Lyle. Either he's different from my friends, or I'm the one who is doing something." With that awareness she helped herself change her mind even more, seeing Lyle's half of the issue with more curiosity and less certainty.

Lyle checked himself to see what he knew about the experience of feeling criticized in the way Janet did. He remembered being intimidated by his high school football coach. Whatever Lyle did was wrong. It got to the point where he was afraid to go to practice and, once there, he made mistake after mistake after mistake.

"I used to tell myself there's no reason to be afraid, but I was scared anyway. I'd just freeze up and I couldn't hear. I mean I could with my ears but not with my mind." When Janet told him that was the same way she felt, Lyle's heart opened to her. He could see how he had been insensitive, "regardless of how caring I thought I was."

They both felt sadness and remorse for how they had been treating one another, and they promised they would actively find new ways to respond to their issues. They could see their whole experience in a new, more expansive, more hopeful light—and a more expansive and deeper intimacy opened to them.

Until they could imagine other possibilities, their conflict was locked in place. They had no choice. They were
unaware of being trapped in self-centered feelings and
beliefs based in the past that had little actual connection
to the real situation they shared.

*Changing your mind does not mean merely re-
arranging what you already believe. It means seeing
the issue differently, from a larger point of view than
was previously available.* It means you have to change,
to literally become someone different from who you
were. You must expand your point of view to explore the
issues more deeply and inclusively so you can become
more conscious and creative.

Regarding your own issue, what other interpretations
can you give to your and your partner's responses? What
do you know from within yourself about the truth of what
your partner is saying? Pay attention to any resistance you
may feel toward letting go of your dedicated stance.

Step Six: Take Personal Responsibility

Rarely, if ever, in an ongoing relationship does a difficulty arise that has not been contributed to by both partners. This fact is critical to the creative resolution of
differences and conflict. Neither party is off the hook.
Both are responsible. The question is, for what?

Intimate relationships weave together conscious and
unconscious elements to create patterns and dynamics—the character of each relationship. To illustrate this
we ask you to bring to mind several couples you know.
Notice how different the couples are, as couples. Every

relationship, every "couple-ing" will have its own identity expressed through the patterns that emerge from the "stuff" each partner brings.

When it came to feeling criticized, Janet had to acknowledge her hypersensitivity. She had to admit her response was less dependent upon what Lyle wanted or the way he asked but rather more on how she unconsciously confused Lyle with the painful ordeal she'd suffered with her father.

This did not exonerate Lyle for his participation in their problem. But he felt utterly impotent in the face of her terror, having to walk on eggshells every time he wanted something different. She came to realize that her impact on him was far more powerful and influential than she could have ever imagined.

Furthermore, she was trapped in being a child, unable to live in the reality of mature intimacy. Unless she got hold of her fear, any real relationship with a real man would be doomed. Janet was responsible for her half of the problem.

Lyle did not take Janet's fearful responses seriously. He unwittingly dismissed her fears, fully believing that, "If she could only see what I'm saying, she'd be a lot better off." His concern, though genuine, was only partial. He responded to her primarily on the basis of his perceptions and his interpretations. In short, he left her out in his attempts to include her.

Additionally, he discovered he was frightened of her fear. On the surface, he wanted to help her. Beneath the surface, he wanted her "to not be scared." It touched in him a sense of helplessness, a concern that he could never be enough of a man for her. Lyle was responsible for his half of the problem.

In what way or ways do you contribute to the situation that upsets you? Do your behaviors have their roots, even slightly, in your own family or relationship history—making you even more vulnerable to shame, anger, embarrassment or whatever it is you feel?

How can you tell if you are being governed by your past?

When something from your past that hasn't been resolved is touched, all the old woundedness comes rushing forward demanding attention. You feel impotent, both in yourself and in the relationship, because that's exactly how it was when you were a child and unable to be seen or heard, to be recognized for the truth of who you were. All of that pent-up emotional energy—deep frustration and rage and a sense that "nothing I can do will make a difference"—gets released into the present situation with your partner. If your response is out of proportion to your partner's attitude or behavior, that's a sure sign.

Step Seven: Remember Your Partner Is Not You

As obvious as it sounds, recognizing that your partner is not you is a critical step in the process. Many people cannot see beyond themselves. They don't truly recognize that other people are different from them. They translate everything and everyone in terms of how they view themselves and the world. This narrow-minded perspective is called "narcissism."

For example, bring to mind any of the times you were with another person and felt like you were not being seen or heard. Whatever you said was somehow dismissed or ignored. Only the other person's thoughts, ideas, beliefs, feelings were relevant. Sometimes the other person's narcissism was gross and repulsive. Other times it was subtle and hard to detect.

At its root, narcissism is the inability to recognize and acknowledge another as an other, as someone who is distinctly different and whole in his or her own right. Have you heard the joke, "Alright, I've said enough about me. Now, what do you think about me?"

In order to have fulfillment in relationship, to have real romance and long-lasting intimacy, you must internalize the fact that your partner is not you. As a result, you will have to pay attention. You can't take her or him for granted. You'll have to become deeply and sincerely curious about who she or he is and what he or she is thinking and feeling. When he or she is different from you, especially in a conflict, it is critical that you respect that difference in the same way you want your own distinctiveness respected.

In Janet and Lyle's relationship, she had a tendency to talk while they were watching television together. When they came to see us they described an instance when Lyle asked her, "Why do you do that?"

"Do what?"

"Talk while we're watching."

"Because I want to share what I'm feeling."

"But that breaks my connection with the movie."

"There you go, being critical again."

"I'm not. It's just that you're being inconsiderate."

This moment led to an argument that left them both filled with anger and resentment.

One afternoon, in our office, after they'd committed to the process of Conscious Creativity, we all focused on what we called their "TV fight." Janet kept in mind her hair trigger for criticism. Instead of reacting as though Lyle were being critical, she learned to ask him, "If you're not being critical, what are you doing?"

"I want you to know you're being inconsiderate of me."

"How?"

"When I get wrapped up in a story and you talk, I get pulled out of it. It's jarring."

"I don't understand. That's not how it is for me."

"I know. . . . But I'm not you. It's jarring for me and disruptive, and I don't like it."

Janet's response is narcissistic because she cannot appreciate any other way of reacting. Because she wouldn't be disrupted if Lyle spoke during a movie she was watching, she doesn't recognize and, therefore, doesn't value Lyle's point of view. She doesn't understand and so has no reason to stop. More importantly, because she sees no other possibility but her own, his calling her "inconsiderate" feels like a slap in the face.

"Okay, so where does that leave me?" Janet asked. "Do we just do it your way?"

Janet's question is right on point. If she's supposed to appreciate Lyle's experience, shouldn't he be asked to equally appreciate hers? Even though it was Janet's tendency to talk that sparked these particular confrontations, it was also Lyle's tendency to feel jarred that contributed to the conflict. If Lyle truly wanted to be taken seriously, wouldn't it be in his own best interest to take Janet's different experience seriously? Otherwise he's just as narcissistic.

"What's your need to talk all about?" Lyle opened. "Do you just need to comment on what's happening?"

"No. I want to feel connected. I want to know what's going on with you."

"What do you mean?"

"Well, when we watch a movie in silence I feel a distance between us and I don't like it. We feel apart. You don't feel that, do you?"

"No. I don't."

Janet and Lyle are different. Very different. What are they to do?

Learning to internalize and understand that your partner is not you happens through your curiosity and inquiry in each situation. Your resolutions will be respectful of your differences only when you both find ways to empathize with the other's point of view.

In her own life, Janet understood the experience of feeling jarred. Her father was a master at taking her off guard. She remembered how invaded she had felt. "That's what Lyle's feeling," she realized. "That feels horrible."

Lyle certainly had moments when he felt distant from Janet and wanted her close. When that happened he would hug her. Recalling his similar need, he could feel what she felt when she started talking. After all, he never really considered what she was doing when he wanted a hug. "Why would she resist. We all want hugs." But that was irrelevant. "I've interrupted her in the same way and for the same reason. I know what she's doing."

They both found a way from within their own experience to extend out beyond their self-centered isolation to appreciate the other's point of view. They were not merely coping with one another, that is, tolerating their differences and staying out of each other's way. They were learning how to transcend a merely intellectual understanding to include an emotional identification with the other's experience without losing their own. That was the ground upon which they could reach a mutual resolution, one in which neither felt any loss and both felt a deeper and richer intimacy.

How well can you appreciate your partner's experience? How open are you to acknowledging that your partner's reality is different and just as important to her or him as yours is to you?

Step Eight: Be Consciously Creative

Now you begin to look for a mutually respectful and satisfactory resolution to your differences. Here, you can have the creative pleasure of exploring possibilities that will get both of you what you want.

As the first suggestion, Lyle offered that when they watched movies together they could cuddle or hold hands or Janet could drape her legs over his. When he offered these suggestions, his intent was not just to solve the problem, but to let Janet know that he acknowledged her reality, that he respected and valued her need to feel connected.

She was delighted and said that she wouldn't talk until the commercial breaks or perhaps after the movie was over. In the same way, she wasn't just solving the problem, but was accepting Lyle's experience and treating it with the same care that she wanted for her own concerns.

The simplest gesture can be a doorway to discovering deeper intimacy at the heart of your relationship.

Ultimately, it didn't matter if they held hands or kept silent. Those were just possibilities. Through their caring intimacy they were opened to any number of solutions that recognized and respected them both. Instead of an either/or outcome, they were on the track to finding new options that could be valuable and satisfying for both of them.

Hold the other in your consciousness as you would want to be held. Appreciate and value the other's experience in the ways that it is different from yours. Conscious Creativity asks you to become more conscious, to truly know that your partner is not you, and, indeed, to become curious and flexible and interested in differences. When you do you will discover an unexpected boon— you'll become more alive to yourself as well as to those you love.

Step Nine: Seek Both/And Solutions

As you look for new approaches, remember that you must neither abandon nor dismiss your own upset feelings nor expect your partner to just give in. As you reach resolution, a deep benefit emerges from the process. Since you are two different people, and your being together is important, your mutual resolutions will reveal a both/and quality. Not either/or. That's a win/lose result in which neither participant is ultimately satisfied. Nor are we suggesting a win/win resolution.

Conscious Creativity has nothing to do with winning.

It is a process of respect and intimacy, growth and emergence. When you are consciously creative, you are both acknowledged and satisfied. Yet this process goes even further. You both meet the issue directly and enter a field of possibilities that arises out of your deepening intimacy, a field that would not otherwise be available. Your resolutions satisfy both of your grievances as each of you grows into new awareness. Your determination to live together in a commitment to both/and resolutions continually broadens your field of discovery, fun and joy.

The Promise

When you use Conscious Creativity to address any disagreement or difficulty, you can be assured that you will reap the emotional and spiritual benefits of this balanced, inclusive approach. You will neither betray your own needs or those of your partner. You will expand in consciousness by learning more about emotional responses to a situation that is different from your own. You will enlist and direct your compassion and creativity to arrive at a resolution—one in which no one loses. In fact, through the process you both are made more whole.

To become adept at Conscious Creativity requires practice, taking it step by step each time, to learn the process by heart. But you will know that approaching any issue, especially a conflict, using this method will be an illuminating, healing and spiritually enriching experience.

That is the promise of Conscious Creativity.

Chapter 7

SACRED TRUST:
SECURE IN THE
DIFFERENCES

Without trust you'll never be free
to love and be loved.

—Pat Feinman

Trust enables you to put
your deepest feelings and fears in the
palm of your partner's hand, knowing
they will be handled with care.

—Carl S. Avery

*T*rust is like a vine that wraps itself around and through every corner of a relationship. At first it is delicate, easily bruised or wounded. But over time it becomes strong and hearty and can withstand even the fiercest storms. Trust holds a relationship together.

But trust is not automatic. In a world where misgivings and doubt, suspicion and hesitation are common, trust must be cultivated and nourished. It must be strengthened through patience and sincerity and tested through direct and honest communication.

When two people become conscious of their trust they can rely upon it to ensure their safety when they move out and explore the unknown or when they reveal the tenderest parts of themselves. When they realize how powerful their trust is, they can celebrate it, hallowing the weave, the intimate connection they have built between them.

Vows Without Trust

Every day, in countless churches, synagogues, judges' chambers and Las Vegas chapels, men and women get married. They speak their vows, exchange rings, pledge their fidelity and enter into the legal commitment of matrimony.

Of all the promises these couples make, the one we're most familiar with is "to love and to cherish, in sickness and in health, from this day forward." They also pledge "to love, to comfort and to keep until death do us part." When the words are spoken, "By the authority vested in me, I now pronounce you husband and wife," the ritual is finished.

The wedding is an ancient rite, standing at the center of community life. It has assured stable families and identifiable kinship ties. Marriage vows are so sacred many ceremonies include the warning, "What God hath brought together let no man put asunder."

But the one word conspicuously absent is "trust." While you commonly hear the words love, honor, cherish, promise, respect, provide, protect and keep, trust is curiously missing. Yet without trust how can any of us reveal our intimate self? How can we ever feel comfortable with our differences? Without trust, what does intimacy mean?

If you are choosing to be with me
in a committed partnership, I implicitly trust
that it's me you want to be with.

—John Amodeo

What Is Trust?

Trust is defined as "having confidence in and assured reliance on the honesty, reliability and integrity of another." In other words, trust lets you feel secure and confident in your dealings with someone. But how do you get to trust and be trusted?

For starters, a simple and inevitable truth of all relationships is that we're always teaching each other what to expect and how to behave. We make clear what we accept and what we refuse to put up with—and we do that right from the first moment. That's what creates the shape and feel of a relationship and keeps it in place. If the person you are with changed personalities every week, you couldn't be confident enough to build trust. Without a certain stability trust is impossible.

Trust can never be immediate, no matter what you feel when you first meet someone. Real trust takes time. It needs to be tested. You have to open yourself, show your vulnerability and pay attention to how the other person responds. Even after marriage, trust needs to be tested, because many people think once they're married they can take each other for granted.

Don't Be Victimized by Terminal "Nice"

"You're not supposed to test someone. It's not nice."

"You should just trust people until you learn otherwise."

"Trust is something that you don't think about. You'll know it if it's there."

Many of us grow up accepting some version of these naive beliefs. But a solid, fulfilling and trustworthy relationship cannot be built on "nice." You have to be involved, emotionally connected and spiritually available. You have to show up, whether you're loving or angry, affectionate or wary, exposed and yielding or self-protected, ready to stand up for what you want. You have to confront your partner when she or he is out of line and insist upon respectful, caring treatment.

When Judith was in graduate school one of her professors told his class, "Nice guys leave a wake of destruction in their path." He explained that when we're intent on being nice, we avoid conflicts, and the problems only get worse. An attachment to nice will cloud your ability to see when someone is mistreating you or even being cruel and abusive.

Love means that I am
confident enough about the other that
I can trust him with my gift.

—Carol Travis

Positive Trust

Most people want their relationships to support them and help them grow. That takes what we call "positive trust." Positive trust develops whenever two people share a commitment to the following experiences:

- An acceptance of life's complexity and challenges;
- An understanding of relationship as a cocreated process;
- Respect and value for the differences between the genders;
- Feeling alive through the emotional risk-taking of intimacy;
- Concern for the well-being of both you and your partner;

- Responsibility for the growth and healing inherent in differences;

- A willingness to be accountable for your dark side.

Positive trust grows as you deepen your commitment to living the full scope of who you are—taking responsibility for your desires and disappointments. By communicating your needs and your appreciation, you take care of yourself as an individual and each other as a couple.

Later in this chapter we'll also address what we call "negative trust."

Whether you develop positive or negative trust depends on what you want and the intentions and expectations you bring to your relationship.

Ty and Ramona

Responding to our web page, Ty and Ramona told us their story.

When Ty began dating, his favorite uncle took him aside to teach him a couple of things. "What'cha gotta know about women is, if you wanna keep 'em in line, you gotta keep 'em guessing." Ty's uncle proudly told everyone, "I'm the only one ever talked with the kid about sex, dating, all that stuff." Ty was grateful and a good student.

His uncle's strategy worked pretty well until Ty was 30. He met Ramona at an awards banquet for their company where he was being honored for his work in research and development. She worked in the CEO's office as part of the strategic planning team. Ramona was different from any other woman he'd ever known. He loved being with her, making her laugh, dancing to the car radio in her garage, taking her to rock concerts she'd missed as a teen. Ramona loved being with him as well, but she never hesitated to challenge him when he said he'd call and didn't, when he showed up late for a date, or the time in the beginning when he went home right after they had enjoyed delicious sex. She also didn't chase after him as other women had.

Ty was becoming serious about her, but at the same time he struggled with a fear that had never been part of his other relationships. After a few months of dating, he was stunned when Ramona respectfully told him that he needed to grow up, and if he didn't "get it together" their relationship was over. She wasn't taken in by Ty's shenanigans and trusted herself to call it the way she saw it.

No one had ever confronted Ty's "keep 'em dangling" bad-boy behavior. He found himself admiring her for not putting up with it. This was a strong woman, a woman he could love.

What did Ramona see in Ty? She enjoyed his charm and high energy, his fun-loving style. She'd grown up with a strict, straight-laced father and was usually drawn to predictably serious men. She invariably left them because she felt oppressed and starved for fun. With Ty she felt energized and vital but "scared to death of his antics."

Being on new ground, they slowly and cautiously talked about what was happening. Ty knew he would have to come clean. He told her about his uncle. Then he screwed up his courage and told Ramona, "I've never felt this way for any other woman. I'm willing to change if we can make this work. What do you think?"

It was Ramona's turn to be surprised. Instead of delight, she was overwhelmed by Ty's intensity and scared of the importance she had in his life. She'd never known this kind of passion and intimacy before, never felt such a mix of fear and hope. She told him so and also that she was not sure he would actually be able to change. "But I have to confess, you're not the only one who has to change."

Their trust grew gradually. Ty did what he said he'd do. He stopped game playing. Gradually, Ramona opened herself to Ty's emotional intensity.

The growth of their love was also gradual. It was an adventure into the unknown as they continued to bring their baggage out into the open and discover their increasing desire and respect for one another.

Ty and Ramona learned what they had to do, as the unique couple they were, to express and develop their love and build their relationship. Walking shoulder to shoulder they met the future with resolve and courage, caring for themselves and one another, creating a spiritually gratifying positive trust.

Relationships are like a dance,
with visible energy racing back and forth
between the partners. Some relationships
are the slow, dark dance of death.

—Colette Dowling

Negative Trust

Although it may sound like an oxymoron, "negative trust" is just as real.

The television sitcom, *Married with Children,* epitomizes negative trust. Husband and wife, Al and Peg Bundy, loathe each other. He rejects sex. She rejects work. Their life is built around trading insults and sexual put-downs. Their children, Kelly and Bud, do likewise, not knowing any other way to relate.

Married with Children is extremely popular because the Bundys' behavior is so very familiar. Millions of fans from more than 60 countries love and identify with the Bundys. They've been described as a family "in hate" with each other. The Bundys have given up on life and themselves. They don't believe they deserve better treatment, or else they couldn't put up with what they go through. Seeing nothing but disappointment with each other and their relationship, Al and Peg mercilessly compare one another to other people or to their fantasies. They've taught each other that it's okay to be disrespectful and mean. Through it all they can trust each other, wholeheartedly and forever. They can count on one another's barbs, backbiting and disgust with certainty. They can depend on the predictability of being belittled. The Bundys are a model of negative trust.

Scott and His Mother

We met Scott, a 59-year-old bookkeeper, at a men's conference in Texas. He came to our workshop on The Healing Power of Relationship. Afterwards he told us his story.

Scott's mother went beyond being merely seductive with him. He became her sexual plaything. When he was a child, she would kiss and fondle him, occasionally making him stay home from school to "keep her company" and play sex games. As is typical in such cases, she warned him never to reveal "their little secret."

To make certain he would be silent, she teased him, telling him that it was his desire for her that was "the original sin." She convinced him that there was something wrong with him, but that she forgave him for it.

As he grew older, the sex games stopped, but Scott could never quite articulate his constant feeling of being cheated and abused. He was never without it. While he also lived with a chronic, subdued rage, he could not ever allow himself to direct it at his mother. She was out of bounds. According to Scott, "She did the best she could." So he turned his rage against "the church and their god-damned 'original sin.'"

Having never married, he continued to live with his mother, even though they frequently fought about her attempts to control him. When he tried to date, she flew into rages or feigned illness to try and stop him.

Scott felt driven to prove his sexuality, but he would always return home feeling inadequate and dirty after being with those "disgusting" women who would have him. Then his mother scolded him for "being just another goddamn man."

Scott and his mother shared a mutual fear of and contempt for the world. "It's a den of sinners," she'd howl.

They stayed together until she died. Bonded in an orbit of rage and revulsion, they were as deeply entwined as any couple. They colluded to perpetuate their stunted shadow world, defining their relationship in ways that continually diminished them. They could always count on each other to produce the emotional crises, the bitterness and spiritual violence that was their way of feeling alive. Theirs was a negative trust—dark and deadly—but trust nonetheless.

After his mother's death, Scott's emptiness was overwhelming. He didn't know where to turn. He would take himself to the library and spend afternoons thumbing through magazines or just sitting silently. That's where he met Marnie. She felt for his recent loss and was very comforting. She invited him to her home for dinner, took him for walks along the beach. He told her nothing about his mother.

When he permitted himself to realize he was enjoying Marnie's company, he broke it off. Being with her was too much for him. Not because she was so bad. Hardly. What he couldn't stand was the care he saw in her eyes because it forced him to see that he had lived a life of lies. Rather than allow himself to take that in, to acknowledge the distorted web he and his mother had woven, he turned on Marnie, hating her for her compassion, disgusted by her "weaknesses." He convinced himself that she was manipulative and needy and that he barely escaped being seduced by her deceits.

Not long after that he met Sally, a coffee shop waitress. From their first date, Sally wanted more than he could deliver. She wanted her three-year-old daughter to be included in their nights out. She berated him when he became impotent. She wanted him to promise that he wouldn't see any other women.

Scott couldn't turn away from Sally. Her demands brought him home to a familiar relationship. He fought her for what felt like his life, but he knew he would never leave her. Her "love" was safe, something he could count on. Theirs was a relationship founded on negative trust.

Negative trust develops whenever two people share a commitment to the following experiences:

- Bitter dissatisfaction with life;
- Distrust of love;
- Hatred and fear of the other gender;
- Feeling alive through fighting or competition;
- The need to win;
- Martyrdom and suffering;
- Self-hatred projected onto the other person.

It's no surprise that much of what young women and men learn about dating and about one another serves to teach and reinforce many of the patterns of negative trust. Sadly, too many people have no idea that there can be anything better.

He is playing the kind of man
that she thinks the kind of woman she is
playing ought to admire. She is playing the
kind of woman that he thinks the kind
of man he is playing ought to desire.

—Theodore and Betty Roszak

Games We Are Taught

Surely you've heard the phrase, "It's the '90s." It usually means that we're advanced, aware, much more conscious, at the leading edge. Of course we are, in some ways. However, when it comes to interpersonal skills, we're woefully lagging. We need to teach our youngsters that the skills of paying conscious attention to how they're treated and expressing what they really feel are essential to their well-being and the success of their intimate relationships. Instead, most girls and boys are still being taught the same destructive ideas that have been passed down for years.

Never mind 30 years of women's liberation, mothers still teach their daughters the rules for getting a Prince Charming. The language may be different but the messages remain the same.

- Play hard to get—men love a challenge.
- Don't reveal too much about yourself—men love a mystery.
- Never beat a man in sports or cards—men need to feel like the winner.
- Build up a man's ego—especially in public.
- Don't be so outspoken—men don't like opinionated women.

Perhaps most important to Prince Charming hunters, mothers also include the clincher:

- It's just as easy to love a rich man.

Women are still being taught that they're not desirable as they are. If they want a man they have to mold themselves into some preconceived fabrication of who they are and what they're supposed to do. At the same time, the men who are attracted to them have to be blind not to see through their charade.

On the male side, fathers and older brothers pass on their "words of wisdom" to teenage young men who've got images of Lady Perfect dancing in their heads.

- Get it while the gettin' is easy—once you're married it's the same-old, same-old.
- Take charge—a woman wants to feel a man can protect her.
- Don't let a woman boss you around—you gotta let her know who's wearin' the pants.
- It's all about money—that's what they're really after.
- Take her lots of little gifts—she'll think you're in love and give you anything you want.

Perhaps most important to Lady Perfect chasers, fathers also include the advice:

- Never show a woman your real feelings, she'll eat you alive.

Men aren't desirable as they are. If they want a woman, they have to deform themselves in accordance with silly clichés that strip them of any authenticity. At the same time, the women who are attracted to them have to be blind not to see through their adolescent nonsense. With that kind of preparation, two people are expected to find each other and live happily ever after.

Love is very powerful. Through love we can be healed. We can even be reborn. But not if we're pretending. Then love has nothing to hold on to.

Carl and Jessica

Have you ever known someone who wanted to be loved so badly that she or he overlooked things in their dates or mates that were clearly untrustworthy—just so they could tell themselves, "I'm in love," or "I'm getting married"? After he attended one of our lectures, Carl, a 24-year-old security guard for a film studio, told us his story.

He met Jessica at church. She was gorgeous, easygoing, "a dream come true." When he asked her out and she accepted, he secretly hoped, "Maybe she's the one."

The first time he went to pick her up, she was 40 minutes late. "I had to run over to my mother's," she explained. "That's okay," Carl assured her, "things happen."

He had planned to take her for pizza. When they got in the car, Jessica said she wanted to try a new French restaurant her friends were raving about. Carl hadn't intended to spend that kind of money. "But, I admired how she took charge and was so sure of herself."

During the ride and through most of dinner, Jessica talked about her friends, her work and her excitement about the restaurant. Carl kept quiet, not wanting to seem intrusive or controlling. He noticed that she finished three drinks to his one "but she's probably just nervous, trying to get relaxed." After all, since she was a regular at church, "she couldn't be an alcoholic."

After he dropped her off, his mind danced with dreams of making love with her. His imagination skipped ahead to their wedding day and on to the births of several children. Oh, it was so sweet to be in love!

They dated for three months, never sharing the costs, never staying at home. She expected to be taken out in style. They had sex, but Carl was never allowed to spend the night. She said she didn't want things to go too fast.

Because he wanted her to like him, he was careful not to want anything different. He felt they were meant for each other.

When Jessica started dating another man from the church—without breaking up with Carl or even telling him—he was devastated. "If she could be so cruel," he sighed, "after all the love I've given her ... I don't know if it's worth it to ever love again."

Pay attention whenever the person you're with is unkind, thoughtless or self-centered. Those are danger signals. Respect whatever you feel in response, whether it's doubt, fear, distress or anger. Your feelings are warning you of trouble. And then speak up. *Real love has a chance to develop only when you speak up and discover the real substance of the person you're with.*

A Question of Trust

Whether you are single or married, use the following questions to determine if your relationship is based on positive or negative trust. The questions apply to both genders. Trust is an equal opportunity opportunity.

Does he do what he says he's going to do? Or are promises unkept, dates broken, "facts" changed?

When she offers criticism, does she do it with care and affection for you? Or is her "helpful criticism" delivered with contempt or sarcasm?

Does he consistently show his regard for you? Or do his actions run the gamut from high-intensity romantic performances like sweeping you off for a getaway weekend, to self-indulgent escapades such as getting roaring drunk at your office Christmas party?

When you reveal your imperfections and limitations—your fears, physical illness, dysfunctional family background, disappointment at work and the like—does she make an effort to understand you? Does she feel compassion? Or do you end up being reprimanded, ignored, neglected or demeaned?

When disagreements or fights arise, can you still feel that he cares for you? Or is he simply determined to win?

When you express dissatisfaction with something she does, are you taken seriously? Or are you dismissed—told "it's all your problem"?

Positive and negative trust are very different. Here's how you can distinguish between them.

- Positive trust is expansive. Negative trust is restrictive.
- Positive trust is openhearted and generous. Negative trust is self-protective and punitive.
- Positive trust embraces differences. Negative trust abhors them.
- Positive trust is largely conscious. Negative trust is largely unconscious.
- Positive trust grows in depth, appreciation, cherishment and sacredness. Negative trust is stagnant, repetitive, emotionally miserly and deeply forbidding.

Positive trust is powerful and inclusive. As it grows, it can evolve into sacred trust.

*The gift of a relationship is
not only the intimacy between persons,
but ... the invitation to enter more
deeply into its mysteries.*

—Thomas Moore

The Elements of Sacred Trust

Sacred trust calls you beyond the everyday cooperation and consideration of positive trust. It's available when you're willing to follow your intuition into the unknown, into the untried. As you learn to respect and cherish *the magic of differences,* sacred trust opens right there in front of you. It is yours to develop and evolve. You and your partner discover it as you develop a deepening capacity for the four basic elements of positive trust:

- Revealing your neediness and vulnerability;
- Expressing your desires;
- Opening to receive love;
- Surrendering to a full commitment.

Through practice, you can create a consciously intimate relationship based on a caring connection that empowers the spiritual fulfillment of you both.

*You actually end up getting your
fondest dreams by going through the
portal of your greatest fear.*

—Patricia Sun

Revealing Neediness and Vulnerability

The intimacy of sacred trust flows from your willingness and commitment to bring yourself fully to your relationship. That means sharing your excitement and wonder, your ambitions and determination, the "for better" side of your relationship. But that's usually the easier half of it. You will also need to reveal your private, secret needs and vulnerabilities, your fears and inadequacies, what most of us would probably think of as the "for worse" side.

Every one of us has a *shadow side*. It's where we hide anything we consider ineffectual, offensive or even "too much," "too bright" or "too talented." We sentence to our shadow the wounds that occur when we not only feel but believe we are unwanted, unwelcome, inadequate, stupid, not attractive enough or whatever. *It is precisely those vulnerable aspects of us that so desperately need to be recognized and loved, recovered and healed.*

Yet, how often do you judge your or your partner's tender feelings as "weak," "pathetic," "childish," "desperate"? How often have others criticized or punished you for revealing your vulnerability? Have you ever been told, "You're being childish. You should've gotten over that long ago. Grow up."

It's true that you sometimes feel needy, isn't it? Like everyone else, you can feel unsure, confused, scared or just plain tired. No matter how much you have going for you, life doesn't always turn out the way you would like. It's just natural to sometimes feel bewildered, undone, frustrated, angry or depressed. Anyone who claims to have never felt needy is either lying or is living in a massive delusion. Life on this side of Eden is difficult and some-times overwhelming. Nobody is immune. Most people try to hide these "unacceptable" parts of themselves and con-sequently miss out on the extraordinary freedom of sacred trust at the heart of a rich caring connection.

We encourage you to come out of hiding. That's important lovework. And remember, your partner isn't a mind reader. She or he can only deal with what you reveal. *Only what you show is available to be loved—by the both of you.*

Be as direct as you can in your communication. Hoping that clues, hints or subtle "signs" will convey your needs rarely works. Just like you, your partner is caught up in his or her life and needs you to be responsible for calling attention to whatever's going on with you.

By exposing your neediness and vulnerability, you give the gift of courageous generosity to your partner and your relationship. That's the only way you can ever feel really safe, loved for all that you are.

> *One can give nothing whatever*
> *without giving oneself—that is to say,*
> *risking oneself. If one cannot risk oneself,*
> *then one is simply incapable of giving.*
>
> —James Baldwin

The Healing Connection of Vulnerability

We've all been ignored, dismissed or humiliated. We've all had our sense of self-worth devalued or denied. Those wounds don't merely go away. Unless they are healed, they remain with us. They're called "hot buttons." They undermine our personal power, contentment and our ability to love and be loved.

When you take a physical wound to a doctor, you hope she or he will be caring and respectful, aiding and promoting your healing. Psychic wounds require the same kind of respectful attention. To heal a physical wound, the wounded tissue must develop a new integrity. The same process takes place when healing a psychic wound.

Your wound experience needs to be "reversed." *In other words, whatever you've kept in shadow, rejected and undeserving of love, must now be brought into the light and loved by someone whose love you trust.* When your partner sees the "awful thing" you've been hiding and loves you anyway:

- You can re-see your "fault" through your partner's eyes.

- You can choose to identify with your partner's love and respect for your differences.

- You can begin to undo the negative feelings and beliefs you have lived with.

- You can re-value and integrate the "awful thing" into your overall sense of worth.

- You can opt for your own self-worth and integrity and redefine who you believe yourself to be.

- You can heal as you reverse your belittlement and open yourself to a wider and more active sense of personal worth.

Then when you experience self-love, it's not a superficial affirmation or fantasy. Your experience is believable within your own sense of truth. You can see your value in your own eyes. *You can stand confident in your own worth and in the courage it took to face into, reveal and "reverse" something that you have used to keep yourself feeling unacceptable and imprisoned. All of that can happen when you take the risk of being vulnerable and ask for help.*

When it's your partner who feels needy, just be there. No condemnation. No withdrawal. Don't try to analyze or fix the problem. There's nothing for you to do. Just listen. Because you know what it's like to feel needy, you can share your compassion, empathy and understanding from your own experience. That's the best way to assure your partner that you're fully present even in the face of what feels so awful for her or him. That way, your partner can feel secure in your love and respect even when he or she is feeling so awfully dependent.

Check Yourself Out

How were you made to feel unworthy or undeserving? What failures led you to believe you were incompetent or inadequate? What secrets do you harbor that you believe would be shameful and humiliating if they were exposed?

We all struggle with debilitating self-judgments and are hobbled in allegiance to these "truths." As long as we hide them, we act as the wardens of our own self-imprisonment.

To be released, you need the courage to reveal your shadow *stuff* to someone you trust. You need a second opinion about what you're sure is so horrible. Even if what you're carrying is the result of something you have actually said or done, you won't be able to let it go, to pardon yourself, by keeping it hidden. Only by stepping out beyond your shadow, can you free yourself.

Coming Out from Behind the Shadow

1. **Practice asking for help.** We all need help with our daily affairs. Often we don't ask for help because we fear rejection, obligation or any number of other reasons. But, if you don't ask, you can't know who cares. Power and strength come from simply asking for what you need: a raise, a new job, to go Dutch on your date, to more equally split the chores around the house, for your mother- or father-in-law to stop calling at dinner time. Ask for help with anything that could make your life better. You won't always get what you want, but you will make yourself known and you will learn more about who you can trust and depend on to respond with care.

2. **Learn to ask for emotional support.** We all need to feel recognized and supported for our accomplishments. Ask your spouse to listen when you are making changes. When you've reached an important goal, invite your friends over for a special celebration. Tell your date about a recent success and make it clear it's a big deal and you want to acknowledge it. Find out who's really on your team and who's unable or not interested in supporting you.

3. **Ask for the sympathy and compassion you need when you're struggling or suffering.** You need to

know you're not alone when you are going through tough times. Call somebody you can trust and tell them you need to unload. Ask your spouse for special time together so you can just cry or rage or be held and listened to. It's okay to tell your date when you've had a rough day at work. *Telling the truth is the basis of real intimacy and the only way to find out if someone can be trusted with who you are.*

These are just some examples of how you can begin to establish positive trust as well as receive the kind of love and support you need. If you insist on stuffing your neediness into the shadows, your wounded parts will re-emerge without warning and sabotage your bid for love. But when you step into the unknown with a sincere desire to seek and get help, you can open your heart and move toward new and unimagined connections that can change your life forever.

Exploring Your Shadow—Guided Exploration

Olympic athletes visualize their athletic performance as a significant part of their preparation for the real thing. Initially they are guided in their visualization process by a coach who helps them to locate within themselves the images and feelings that will help them reach their goals. The same guided visualization gives you an excellent way to practice a particular skill in your imagination or to remove obstacles that are in your way. So take this opportunity to explore your experiences of neediness and of receiving help and what it will take for you to allow yourself to be needy and accept help without belittlement or self-punishment.

It is important that, at the outset, you trust whatever arises in your imagination in response to the following suggestions. That way you can gain the most insight and practical awareness from your experience.

1. Take a moment right now and bring to mind a time when you felt needy. Dependence is basic to the experience of neediness. It's a kind of incompleteness. In some way, you don't feel you're enough, that you can't do well on your own. Given the experience you've recalled, in what way (or ways) did you feel inadequate? What made you believe you were incomplete? Can you feel the dependence you felt at that time?

Now, to what degree can you accept your dependence? After all, every one of us is limited in some ways, otherwise we wouldn't need each other. If, at first, you find your dependence intolerable, that's not unusual. But, before trust can deepen in your relationship you will have to accept the fact that you can be needy and sometimes need help. How can you make your very human and natural dependency needs acceptable to yourself?

2. The experience of neediness is, in part, a yearning for a sense of security that comes with someone else's help. Someone else is necessary, because you feel you can't go it alone.

In the experience you are remembering, how did you treat yourself in the face of your need for someone else's help? Did you feel small or less than the other person? Were you able to ask for the help you needed? Can you now see yourself as equal to whomever it is you need help from?

If you're feeling reduced, belittled, shamed or any other similar feeling, you can change that by practicing Conscious Creativity. Real maturity knows that we can't get along without relying on one another. Nothing significant was ever accomplished in isolation.

3. Now imagine asking for the help you need. Do you feel like you are in any danger of selling out? Will you lose your individuality? Will you give yourself away? If merely asking for help causes you to feel indebted or humiliated, you're not certain you deserve help. This is a common reaction. But it is a learned reaction. You now need to outgrow it. Remember, the person you're asking for help also needs help from time to time.

4. Finally, imagine receiving the help you asked for. Can you take it in? Can you make it a part of you? Can you allow yourself to be changed by it, even just a tiny bit?

If not, the problem again is that you feel undeserving, unacceptable or some other debilitating self-judgment. Your self-belittlement is an old story—one you still believe. It's an allegiance that keeps you imprisoned.

Begin to create a new story about how brave you are to want to change. By doing this exercise, you are demonstrating just how willing you are. So take into yourself as much of the help you're receiving as you can. And congratulate yourself for doing it.

We all experience neediness. It's as natural as breathing. It must be lived through. It can only be fulfilled with someone else's help. The spiritual gift of neediness is that, in order to be loved, in order to grow and heal, you have to experience your connection to other people, the inherent need we humans have for one another.

Rainer Maria Rilke, a turn-of-the-century German poet, teaches us—"Perhaps everything terrible is, in its deepest essence, something helpless that needs our love."

The more passions and desires
one has, the more ways one
has of being happy.

—Charlotte-Catherine

Expressing Desire

It is essential to your relationship that you and your partner express your desires. If you don't, you will never get what you want and you will even lose touch with knowing what you want. Then you'll feel betrayed, resentful, victimized and of course, unloved.

Desire is fundamental to communication. Your desires let you know who you are by what attracts you. When you both are open about your desires, you teach each other how you can be fulfilled. Fulfillment works like a feedback loop—the more fulfillment, the more desire.

Even so, many, many people are dedicated to the illusion that, "I shouldn't have to ask. If you really loved me, you'd just know. If I have to spell it out, it spoils everything." This allegiance is a straight road to frustration and failure. As we pointed out earlier, your partner can only deal with what you reveal.

Desire is any impulse that moves you beyond where you are toward something different. It is desire that inspires you to take action. When you feel and express your desire, you become passionate, powerful, in charge of yourself.

Is it easy for you to express your desires? Do you seek out intimate conversation? Do you pursue sexual and romantic interludes? Do you need resolution to your conflicts? When you don't want something that's been suggested, can you easily say no?

It's not always easy to feel desire, to know what we really want, let alone express it. Some of us have been taught that desire is sinful. Others were taught that desire was evidence of selfishness. Still others are frightened of desire because it stirs passion, and passion is too self-revealing. For these and many other reasons, we stuff our desires, don't speak up and back away from the desire we see in other people.

Desire and a sense of self are inextricably linked. Stifle your desire and you diminish your self.

Children who fulfill their parents' conscious or unconscious wishes are "good," but if they ever refuse to do so or express wishes of their own that go against those of their parents, they are called egoistic and inconsiderate.

—Alice Miller

The Terrible Twos

When a child reaches the age of two and has mastered enough speech and movement to feel his or her first sense of independence, what does the child often say? "No!"

"No, I don't want bath," "No, I want Daddy," "Not tired." Over and over again, in a whole assortment of ways, the child announces, "No, I'm not you. I want to be who I am."

What does our culture call this period of self-development? The "Terrible Twos." And why the Terrible Twos? Because most parents don't know what to do. They just fall back on what happened to them. They tell the child she or he is "bad."

The child is not being bad. *It's in the nature of growing up to discover and express our differentness.* The child isn't saying no to be resistant. The two-year-old is doing what it has to—becoming a self.

It would be nice if a two-year-old could say, "Well, you want me to go to bed, huh? Let's talk this over. I see your point about bedtime, but can you understand that I'm having a whee of a time with my toys. After all, you were two once. Under the circumstances, I'd like just 15 minutes more." Many adults can't even be that clear. "No" is all the child has available.

What many children face is punishment. They soon learn that "being good" means "not wanting." What they don't learn until it's too late—and many never do—is that by not wanting they are sacrificing who and what they can become.

We're not suggesting that parents should not discipline their children. We are saying that children are not ours to do with as we will. They are full and sovereign beings in their own right. Anyone who chooses to have children must realize that a parent's job is to help bring out who the child is, distinct from his or her parents. When we force and squash our children, we deny and dis-integrate their wondrous spirits, the unique differences that make them who they are.

Check Yourself Out

When you were growing up, how free were you to say what you wanted, particularly when it was contrary to what everybody else wanted? Were you supported in pursuing your goals or were you brought into line?

Now, as an adult, when you're on a date, how well do you speak up for what you want?

When your spouse wants something different than you do, how does it make you feel? Do you believe you have to give in? Do you pull out the armor and fight for control? Or do differences interest and excite you?

Having a self is not automatic. You have to nurture and develop it. Your intimate relationships are the best place to reclaim what you may have long ago given up—the passion of your deep desires.

Feeling and Following Your Desire

1. **Pay attention to the times when you don't speak up.** What happens? Are you afraid? If so, of what? What keeps you from participating in asking for this level of trust?

2. **Make a choice.** When you find yourself saying, "I don't really care where we eat," or, "It doesn't matter to me what movie we see," or, "No, no, no, I don't have an opinion anyway," make a choice. Even if it's only to say, "I'd prefer fish," or, "No I don't want to see a comedy tonight." Promise yourself that you will speak up. Your body needs exercise. So does your desire.

3. **Trust someone, in the positive sense, only if he or she respects your desires.** Speak up if your date or partner disregards your political opinions, your sexual timing, your need to be heard or anything else that's important to you. Speak up! You will

extend your desire for trust—in yourself and in your partner.

When you don't speak up, you abandon yourself. But it doesn't end there. You will find yourself wanting to point the finger of fault. When you don't speak up, the resentment that builds will poison your relationship as surely as if you used cyanide. Commit yourself to honor your desire and *speak up!*

Desire Enlivens Love: Guided Exploration

For the following guided exploration, bring to mind a desire you're reluctant to reveal.

1. Basic to desire is the impulse to get more, be more, say more. Are you willing to become more of yourself by putting your desire out in the world? Or do you hear an inner voice that warns, "Who do you think you are?" *If so, remember, you are the author of your desire. No one can take it away if you don't let them.*

2. Imagine expressing your desire. Do you feel young, small, in jeopardy of feeling bad about yourself? If so, remember those times when you gave voice to your desire and felt excited about life. Use these experiences now to reaffirm confidence—and ask, ask, ask for what you want.

3. Desire wants to be met with respect, even if it can't be fulfilled. Imagine speaking your desire to someone. Are you comfortable allowing this person to see your hunger, your wanting? Or does it make you feel too exposed, too dependent? And remember, the larger forces of the Universe cannot help you unless you are willing to be helped.

4. What happens if your desire cannot be fulfilled? Sometimes that's just how life is. Can you accept this with no loss of self? If not, what do you feel? From time to time everyone experiences frustration or disappointment with how hard life can be. We urge you to accept your disappointment and get ready to ask again.

Desire is the source of life. It is creative, expansive, adventurous, bold, hot, powerful and deeply, deeply spiritual. *It is through the vitality and enthusiasm of desire that we are moved to express ourselves, to be alive and outgoing, welcoming life to abide within us.*

The word "enthusiasm" comes from the Greek *entheos,* meaning "God within." When you respect your desires and those of your partner, you cocreate a relationship in which desire and enthusiasm are sacred pathways to the divine.

Love's gift cannot be given,
it waits to be accepted.

—Rabindranath Tagore

Opening to Receive Love

Many people imagine that they'll just meet "the one." It may be his special look across a crowded room, or the unusual lilt in her voice on the telephone, or any number of Hollywood plot lines that promise love will be instantaneous and last forever.

In her 1995 recording of "Dracula Moon," blues and folk-rock singer Joan Osborne describes the arrival of love this way: "Love come down any way it want to/It don't ask for your permission/Open up your arms/Or he will break you in two." There's nothing we can do to start or stop it. In other words, love happens or it doesn't, whether you like it or not. These are hardly new ideas.

Love Happens! Or Not!

According to this line of thinking, if love happens, great! You get to jump into happily ever after. It's all prepackaged and underwritten by Cupid and his consorts. You belong to love. Either follow or it "will break you in two."

From this perspective, what do you do when love's enchantment starts to fade and go away? If you didn't have much say in the beginning, there's not much you can do to stop it, is there?

What if love never happens? What if Cupid's out to lunch? Where does that leave you? In fantasy? Empty and yearning? Watching others have what you don't have—and can't have—because it's all out of your control?

The idea that you can't participate in your own loving, except as a spectator, is deeply fatalistic. No wonder there's so much melancholy surrounding love. Positive trust. Negative trust. Fantasy. Reality. It's all meaningless. If love determines to enter your life, so be it. If not, not!

When we ask women and men about this view of love, many of them tell us, "Yes. That's my experience." We all recognize love as one of life's greatest treasures, yet have almost no training to suggest a more active and conscious alternative. It's no surprise that love and intimacy are left to chance and good luck.

Check Yourself Out

Has love been a mystery for you? Are you open to receive it?

There are a number of obstacles that can block your ability to receive love. The most unforgiving is your fantasy of exactly what love should look like. The more intense your fantasy, the less open you are to receive. If your fantasy expectations dominate, you are more committed to your own ideas of love, more interested in your "ghostly" lover, than in being with someone who is real and different from you. Then when someone's love comes into your life and doesn't match what you've imagined, you may be unable to recognize or feel it.

It's not that you have to be without expectations. That's impossible. Expectations are a natural part of being human. *But, as you open yourself to differences, as you welcome them, you consciously make room for the possibility of receiving real love.* Then, when someone's love comes into your life and doesn't match your expectations, you can rely on your awareness to help you understand where you are and what you are feeling so you can become actively and consciously involved in shaping and guiding your relationship.

It's most important to know that the person who does (or will) love you, can't help but love you in ways you have not anticipated. Why? Because your partner is not you. If she or he doesn't, in some ways, express love differently than you've imagined, your partner is expressing nothing but learned clichés. That will ultimately be unsatisfying.

On the other side of the coin, your lover won't be entirely prepared for the different ways you express love either. Some of his or her expectations are bound to be disappointed when they are not perfectly matched by you. You'll probably feel misunderstood, maybe even rejected. Again you will need to rely on your feelings and your consciousness to help you open yourself to the adventure and discovery of real life love.

In order to make a place for real love to reside in your relationship, you will both have to become trustworthy receivers.

What You Can Do

1. **One simple step is to pay attention to how you react to compliments.** When someone gives you a compliment, do you make excuses? Do you wave it off? Do you feign shyness? Do you say something like, "No, no, not really"?

   Do you discount the person who said it ("It's just the guy in the mail room"), the basis for the compliment ("Big deal, of course I'm organized"), or the way it was said ("How stupid. As I was going into the men's room, she stopped me to compliment my shoes!")?

   A compliment is a mini-version of love. It is a gift of appreciation. It can teach you something you don't already know about yourself and the other person. When you receive it, you complete and enrich the connection.

2. **Stop each time you catch yourself deflecting a compliment.** Why would you rather dismiss a

compliment instead of receiving it? When you deflect the compliment, you're teaching the other person that you don't want positive attention. Don't be surprised when she or he obliges you.

Stay focused on what's being said and given to you. Notice the feelings you want to hide: guilt, shyness, embarrassment, fear, concern about envy, etc. They are like treasure maps leading you to hidden allegiances.

3. **Each time you're given a compliment, practice receiving it.** Trust that the person means it, especially when you want to deflect it. Let yourself be moved, even if just a little, by the giver's generosity. And then say, "Thank you." That's not much, but it acknowledges the giver and closes the circle of giving and receiving.

If you won't receive love, you can't be trusted with it.

Giving Love—Exercise

Love is uniquely expressed by each of us. Every relationship has its own spiritual way of being. Lovers must learn to participate in the intimacy that comes alive between them like dancers learn to dance together.

Instead of a guided exploration, this time we suggest that you consciously pay compliments to your date or spouse. Pay attention to how you are received. Whenever the other person doesn't take in what you're giving, don't let it slide by. Make it clear that you really meant what you said, and you want to be taken seriously. If your partner is shy, awkward or uncomfortable, that's okay. Most people are. When we're unaccustomed to being loved, we just don't know what to do. But, if you are still dismissed, there's a problem. Pay attention to the fact that he or she refuses to receive you, refuses to be loved. Love, like all other human experiences, has to be learned. Many relationships, even between well-intended couples, flounder or crash because they don't know what to do with love.

A lot of it is about saying,
"Hey, I'm going to be committed to this.
I'm not going to be constantly looking for
where the grass is greener." You have to finally
say, "this is it. And this is what I'm going
to commit to and deal with."

—Nicole Kidman

Surrendering to Full Partnership

Commitment is the soul of a trustworthy relationship. It's your pledge to stay, to be a full participant in all the challenges and ecstasies the relationship will bring.

Traditionally, staying simply meant not physically leaving the marriage. That isn't enough. To foster spiritual aliveness and a new intimacy, you have to commit to the long-term, creative adventure of building something together. When things are bad, it's your commitment you can trust to support you in rooting out whatever's going on. This lovework will enable you to open up and discover the treasures buried in the depths of your being together. When things are good, it's your commitment that sweetens your celebration, allowing you to relax and harvest your blessings with confidence and excitement toward your future.

Your commitment means much more than just physically being there. It's all about involvement and deepening intimacy. It's the same as saying, "I will reveal myself and enter into the discovery of who I am and who you are." Without a commitment, this ongoing process is far too risky.

Our Commitment to Each Other

When we were married, we wrote our own ceremony. We each composed our own vows and then we offered them to each other. The two regarding commitment were:

JIM:

I offer to you my vow of commitment.
I promise to stand with you and build a future
To which I commit my energies and dreams
My most closely held treasures
My just plain everyday self
All of who I am.
I commit to bring to our life together
My spirit
My soul
My feelings
My thoughts
My words
My actions
My mind and body and
My pledge of trust and love.

JUDITH:

I accept this vow you offer to me and return it to you in kind.

I offer to you my vow not to leave in any way when we experience difficulty between us.

I vow to stay open to you emotionally and viscerally and express my experience to you so that you do not feel shut out or abandoned. I promise to keep in mind that I love you even when I'm furious with you. And I accept that achieving a resolution on some issues may take a long time. But maintaining my integrity and yours makes the struggle most worthwhile.

JIM:

I accept this vow you offer to me and return it to you in kind.

When you make a commitment, you give your promise in trust to your partner. You hold each other's word, confidently, and rest your hopes with the assurance that they will be well cared for.

Check Yourself Out

What comes up for you when you hear the word commitment? Does it mean something permanent? Does it mean security and freedom? Or are you worried about being tied down?

When you make a commitment, is it to your partner? Is it to the relationship?

Does commitment close the door to new possibilities? Are you confined? Does it make your life smaller? Or can your commitment be the basis for growth and change? Can it be an opportunity to expand far beyond how you have been?

When you surrender to a full commitment with another person, the two of you begin to create something larger than you both. Then your relationship is a synthesis of your mutual and ongoing physical, emotional, psychological and spiritual dialogue. It's your living, breathing work of art.

Moving Toward Commitment

1. **You are one-half of your relationship.** When you know that your relationship can foster deep and very personal expression, you won't have to worry about becoming invisible or losing yourself, because 50 percent of your relationship is formed by your input.

2. **You will change.** Understand that each of you will be changed, merely by being involved. As you change, your relationship follows. As your relationship changes, it will cause each of you to change even more. *A relationship is a change agent of the first order.*

3. **Be present as you are.** Who you are is the necessary stuff of intimacy and trust. If you take your intimate self only to your parents, friends, your therapist, your sponsor or even an affair, you're cheating on the connection with your partner. Without your truth and your partner's truth, what you have is watered down, at best and, at worst, a charade. It's counterfeit, unworthy of sacred commitment. Because you want a vital and spiritually intimate relationship, commit yourself to being present as you are.

Opening to the Future: Guided Exploration

Inherent in the spirit of commitment is the sense of a long-term vision. *Your commitment energizes the here and now by promising a future.* If your relationship has no sense of a future, if you and your partner don't feel that you're moving, heading somewhere, even if you aren't sure where that might be, then your relationship is stunted by a lack of commitment.

Visualize yourself in a committed relationship. Either the one you're already in or one you imagine.

1. See yourself surrendering to commitment. See it as an act of practical spirituality, an act of faith in your partner, in yourself and in the love and intimacy that is alive between you. Know that change will be inevitable. Your relationship will live and grow. As you stay conscious, that change will most always be for the better.

   If you are struggling with doubt, wanting to withdraw from commitment, your feelings are echoing old allegiances that want to claim your heart—allegiances that keep you within their grip. Remember, you have the power to change your mind.

2. Can you sense a future? Do you see a path or direction that calls you? Can you feel that "commitment" means long-term?

   What happens when you think about finances, having children, or doing the lovework necessary to continually re-kindle your love? Can you see that these issues actually help you to direct the course of your being together?

3. See how your individual commitments join together and expand into a co-commitment, a greater love you've accepted and given yourselves to. Your loving relationship begins to take on a life of its own. And, though greater than each of you, a life you actively participate in. One that you both learn from and guide, nurture and are supported by. A life you cocreate as it creates you. In faith and confidence, with an open mind and heart, you both follow wherever your path leads. Stay conscious as your love flows through you and remember, your commitment paves the road.

4. Now commit yourself to expressing this vision of commitment in your real, everyday life. Let it live and grow within
you. *You can create and sustain a sacred trust when you
and your partner are consciously willing to meet at the intersection of your courage and care.*

When you unite in the commitment of sacred trust—
revealing your vulnerability, expressing your desires, opening
to receive love and surrendering to a full commitment—you
can create and live in an atmosphere of relaxation, security,
freedom and fun.

"That's Really True!"

After a lecture we gave on The Healing Power of
Relationship, we were approached by an older couple, both
in their seventies. They were lively and vibrant, radiating an
excitement that was enviable. "We've been married for 58
years," the man announced, his eyes wide and eager. "I love
her more now than when we first met," he beamed. "That's
because I know her and trust her far better than I did in the
beginning, so there's more for me to love."

The woman reached out and took each of us by the
hand. "What you say is true about a relationship helping
you practice spirituality. It helps you develop yourself and
get beyond your own small reality. That's really true. And
I feel the same way about him. We have so much more
than at the beginning of our marriage."

We felt honored, as though we'd been visited by
guardian angels. Who knows, perhaps we had.

Chapter 8

BEHIND YOUR MASKS: BEING LOVED FOR YOUR DIFFERENCES

Our strength is often composed of
the weaknesses we're damned if
we're going to show.

—Mignon McLaughlin

We are all like the clay Buddha
covered with a shell of hardness created out
of fear, and yet underneath each of us is a golden
Buddha, a golden Christ or a golden
essence, which is our real self.

—Jack Canfield

A mask is a symptom of a conscious or unconscious assumption that others will not accept you for who you are. Its job is to change how you appear to others, to stand in for or replace who you are, in the hope that people will accept your made-to-order self.

Masks are often necessary. It would be foolish, if not dangerous, to suggest that you just drop your masks and go out into the world soul-naked. But as your masks successfully keep you distant from those around you, they also keep you distant from yourself. To create the kind of relationship you want, you will have to risk going behind your masks. Only there can you experience the riches of deep intimacy.

---

*The first half of my life
I worked so hard to deny the hillbilly
that was me, and now the second half of
my life I find that I am totally
enshrining it.*

—Roseanne

Masks

How They Come About

Whenever you express yourself and are met with rejection, ridicule or any response that devalues who you are, you stand at a crossroads needing to make a choice. You can decide that the response is inaccurate and meaningless and go about your business with confidence and pleasure. Or you can take the rejection to heart, agree that there must be something wrong with you and decide to protect yourself by creating a false but acceptable front. That front we call a mask.

Masks hide all kinds of perceived inadequacies. You may not feel attractive enough, so you wear heavy makeup or drive an expensive car you can't afford. You may think you are not smart enough so you purposely limit your discussions with friends to a narrow range of topics. You may feel you need to compensate for being overweight or underweight, too sensitive or not sensitive enough, frightened, indecisive or anything else you feel you need to conceal.

But masks don't hide just the bad things. We often use them to hide our talents and dreams, our skills and abilities in order to purchase acceptability. In our culture, women have often had to deny their own competence in the workplace in order to appear "ladylike." Many men have had to suppress their tender feelings to protect themselves from being called "wimps." It's not uncommon for teenagers to sabotage or deny their academic excellence in order to belong. *Mask wearing is always a performance calculated to produce a specific result.*

Masks come in many different forms. Sometimes we use masks to manipulate. Other times we use them to rationalize our own behavior. We go into hiding the moment we identify with our arrogance or self-righteousness; when we ingratiatingly cater to others; when we lie, cheat and steal emotionally; when we refuse to ask for help; when we deny responsibility for what we do and then cry victim when things "just happen" not to go our way. Masks will cover anything we want them to.

Once you decide to put on a mask, you've decided to stay in allegiance with those who have rejected you, because the whole point of your mask is to gain their acceptance. You twist and turn, making yourself into whatever you believe will gain their favor, so much so that who you are is thereafter determined by someone else. All that energy and effort only to end up without a self of your own.

Throughout our lives we are surrounded by masks so that living authentically—living true to yourself—requires conscious attention. But if you don't live true to who you are, if you don't live within your own skin, you are destined to a life of nagging insecurity and constant longing—for something you cannot even define.

The longer you keep the mask on, the more practiced you become at being what you imagine someone else thinks is acceptable. You become increasingly dulled to your own impulses, feelings and responses and are finally unable, for all practical purposes, to distinguish between who you are and who you are trying to be.

But, even so, the truth that was buried alive never dies. It echoes out through a vague sense of fraudulence and through an almost silent guilt. Somewhere within you know you are acting out a deceit. You know you are accountable for the self-rejection that initiated the whole process, the self-rejection you are doomed to perpetuate as long as you keep concealed.

Furthermore, it doesn't matter how successful you are with your disguise. You still lose yourself. In fact, your success is a death sentence, creating more and more emptiness, more and more loneliness, more and more spiritual hunger, because your mask cannot ever fulfill those you are trying to please nor can it be fulfilled by them. *You can only come back to life by reclaiming your self and that's one of the primary rewards of lovework.*

If you tell the truth, you have infinite power supporting you, but if not, you have infinite power against you.

—Charles Gordon

Getting to Know Your Masks

If you do not recognize the masks you wear, they will sabotage your intimate relationships, damage your self-esteem and prevent you from ever getting what you really want. Here's one way you can distinguish between what is real and what is a mask.

Think about those times when you are with someone and you're comfortable. You know what you feel and what you want. Your interaction is spontaneous, alive and lively. You speak the truth, even if what you're saying is difficult.

When the other person responds positively to who you are, you feel an energy shift in your body. It could be a feeling of warmth or fullness or enthusiasm. You know you've touched that person and you are open to be touched in return. You emotionally welcome each other, in effect saying, "I want more from you and I'm willing to give more to you."

Now, what about those times when you are with someone and you're not really present. You might feel hollow, anxious, maybe even scared. You might be trying to figure out what to say next or worrying about how to say it. You might be thinking about other things, such as comforting yourself with alcohol or food or asking yourself, "What am I doing here?" There is a distance between you and the other person. Your interaction is stilted and awkward. You know that if the other person were to realize what was really going on with you, you would be exposed. You may silently wonder "What's the point?" because nothing is really happening.

We're all familiar with this experience, to some degree or another. It's what makes dating such a waste of time when only masks show up to impress each other, compete with each other or perform the ritual dance of seduction. It's what turns families into breeding grounds for depression and loneliness, substance abuse and violence.

As threatening as it may seem, you have nothing to lose by letting go of your masks. If someone accepts you for who you are, you both have made a meaningful connection. If someone accepts you for your mask, you both have nothing. If you are rejected for who you are, you still have yourself. If you are rejected for your mask, you end up with nothing—no secure protective façade and no truth. *Remember, when you put on a mask, you are saying to the world, and to yourself, that who you are isn't good enough as is.*

The Price You Pay

The danger of mask wearing goes very deep. In *Doctor Zhivago,* Boris Pasternak warns:

> *The great majority of us are required to live a life of constant, systematic duplicity. Your health is bound to be affected if, day after day, you say the opposite of what you feel, if you grovel before what you dislike and rejoice at what brings you nothing but misfortune. Our nervous system isn't just a fiction, it's part of our physical body, and our soul exists in space and is inside us, like the teeth in our mouth. It can't be forever violated with impunity.*

You pay a steep and dreadful price to wear a mask, a price that is inescapable because it's built into the process of choosing a mask in the first place. *Whenever you decide to wear a mask you suffer a loss of self after which you must endure living within the prison of your own self-contempt.*

When I was under contract to Warner Brothers, word would come down from Jack Warner that we had to look and act in a certain way. The message was clear: You're not good enough the way you are.

—Jane Fonda

Do as You're Told: Be What We Want

To be fair, isn't it true that every day we are all bombarded by messages, especially through advertising, telling us the best way to be or the right way to be?

When we are growing up we're all told some version of, "No matter what, put on a happy face." Sounds innocent enough, doesn't it? And wasn't it always meant for your own good? So, what's the big deal? The big deal is that you're really being told to bury yourself, to become invisible. In spite of how you feel or what you think, be sure to show only your "best side"—no problems, never feeling bad, always up and positive. Furthermore, make sure your performance is believable—no matter what.

How about, "You never get a second chance to make a good first impression"? This is actually a sound piece of advice when it means, "Be who you are." But what it usually means is, "Keep your eye on the other person and be whatever you think she or he is looking for." That sets you up for a pretty big risk. If at first you don't succeed, you fail.

Judith: When I was growing up, my parents were always stressing how important it was to make a good first impression. When Gary, my date for my first high school formal, arrived to pick me up, he spent a few minutes with my parents. They asked him how he felt. "I'm nervous," he stammered. That's all it took.

They were too polite to say anything to him. But the next day they went on and on about how "such a big, strong guy, a football player, all dressed up" could be so inept. "Didn't his parents teach him any better? You never let anyone know you're nervous." The truth was, I had a wonderful time at the dance. I'd been nervous, too. Probably a lot more than Gary. When I heard about what he'd said, I thought he was sweet for being so vulnerable.

Here's another one. "Smile, though your heart is breaking." That may seem heroic and very romantic, but, in the long run, it will keep you unknown and lonely.

The advertising industry is a conspicuous voice telling you how to be. "Do this, you'll be sexy." "Do that, you'll be rich." "Do this and that, you'll be powerful." And on, and on, and on. The end result of all this "good advice" is that you vanish. The better you are at these games, the less lovable you become, because you're not present to be loved.

Bring to mind someone you've known who is always "on." It's really difficult to be with that person, isn't it? People like that usually dominate the conversation because they have to keep their performance going. If not, they don't know what to do. They will tell you that they're both capable of and ready for intimacy. But that's not true. They are terrified of it. *The fact is, it's not possible to be intimate with a mask, because there is no way to make real contact.*

It's not just in dating and romance that we're told to hide who we really are. What about school? Was it safe to say that you didn't understand something? Could you feel comfortable being brilliant in class? Were you invited to challenge or disagree with any of your teachers? Most people would answer no to all of the above.

What about religion, politics, work or the culture of your neighborhood? How often were you asked, "What do you think about . . .?" or "How do you feel about . . .?" by someone who really listened and wanted to know? Most likely, not often . . . if ever.

What we're told is that we will be accepted and loved if we "put on a happy face," "do it right," and "have a nice day." If not, "Who do you think you are?"

"I'm a Hell's Angel," some would say, hiding behind a Harley and a tough veneer. Others might not say a word. They'll dye their hair purple or pierce their nose, lips, tongue and ears and/or cover themselves with tattoos to be hip. More common, but less obvious, are those people who are usually aloof, angry or contemptuous. Their masks tell us, "Don't come close." It doesn't matter if all they're doing is protecting themselves. It doesn't matter how sensitive and good-hearted they may be inside. They tell others to stay away, and we generally oblige them. But underneath it all, the sad truth is that, for many of them, what they really want is to be touched, to connect. They just don't know how.

This last mask pattern is common enough that playwright Jules Feiffer memorialized it in his play, *Hold Me.* During the last scene, the lead character cries out:

I live inside a shell,
that is inside a wall,
that is inside a fort,
that is inside a tunnel,
that is under the sea—
where I am safe from you.
If you really loved me, you'd find me.

Whatever your mask hides, the simple fact is that one way something surely becomes hideous is when you hide it. That's the root of the word and the problem.

Something Has to Give

When you choose to wear a mask, you choose to deceive others. More importantly, you try to deceive yourself. Even so, behind every mask there is a soul wanting to be known in its fullness, to be recognized, valued and loved for its true expression.

But what about the self-judgment that starts the whole process, the self-contempt you feel that drives the need to hide yourself? What about the terror of being revealed? What do you imagine would happen if love entered your life? What if someone took you into her or his heart? Would you survive?

In the *Duino Elegies,* Rainer Maria Rilke wrote of fear and desire.

> *Who, if I shouted, among the hierarchy of angels would hear me? And supposing one of them took me suddenly to his heart, I would perish before his stronger existence. For beauty is nothing but the beginning of terror we can just barely endure, and we admire it so because it calmly disdains to destroy us. Every angel is terrible. And so I restrain myself and swallow the luring call of dark sobbing.*

What does Rilke's elegy have to do with masks? What does it have to do with being who you are?

If you are living an illusion, then love's power will be "terrible." It will take you into its "stronger existence." It will penetrate your mask. It will expose your deceit and "destroy" your performance. When you let yourself be seen, you will have to go forward into the "dark sobbing" that comes when you admit what you've done to yourself.

Or you may withdraw in "terror," and slip back into the shadows, safe and unknown.

Does this sound all too poetic? Not part of the real world? Advice columnist Abigail Van Buren received a letter from a woman in Houston, Texas who characterized herself as, "On Hold in Houston," and she wrote:

> *I am a woman in my late sixties. My husband and I were very friendly with "Frank" and "Lucy."... In 1963, they moved to Hawaii and I have not seen them since.*
>
> *In recent years both Frank's wife and my husband have passed away. Frank and I have been talking on the telephone since then. We have become very close.*
>
> *So what's my problem? He wants to come here to see me—and I'm terrified.*
>
> *I feel this almost-make-believe "phone romance" is not real, and that to meet in person might spoil it all. The years have not been kind to me, and I also have some medical problems of which he is not aware. On the phone, I can be 35 again, beautiful and sexy.*
>
> *True, Frank is also 32 years older, but to me, that is not important. I just couldn't bear it if he were disappointed when we met. How can I refuse to meet without hurting him? Or am I just being foolish?*

On Hold is immobilized by fear. Instead of facing the possibility of creating a real relationship with Frank, one that might take her through the rest of her life, she wonders if it would be better to "swallow the luring call of dark sobbing" and pretend to be "35 again, beautiful and sexy." Would it be better to keep her almost-make-believe phone romance going and live in a delicious fantasy, uncomplicated by the reality of her life?

On Hold in Houston deserves our compassion. Her self-judgment is tearing her apart. She feels very unlovable. She is consumed by an allegiance to a very limited "idea" of beauty and to solely negative expectations of what would happen if she and Frank were to meet. Still, she had the courage to admit her terror and wrestle with her fear and desire. She knows that make-believe ultimately will not be satisfying. The power and the beauty of her connection with Frank is calling her out to explore her true value. But it's contrary to what she's understood "love" to be, and so she's confused and terrified. She couldn't bear being seen as who she is—or more accurately, who she has consigned herself to be.

On Hold's worries are not entirely unjustified. Frank might not like what he sees. Then what? On Hold might take that as "proof" that she is no longer attractive, and probably end up punishing herself for being so naive, and for risking such heartache. Put yourself in her shoes. Wouldn't you be skittish?

But what if Frank does like her? What if he wants to be with her as she is? What masks does the "terrible angel" of Frank's love force her to drop? What if she can see that she is beautiful in his eyes? That would be "nothing but the beginning of terror," cutting through illusion to a new discovery of herself. She will have to give up her fantasies, risk entering into the beauty of being accepted for who she really is and "perish" in the presence of a new image of herself. Suppose he takes her into his heart? She will have to "endure" being loved in all her "imperfection," all her humanness.

When you conceal your personal value with a false identity, love becomes an adversary, a threat to the life you have carefully, if fearfully, constructed.

Fantasy Is Never Enough

Fast food is never enough. It's made to satisfy your hunger, but only in the moment. Its real job is to hook you so you'll keep coming back for more. Yes, it's actual food—potatoes, fish, beef, bread—but it's filled with fat and salt and sugar. That's what gives it the habit-forming taste. However, it's also very low in nutrient value, so it does not give your body what it really needs. In the long run, the more you eat, the more you need, and you don't even know why.

You might say fast food is not really food but rather a profit-generating commodity. In that same sense, fantasy love is not actually love. It's a substitute. It only seems to be what we want.

On Hold in Houston is seriously considering the option of a "phone romance," substituting long-distance for a face-to-face meeting. She's a classic example of—"If he really got to know me, he'd find me wanting." Sadly, whatever love she might receive through the phone lines will only be a substitute. The more she gets, the less satisfied she'll be, so the more she'll need. Her dilemma was exquisitely described by Eric Hoffer, an American longshoreman and philosopher, when he wrote, "You can never get enough of what you really don't want."

It's a Closed Loop

If On Hold chooses to continue the mask of her phone romance, she'll find herself in a veiled trap. What she doesn't realize—what few people realize—is that every mask has its own hidden agenda.

You developed your masks to protect yourself against disappointment, fear, loneliness, confusion, whatever. *As long as your mask is in place, the danger it was developed to protect against must also remain in place.* In other words, for your mask to have purpose, you have to be in allegiance to some kind of threat, real or imagined. Otherwise, there is no need for your cover.

On Hold's phone romance would become a mask built on the threat that "the years have not been kind to me." As long as she resists meeting Frank, she unconsciously perpetuates her own fear of the aging process, and thus, her humiliation at no longer being 35. She must continue to believe that she is unattractive, otherwise, what would be the point of remaining at long-distance.

Because On Hold would unconsciously be in allegiance to her self-rejection, she'd find it very difficult, if not impossible, to believe that anyone else might think she is attractive. So, the only men who could fit with her self-image would be those who would support her self-degradation. Then On Hold either ends up associating with men who are not really good for her or she stays alone. From this point of view, it's sadly ironic that she chose On Hold as her pseudonym.

For their relationship to have a chance, On Hold will have to drop her mask and give up her allegiance to the cliché that there is only one kind of beauty. If she lets the "terrible angel" in, he will arrive from a place *beyond her imagination.* In other words, On Hold cannot now imagine what Frank may want and have to offer. She will have to discover that with him, because she'll have to reverse her current point of view and re-see herself through his eyes. As long as she maintains her mask, she'll be trapped. She will never get the intimacy she really wants because she will be the source of her own disappointment. That's a closed and terminal loop.

If On Hold breaks her allegiance to self-hatred and invites Frank to visit, whether he finds her attractive or not, she will take a courageous plunge into creating herself as acceptable in her own eyes. She will have the opportunity to take stock of her qualities beyond beauty or health: what she's learned during her years on the planet; what compassion and care live in her heart; what wisdom she's accumulated. As long as On Hold wants Frank to see her as she was at 35, she can only fail. However, she will succeed at her self-fulfilling prophecy that he will not find her attractive. If she can move into emotional and spiritual maturity, she can give herself the chance to live a long, good, loving life together with Frank or with someone else.

Ten Rewards for Dropping Your Masks

When you're trying to change and learn something new, it's easy to forget what you desire and slip back into old habits. The following list will remind you of the important points to remember as you work to change and cast off your masks.

1. Masks cover your fear of feeling unlovable. By dropping your masks, you claim self-respect.

2. As long as you feel unlovable, there's no place inside you that can sincerely receive love. By dropping

your masks, you create a space *inside* for love to enter.

3. Your masks block any real connection. By dropping your masks, you open the way for a real relationship.

4. With your masks in place, your relationship remains static. You can never be spontaneous or open to what you don't already know. By dropping your masks, you can tap your imagination and creativity.

5. Masks prevent you from revealing anything that is meaningful or vulnerable. By dropping your masks, the truth of who you are becomes available to be loved by you and your partner.

6. With your masks on, you feel emotionally hungry and never satisfied. By dropping your masks, your human need to be recognized and valued can be fulfilled.

7. Your masks keep you dedicated to your past, and perpetuate the pain you're trying to escape. By dropping your masks, you make the courageous move to leave home and become your own person.

8. Your masks keep you emotionally cut off from yourself. By dropping your masks, you open to the truth of yourself, allowing you to become truly intimate.

9. Your masks attract only those who support your pretense. By dropping your masks, you can attract someone who loves you for who you are.

10. Most importantly, masks force you into fantasy, because they put real intimacy and real love far beyond your reach. By dropping your masks, you set

yourself free and make way for the possibility of intimacy and real life love.

Having just read this, take a moment and look inside. Are you willing to drop your masks, even just a little, and invite people to really know you? Are you willing to find out how people would actually respond to *you?* Will you concede that their acceptance would be more meaningful than liking you for your performance?

Honesty ... makes me feel powerful
in a difficult world.

—Cher

Beyond Your Masks: Exercise

Pick one of the masks you know you wear. Then choose someone with whom you use this mask. As an experiment, we encourage you to drop your mask with this person and reveal your truth. Find out what will happen.

Of course there is risk involved, but it's not what you probably fear—that the other person will reject you. If that were the case, what would you really lose? Just someone who doesn't have the capacity to like you in the first place.

The real risk is to face whatever discomfort you feel. You may have to deal with what it was that caused you to put on the mask in the first place. Then, you will have to face the fact that you've been rejecting yourself for years, losing out on life and love, and using your mask to hide that from yourself.

You also risk finding out that the other person actually prefers being with you, rather than your mask. It's always so baffling, at first, to discover that love actually works the opposite of what you've been taught. *The perfect mask reaps distance and self-rejection. The imperfect real self invites and attracts compassion, respect, love and intimacy.*

One of the spiritual challenges we all face is how to experience the kind of self-acceptance—*for all that we are*—that allows even imperfection to be beautiful. Accepting our invitation to come out from behind your masks is one way you can meet this challenge. You can decide to change. You can decide to be who you are. And why not? It's got to be better than the nothingness of illusion that makes you depressed, lonely and anxious. Life is much richer and ultimately more fulfilling without masks. But the only way you'll know that is to find out for yourself.

---

*If you bring forth what is
within you, what you bring forth
will save you. If you do not bring forth
what is within you, what you do not
bring forth will destroy you.*

—Jesus of Nazareth

Spiritual Intimacy

If you could have only one thing from a relationship what would it be? We've asked many people this question. They've told us that they would like to be known. They would like to be witnessed and accepted for who they are. "If somebody actually sees me, all the way, good and bad," a woman in Melbourne shared with our workshop group, "and he accepts me, everything else will follow."

We asked if it was easy for her to share herself with a man. "Well, no it's not," she blushed, revealing her version of On Hold's dilemma. "I say I want someone to see me and yet I won't show myself. It's so confusing."

"You're not hiding now," Jim said, supporting her. "Is it so bad?"

"Scary," she whispered.

"Yes, it can be," he comforted, "Coming out into the light . . . that's serious. Not only will we get to see you . . . you'll run into things about yourself that you've locked away."

"Yeah," she sat up, smiling slightly, "I know."

Her desire to be seen is hardly uncommon. But fulfilling it? That's something else again.

When you decide to hide, that amounts to settling for being loved for your façade. Then, even if somebody finds you attractive, they're stuck planting seeds in artificial soil. Whatever they have to offer can't take root. When you open up and reveal yourself, you begin to build a bridge across the distance and alienation many of us accept as normal. When you break the silence you begin to create intimacy.

Frostbitten Heart

In snow country, if you stay out too long, you can get frostbitten. You won't even know it's happening until you lose feeling. The treatment for frostbite is to use cold and then progressively warmer water. As the frostbitten area thaws and receives blood flow, it hurts. That pain is the signal that life is returning.

Masks are a form of frostbite. They are the outward sign of those frozen parts of your heart. The more you rely on masks, the more frozen you become. The more frozen you become the less you can feel. Then when love enters your heart, it acts like warm water, defrosting your heart, releasing long-held pain, and that can come as quite a shock. It reawakens the wounds that caused you to withdraw in the first place, and, rather than rejoice, you may even cry. It also brings into vivid, painful awareness all the time you've spent numb behind your masks. You get to see the love and intimacy you wanted and could never get. You recognize in yourself what has gone unrecognized, unappreciated and unaccepted.

It is important to understand that opening up to love and life again is painful, especially at first. That's why so many of us resort to "effortless, happily-ever-after" fantasies. But they can't go very far, even though they seem to be so easy and painless.

Real life love spreads its warmth into all parts of us— our joys and our sorrows, our genius and our scars, our delight and despair. In the light of its fullness, we can live in clarity and simplicity, relaxed and at ease.

Let Love In: Guided Exploration

Bring to mind something about yourself you know is hidden away. Perhaps it's been buried for a long time. Perhaps it's recent. What caused you to freeze up? Were you frightened? Enraged? Where was the threat coming from? Were you rejected? Abandoned? Wrongfully accused? Pay attention to how you were overwhelmed. Whatever happened was beyond your ability to handle. So you froze.

What decisions did you make at that time? About yourself? About those around you? About life? What commitments did you make? Never to show yourself? Never to trust? Never to expect anything good? See yourself. Frozen. Stiff.

And now, bring to mind someone who loves you. Let them see you frozen. See them beaming their love toward you. What happens? Let their love become more intense. See it working its way deep into your withdrawal. How do you feel? Experience the warmth of their love, warmer and warmer. Thawing you. Melting your masks. Warmer and warmer until it's hot. So hot that it becomes alchemical—it can change you from carbon to the beginnings of a radiant diamond.

What happens to you? Can you stand it? Can you open yourself to be changed? Can you allow love? Can you let yourself feel the intimacy?

Too many of us turn away from the pain of love, thinking that, if it hurts, it must not be love. "She can't be right for me. If she were, I wouldn't feel this way."

When you understand the transformational powers of love, when you can step into its "stronger existence" and welcome its "beauty," you can let your masks go. You can let love enter the shadows and bring you the rich intimacy you've always desired.

Marlene and Roger

Too often people associate intimacy only with sexuality. It's so much more than that. *To be intimate is to allow yourself to be seen and be willing to see what the other person is showing you.* That takes security in yourself, an ability to respond sensitively and creatively, and a willingness to enter into the unknown that exists between you. But for love to be truly fulfilling, intimacy needs to be part of the everyday fabric of your being together. Allowing yourself to be available with confidence and openness is a large part of growing into maturity and developing real life love.

Friends of ours, Marlene and Roger had been married for 31 years when Roger was diagnosed with a very aggressive lung cancer. He told us that as he left the oncologist's office, surgery date in hand, he felt utterly alone. All his life he believed it was "the mark of a man not to bother anyone with my problems." But his life had never been on the line before. He was terrified.

As soon as he came home, Marlene asked him for the results. True to form, he did not tell her. He wanted to, but he couldn't. "Nothing major. I just need to watch myself. You know. Diet. Exercise. If I do, everything'll be okay." Marlene hugged him in relief.

During the next several days, Roger withdrew. He assured Marlene he was just tired. "But whenever I look at her across the room," he thought, "it seems like she's a million miles away. I don't know how to reach her. And I feel like she's falling farther away."

Then it dawned on him, "It's not her, it's me. I'm the one who's falling away." That realization shot through him with a jolt. Suddenly he saw that he'd been that way for a good part of their life together, keeping things to himself, dealing with his problems alone. He felt ashamed and embarrassed and knew he had to tell her about the cancer.

Marlene was deeply hurt and very angry. "Damn it, Roger, who the hell do you think you are! Who do you think I am! The next-door neighbor? Did you think you could just keep this a secret? I could just . . . slap you and slap you and slap you."

It was Marlene's turn to withdraw. She sat alone, or went for walks, or stayed up late into the night. She had to admit that Roger had always kept things to himself. That was part of what she admired about him. "He was strong and unflappable," she thought. But then her rage would erupt, "This is life and death, damn it. This is not about being a hero."

"I'm deeply sorry," Roger said, approaching her one afternoon.

"What about?" Marlene responded cautiously.

"For all the ways I haven't included you. For treating you like someone who needs to be shielded. I had no idea." Roger's admission opened a talk that lasted well into the evening. With the possibility of death in the room, there wasn't time to pretend.

"Well," Marlene acknowledged, "it's not entirely your responsibility. I've accepted it all these years. I knew what you were doing and I accepted it. Truthfully, I don't know what I would've done with someone who kept telling me everything."

Then they spoke of their fears and resentments, their disappointments and regrets. They mustered their courage and spoke the unspeakable. They both cried. And they laughed. They could feel the love they had for each other. But a terrible angel had descended upon them, and they could not shrink from the call of dark sobbing.

Roger survived the surgery and the follow-up radiation treatments and the next three years were the richest of their lives. They remembered what they saw in one another before the years piled on. They uprooted allegiances and dropped masks. They held each other in consciousness and felt connected. Their love-making was never better. "I even keep my eyes open," Marlene blushed. "That's incredible."

Suddenly, the cancer reappeared. Tests showed that it had spread. The prognosis was terminal. They both were shocked, then enraged, then depressed. But this time, they were in it together. Instead of fighting the reality, they opened to it. They spoke of their life together. How they had loved and appreciated each other. They spoke of death and separation and what Marlene would do after Roger died.

He deteriorated quickly. Roger told her, "It's as though everything's shutting down. I guess my business here is over." He laughed, "Sort of like I'm packing to leave."

"I've always admired your spirit," she whispered, holding his hand. "And I feel privileged to be with you now."

"It's funny," he smiled, "It is a privilege isn't it? That we're together . . . who'd of thought?"

Near the end, Roger became frightened. "I don't want to leave you alone."

"There you go . . . protecting me again," she gently chided. "Have you forgotten that I'm a big girl?"

"If I only knew you'd be alright."

"Well you don't and you can't. I suppose the deepest things are the last to go." They both laughed. "I'll be alright."

During his final night he was in and out of consciousness. When she began to feel that he was hanging on, she whispered, "Let go, Roger. It's okay. Just let go." She told him again about all he'd given her, and how special their last three years were. She also told him that she would honor the openness and joy of their final years by living her life in the same spirit. That's what he would want. That's what they wanted. She would live fully, holding him in her heart until it was her time to go.

It's deeply sad and true that we are so layered over with masks and caught up in our allegiances that it takes a lot to remind us of who we really are. We spend so much energy on camouflage. But we don't have to wait for the threat of death to make us conscious of our masks and defenses. There are opportunities in everyday life to drop our masks and become more intimate.

For example, you might be in an argument or a fight with your partner and you realize that what she or he is saying is true and your position is off the mark. In that moment a door opens and you are faced with the opportunity to change, or not. You can resist walking through the door, defend your position and keep fighting. But to do so would require that you break integrity with what you know to be true and continue to struggle only for the sake of preserving your mask. Or, by walking through the door, you announce to yourself and your partner that you are willing to change. You are willing to surrender your mask and accept the truth. And as soon as you do, you are more genuinely present, more of you is available in the exchange, and that, in itself, is a position of deeper and more vivid intimacy.

Marlene and Roger did not back away from reality. They opened to it. And because they did they were able to connect more and more honestly with one another, deepening their intimacy and filling out their love.

Life is to be lived. We cannot know how things will turn out in advance. All we can do is commit to being as present as we can and finding out what is in store for us.

> *There is no coming to heaven*
> *with dry eyes.*
>
> —Thomas Fuller

Loving Awareness

In general, intimacy is a feeling of close connectedness. As an adult you have the background of your lifetime that, like clutter or interference, can diminish the connection. You might feel self-conscious, uneasy, worried about what might happen. The sense of immediacy, which is essential to real intimacy, is harder for adults to experience.

That doesn't mean that you have to go back to being an infant. Aside from the fact that you can't, it would not do much good. In order for there to be adult intimacy, you have to have an awareness of being close and in touch. You don't become lost or dissolve into the other person. Quite the contrary! You have to retain a sense of yourself as distinct and different. That's what makes gazing on someone else and, at the same time, being seen in return, so magical. Like Marlene and Roger, you're both present, as you both are, open to one another, aware and unrestricted. Then the deep connectedness that ties all of life together is revealed.

But, although intimacy is always very touching, that doesn't mean you have to do something big.

Jim: Over the 10 years we've been together, we have experienced the powerful beauty of intimacy in many forms. One of our favorites has become a ritual that occurs when one of us is leaving the house. In place of saying good-bye, whoever is leaving calls out the other's name. I will say, "Judith?" As she looks up, I'll hold my hand over my heart. When we make eye contact, I will pat my heart and then, extending my hand toward Judith, I send over my love and affection. After a moment, Judith sends back her love, with the same simple gesture.

Judith: Sometimes we don't even get that far. If I'm leaving, and we're out of each other's sight, I'll call out, "Jim?" By the tone of my voice, he knows what I'm saying. So Jim will just call back, "I know, Judith. I know."

Intimate moments like these can happen any time, anywhere. They are personal, private and they keep your relationship alive in your consciousness. They are the expression of real romance. They don't just happen. You have to consciously participate in nourishing your relationship and maintaining it as part of the focus of your life.

Chapter 9

FAIR FIGHTING AS A SPIRITUAL WORKOUT: RESOLVING DIFFERENCES

If you're angry, be angry
and deal with it. Don't go eat
a bag of Ruffles.

—Oprah Winfrey

One reason that there is so much
aggressive and destructive confrontation in
the world is that there is too little mature,
solid and thoughtful confrontation.

—Brian Muldoon

*I*n any intimate relationship, no matter how wonderful, fighting is unavoidable. Two unique people cannot live together over a long period without clashing
from time to time. They might fight about each other's
ways of disciplining the children, or how to spend money.
They might fight when one feels neglected or the other
feels invaded. *Fighting is like a flare, shot up from the
depths. It warns both partners that something needs
attention. Something in their relationship is calling out
for care and healing.*

Fighting Is Not Optional

Mario Andretti and the Terrified Munchkin

Jim: I've been an aggressive driver. I admit that. Judith
preferred the adjective "reckless." I wouldn't accept that. In
our years together, a recurrent fight happened, as you might
imagine, in traffic.

When Judith saw what seemed to her to be disaster ahead,
she would yelp, suck in her breath, grab onto the door,
preparing for what she believed was just about to happen.

"What?" I'd shout, jamming on the brakes, checking traffic in all directions.

"Those brake lights!"

"Damn it, Judith, that car is at least 60 or 70 feet ahead."

"But his brake lights went on. You weren't putting your brakes on, so I thought . . ."

"There wasn't any need for me to brake."

"Don't yell at me."

"Then don't scare me. If there's any danger here, Judith, it's you."

"That's not fair."

"Maybe. But it's the truth. And besides, I've never even come close to an accident. Doesn't that mean anything to you?"

"Jim, you were looking at that billboard. How did I know if you were paying attention?"

"Was I out of control?"

"I'm not going to wait until we're right on top of a car before I get your attention."

"Then why don't you just say something? Why do you have to panic?"

"Because I'm scared."

This clash always erupted unexpectedly. Each of us was convinced of our own rightness and how wrong and out-of-line the other was. Sometimes it was the beginning of a full-blown set-to.

Do you believe fighting is wrong? Do you believe it is unloving or unenlightened? Well, if you want to ruin your relationship, just avoid fighting. That'll do it. At the other end of the spectrum, just escalate every conflict into all-out war. That will ruin things, too.

> *People who hate trouble generally*
> *get a good deal of it.*
>
> —Harriet Beecher Stowe

Fear of Conflict

Most of us are afraid of conflict. We avoid differences. We suffer in silence to prevent an argument. We'll concede something if that will quiet things. We'll humor somebody even if we don't agree. We'll "shine it on, 'cause it's no biggie." And we'll do just about anything to stave off a fight, because we're afraid of:

- Losing control;
- Physical violence;
- Getting our feelings hurt;
- Driving the other person away;
- Feeling wrong, shamed or stupid when it's over.

There are those who try to live in a world where only harmony and peace should prevail. When that means they avoid conflict, we call it "premature spirituality." They are reaching for heaven, trying to be saints, long before they have accepted their humanity.

Others believe if you love someone, you should never get angry with them. That's a very crippling fantasy, because it demands keeping the relationship as it is, and at all costs. It's also a very expensive fantasy. It costs two people the vitality of what they have together.

Other people are filled with resentment and disappointment. Never having learned that these feelings can provide rich channels of communication for new and sustaining intimacy, and terrified they'll just blow up if they unload, they consciously or unconsciously choose to numb out with romance novels, alcohol and drugs, cheat on their spouses, escape into the drone of sitcoms and talk shows or spend hours surfing the Internet.

Those who profess to favor freedom and yet depreciate agitation, are those who want crops without plowing up the ground, they want rain without thunder and lightning.

—Frederick Douglass

Blessed by the Challenge

Throughout history, our foremost spiritual teachers have understood that to expand your consciousness, you have to go through some kind of personal ordeal. *An awakened vision comes only after you squarely face into a demanding challenge, release and let go of whatever limiting beliefs stand in your way, even if they are those you treasure, and open yourself to the new and different awareness that awaits on the other side of your trial.* When you do that, you move into a larger and more encompassing consciousness, one that inspires more empathy, more compassion, more of a sense of unity with the diversity of life. You grow as you are able to embrace that which is different from you.

We're not suggesting that you have to become a mystic or a religious leader to experience the spiritual dimensions of your relationship. We are saying that when you embrace the challenge of differences—which is at the core of spiritual awakening—you have the opportunity to grow each time you and your partner find yourselves in a conflict.

Spiritual change is not merely a change in appearance. It is a metamorphosis, like carbon becoming diamond. That kind of change cannot take place without struggle, without a spiritual workout. Sometimes it takes a serious struggle with a well-intentioned partner to wake us up.

Jim: After a number of our on-the-road encounters, Judith could clearly see that I was right. I had almost never come close to an accident. But I had to admit my driving could be frightening, even to someone other than her. Still, the fight erupted and nothing changed. So we agreed that the next time it happened, we would pay attention to the details to really understand what was going on. Our intention was to devise a mutually respectful and beneficial resolution.

As it turned out, I realized my aggressive driving had to do with a deep contempt for what I initially believed was weakness. "I can't tolerate drivers who are timid," I explained.

"But, Jim, we're not talking about a race. We're on city streets. There's no rule that says other drivers shouldn't be timid," Judith responded.

"Well, I get bored just following behind."

"Maybe . . ."

"No. Not maybe. I do."

"I know. I know you do. But that's not really the point. You get angry. Even hostile. What's that about?"

"They are so unconscious. They drive as though they're the only ones on the road. That's what gets to me. I don't get considered. They can have anything they want, and not because they choose to drive the way they do, but because they aren't aware enough to even know that how they drive impacts other people. That's infuriating."

"It's not about them. They don't even know you exist."

"That is exactly my point. So I'm forced to shift and maneuver just because they're not with it enough to know there's a world outside their own lives."

"But when you drive aggressively, I get scared."

"That doesn't make any sense to me. What scares you so?"

"Well, when you drive like that I feel out of control."

"How?"

"Since I would be braking, you should too."

"Wait a minute, Judith. Can't I have my own way of driving? There's no room here for differences?"

"You should talk!"

"I should talk?! What do you mean?"

"Is there any room in your world for the way other people drive?" We both burst out laughing.

"Oh. You mean the magic of differences." We laughed even harder. "For all we say, when our own buttons get pushed, there's not much room for magic, is there?"

"That's not true Jim. Don't go overboard. But we can be just as blind as anyone else."

"Boy, isn't that the truth."

Our driving fights were a signal and a blessing. They called us to pay attention. We had to look to the source of our anger and upset. They eventually forced us to face into things about ourselves, our own limits and unconsciousness, that were expressed through aggressive driving and unwarranted fears.

When you avoid conflict, you pass up the chance to know yourself and your partner better. Since such knowledge is required for intimate love, conflict can be a special blessing. It's an adventure of practical spirituality compelling you to move beyond being self-centered. Yet, at the same time, you surely don't want to lose your independence. You like your own habits, attitudes and quirky ways of doing things. But here's the catch. Your partner feels exactly the same way about his or her habits, attitudes and quirky ways. So how can you balance intimacy and the desire to love and be loved with your need for independence and autonomy? What do you do with the ways the two of you are different, especially when those differences spark anger and conflict?

Coming to Terms with Conflict

Human blood is classified into four different types: A, B, O and Rh. People of one blood type can donate their blood to others of the same type without any problem. Their blood is compatible. However, it's very dangerous to mix two different types. They are incompatible and they can kill the recipient.

This lethal incompatibility can serve as a model for conflict at the purely physical level. It's the one most people know and use. It states that where two elements are different, they cannot coexist in the same system. It's as simple as that. When two people experience their beliefs or behaviors as incompatible, they can feel threatened by one another and their relationship becomes unstable. If, like blood types, they can't or won't change, they end up in separate camps. Tensions rise, anger increases and, before long, they're at each other. Their differences have become dangerous.

At the heart of this traditional view of conflict is the belief that there must be a winner and a loser. Somebody must dominate. Sports is another example of conflict at the physical level. Somebody has to win and somebody has to lose.

Imagine what would happen if two football teams played hard and long and at the end of regulation time the score was tied. Instead of battling until there was a winner, what if they decided to accept the tie score as a symbol of their individual and mutual excellence. In the world of football, that would be like saying that two different blood types could coexist in the same body. Can you imagine the lead story during the 11 o'clock news?

What if the two teams compromised? Say it was bitter cold and the crowd was dwindling, there were a number of injuries on both sides and, since neither team could reach the playoffs anyway, the game didn't really mean much. The players were weary and wanted to stop struggling. So they agreed that one team would forfeit this game if the other would forfeit their next game together. Even though that goes against everything they believed about sports and competition, and they would regret it later, they decided to do it. So they just walked off the field.

As ridiculous as this forfeit example sounds, that's what most couples do. To keep the peace, they compromise.

Both people agree to give up something they'd rather not in exchange for something that can never be satisfying. Resentment follows and they both end up less than they were before they compromised.

Because the traditional view of conflict holds that two differing points of view cannot coexist in the same system, winning/dominance and losing/submission are the irrevocable outcomes of most disputes. That's why fighting is so frightening to most people. Even so, anger and fighting are part of any relationship in which two people are honest and outspoken. That's the plain truth. If you insist it should be otherwise, you're hopelessly romantic or fatally naive.

Exploring Conflict: Guided Exploration

Bring to mind a fight you experienced that never was satisfactorily resolved. What was the issue? What did you find unacceptable about your partner? What did your partner find unacceptable about you? What prevented you from resolving the issue?

Looking back, why was it so difficult to approach your partner's point of view with respect? Did you want to be the one who defined reality? Was your partner doing the same thing? In fact, you both had to be doing it together, otherwise the fight could not have gone on. You were both caught in your allegiances, battling in a win/lose stand-off. Both angry. Both certain the other had to change.

Now, imagine a compromise. How would you feel if you had to accept a solution that's not to your liking, but that would definitely stop the fight? Would it truly bring an end to the conflict? It's unlikely. *Concession and compromise can't ever touch your emotional injury where the actual struggle is taking place.*

During a fight, most people usually focus on the content of their arguments. She said this. He did that. As a rule of thumb, the difficulty is almost never about the content. It's about the fact that neither is willing to include the other. That's where the real pain comes from. Both feel left out, hurt or betrayed. Both feel powerless to have any impact, as if they are invisible. No matter what they do, they can't get seen or heard.

Is that what the two of you did in the argument you are remembering? Isn't it true that your tension and hurt feelings won't be relieved until you feel understood and appreciated?

There are always three sides to the truth—yours, your partner's and the whole truth. No one has a God's-eye view on the whole truth. *But because each of you is seeing the conflict from a different point of view, there is some truth to what each of you is fighting for.* So, you are both right and you are both wrong. Insisting that your point of view is the only one is as much a miscarriage of the truth as letting your partner dominate.

What Fighting Is Not

Any time you intend to hurt, wound or damage your partner, you are no longer fighting. You are killing. We don't use "killing" to be dramatic. We mean it quite specifically. When you decide to do damage, you break the connection. Even though you may be filled with rage, you are emotionally detached. Only your view has value. Only your feelings and beliefs are important. Only your reality is real. Once you have dehumanized your partner, you have become a killer. You know how it goes after that. You start name-calling. "Butthead." "Ditzo." "Freak." "Bitch." You attack with words like "ridiculous," "moronic," "insane." Your partner means little or nothing to you.

Killing is not always dramatic, open and obvious. Many of our attacks are hardly visible. A moment's contempt. A silent derision. A belittling gesture. A taunting remark. At that point, enthusiasm wilts, self-esteem crumbles, hope fades and desire recedes into self-protection. All little deaths. You've broken the caring connection.

In the Wilderness of Your Relationship

Conflict, especially fighting, takes place in the wilderness of your relationship, out at the edges where you haven't yet created a mutually beneficial way to be together. You can't see things clearly. It's very easy to misunderstand and misinterpret what's happening. You are both on unstable and insecure ground. The fear of losing your way or being overrun is intense. So you fiercely hold onto your certainty. Without training and preparation for respecting and negotiating differences and fighting fairly, you can't help but be scared of each other. You become angry and self-protective, even lethal—though you know that's not really what you want. The more angry and closed-off you become, the more threatened and isolated you are and the wilder things get. *It's not fighting that's wrong, it's doing it badly that's so destructive.*

---

*Don't be afraid to feel as angry
or as loving as you can.*

—Lena Horne

Six Lessons of Anger

Anger can be healthy. Because it is a response to being hurt, it signals your need for change and decisive action. When you are conscious of and respect your anger, it becomes a wise and powerful teacher. When you know how to read its lessons, you can learn a great deal about yourself and your partner.

Lesson 1: *Anger is necessary to protect yourself from being mistreated.*

You need to express your anger in order to take care of yourself. Use it to declare your needs and to define who you are—what you will put up with and what you won't.

Anger lives at the boundary between you and the outside world. Without anger you cannot know to say stop when someone is mistreating you. This is true whether it is physical abuse or just someone who keeps interrupting you while you're telling a story. Your anger will help you assert your presence and prevent you from becoming invisible.

Lesson 2: *Anger helps you request better treatment.*

Your partner can only deal with what you reveal. If you don't express your anger, your partner may not really understand how important your complaint is to you. Furthermore, your anger will help support you to speak with bold directness.

Lesson 3: *Anger clears the air of unspoken tensions and unmet needs.*

It's helpful to look at conflict as a spiritual house cleaning.

When you express your anger, you free yourself of tensions and prevent emotional buildup. Even at your most conscious, you won't catch everything that may disturb you as you and your partner go through your life together. But that's okay. Because as you practice clearing the air, more and more of your needs can be met. That's how speaking up keeps you healthy.

Lesson 4: *Expressing anger overcomes the fear of confrontation and conflict.*

Anger tells you there is a problem. If you don't speak up, the problem becomes larger. You will have to deal with pressure building up inside. You may become chronically ill, moody or depressed. Anger needs an outlet, because, in one way or another, it will have its say.

As you learn to respectfully express your anger, even if your partner becomes defensive or scared, you will discover that nobody dies. When you know that, then confrontation is just one of the ways you have to express your passion. You'll come to understand that by giving voice to your anger, even if that results in a conflict, you're doing what is useful and necessary for you, your partner and the relationship. Your partner can only deal with what you reveal. Keep the caring connection open.

Lesson 5: *Anger opens the way to a deeper intimacy.*

There is an alchemical power in confronting your differences. Trouble, which you can think of as a rough piece of carbon, is transformed into something valuable through the pressure of anger and the cutting and shaping of a fair and productive fight. *Every time you resolve a conflict, each of you is made emotionally and spiritually stronger.* Together you have come through a "trial by fire." You know each other better, and you both feel seen and heard.

Lesson 6: *Anger motivates you to create a better life.*

With trust and love and with an appreciation for your differences, your conflicts will lead you to discover how strong and resilient you actually are. You will develop courage and confidence, so that the wilderness in your relationship becomes an open space, calling you to expand your consciousness and grow in wisdom and grace. You will move together in ever-changing rhythms to re-create your relationship.

Freely expressed anger is not your enemy. In fact, it is your ally. It is a feeling that moves you out toward your partner to do the bold lovework of maintaining yourselves, your relationship and the differences that make being together so rich and exciting—so powerfully intimate.

---

*I don't want the same season
twice in a row; I don't want to know
I'm getting last week's weather, used weather,
weather broadcast up and down
the coast, old-hat weather.*

—Annie Dillard

Changing the Meaning of "Differences"

Historically, groups of people—families, tribes, nation-states—believed their differences were absolute and unalterable. Consequently, they had little choice but to feel alienated, incompatible and entrenched, defending each of their separate ways as the only true way. Beliefs that exclude differences have been as much a part of the human landscape as the battles they inspired.

And beneath this ancient legacy of struggle and resistance is the most basic fight of all, the war between the sexes. It has been going on for centuries. In today's language, women claim the men "don't get it" while men believe the women "are getting it all." History is one long lamentation over the disrespect of differences.

But what if there were no differences—every face, every body, every personality, every point of view exactly the same? That's unimaginable, isn't it? Yet in an unfair, unproductive fight, we not only dishonor differences, we try to eliminate them. We try to make the other person believe as we believe, act as we act, imagine and think and feel as we do. *The truth is that differences don't create distance and alienation. Only our attitudes about and our misunderstanding of differences do that.*

Returning to the conflict you've been looking at, how would it change if you redefined the meaning of differences so that they are essential to your mutual well-being? To make this kind of change you will have to get beyond the win/lose physical model of conflict.

In the physical world, you can't redefine things. They are what they are. The physical model of conflict is based on an either/or, win/lose view of the world. There are only two opposing alternatives and one of them must dominate. In the psychological world, your reality is malleable. That means you can redefine things. You can change your mind.

What if you could see your differences as the source of a special bond you have with your partner—even when conflicts arise? What if you have more options than just either/or?

In our on-the-road fights, if there were only two choices, win or lose, then both of us would have to fight to win. But once we understood and appreciated what the situation meant to each of us, we could redefine the conditions and see each other from a different vantage point. We opened our hearts and began to create a resolution based on a new understanding of our differences.

When you respect and value your differences, you will have much more psychological room in which to move around. Your connection can deepen as you both explore the issues underlying your conflict, and that leads to an ever-expanding, new vision of intimacy. You can begin to see that both of your positions contain some validity. Given that, you will need to look for a resolution that's mutually respectful. You won't have to settle for something like, "Well that's just the way she is." Or "You know how men are." You can open up to the treasures that your differences provide, treasures that have been there all along.

From this spiritually transformative conception of differences, which is at the heart of the new intimacy, how would your feelings about your partner and about yourself change? What kind of resolution would you try to achieve? Remember, we're not talking about compromise where you both give up something important just to stop the tension. That tack can only be temporary. We are talking about a resolution process in which you both:

- Have each other's well-being at heart;
- Are respectful that you're both in the wilderness of your relationship so that you must take care as you proceed;
- Commit to explore the issue in detail so that neither one of you feels slighted;
- Feel understood and respected, so that neither one of you is forced to concede;
- Intend to use the conflict to grow in individual and mutual consciousness;
- Are willing to be patient, allowing the resolution to emerge rather than forcing it, in order to assure a creative new result instead of filling in with something from the past.
- Trust your mutually defined resolution because it both expresses and includes you and points the way to a more expansive, more fulfilling future.

Differences between people are inescapable. Recognizing and appreciating them can provide you with the deepest source of personal development and profound intimacy. Embracing them makes a spiritual relationship possible.

Trouble is part of your life,
and if you don't share it, you don't
give the person who loves you enough
chance to love you enough.

—Dinah Shore

How to Fight Fair

Since differences and fighting are unavoidable, how can you make them productive? While physical reality is fixed, your mind is pliable, ever-changing. You can move from one state of mind to another. You can change your mind to change your life. You can tap the rich source of wisdom that's hidden in the noise and hurt of every fight.

Jim: During one of our fights, I shouted out, "Judith, don't forget I love you. But, damn it, you really make me angry!" We were still very far apart in our idea of what was going on. I was fighting to make sure that my position would be heard and considered. Yet I wanted her to know that, even though we were in conflict about a specific issue, I still loved and embraced her in the rest of our relationship. That's what lovework looks like during a fight! You remember that there's still the rest of your relationship. If you don't, then the fight is likely to overwhelm you with the intensity of the moment and you'll elevate what might otherwise be inconsequential to the level of a catastrophe.

When fighting is lovework it's an invitation to change your mind, as you:

- Expose and heal your limiting beliefs and behaviors;

- Expand your awareness to include new alternatives;

- Explore and improve the character of your relationship;
- Deepen the intimacy of your being together.

Principles of Fair Fighting

Fair fighting is lovework—a fierce expression of love for yourself and your partner. Given that, there are very specific commitments you and your partner can make, before and during a fight, that will assure that you are doing lovework instead of doing damage. Remember, every fight is like a flare, an SOS drawing your attention to what needs healing.

1. **Your purpose is to find a mutually respectful resolution.** To keep a fight fair, you have to keep your focus on finding a resolution that includes and satisfies you both. During a fight, frustrations are high. Voices are loud. Vision is clouded, even distorted. Both of you can feel unseen, unheard and unappreciated. That's the time to remember you do love one another, that the point of the conflict is to make sure neither of you sabotages your love by putting up with less than your love deserves. The purpose of a fight is to reconcile your differences and dissolve the distance between you.

2. **Remember, you're only human.** You're both feeling vulnerable. And, no matter how things appear, you both feel threatened. Otherwise there wouldn't be a fight. Since you both are feeling very fragile, it is essential that you trust each other. Then, even when your hot buttons are pushed, you can count on the

fact that you both truly care for each other and that your connection is still there. But even so, this does not mean that you forfeit your complaint or your needs. That would only submerge the conflict for the moment, leaving it unsettled, ensuring that it will rise again in the future.

3. **Sometimes a fight is necessary.** When your intention is to keep your relationship healthy, fair fighting is always about getting your grievances out in the open. It's a way of saying, "I'm completely committed to our relationship and I won't let this particular problem continue." You can't stay where you are. You can't go backward. You're not sure how to go forward. The pressure of the situation is actually a blessing bringing you together. You're fighting to stay fully alive, to continue to grow and develop with one another. When you both know this, you will know that a fair fight is a godsend—an alarm calling you to put out the fire.

4. **Both of you are being powerful.** In a fair fight, no one is victimized. Whether you're yelling or silent, weeping or walking around the room, insistent or seeking—you are exerting a powerful effect on your partner. The fact that the fight continues is proof of your influence. Even though you may not feel like it, you are having an impact. You have to stay conscious of that.

5. **Every fight is cocreated.** In a fight, no one is entirely innocent. Do you bristle as you read this? Do you want to argue: "When he starts yelling,

there's nothing I can do," or, "When she starts manipulating, I'm powerless"? We understand. Your feeling
of powerlessness may come upon you so quickly
that it feels like you have no control. But you do. In a
fair fight, you both have to take responsibility for
your participation in what created the conflict and
what you are doing to resolve it. Whether you raised
the complaint, or you are feeling defensive, criticized, whatever, it takes both of you to make a fight.
Even when you're angry, threatened, shut down, you
still make choices. You are always part of the process.

6. **Don't harbor discontent.** Commit to speaking
your desire and need, dissatisfaction and hurt, as
soon as you possibly can. What you keep secret acts
like rust and fungus, coat hangers and the stuff in
your garage. It keeps growing in the dark. It extends
its contagion into more and more areas of your relationship until there is no more room for love. It's
been consumed by unspoken wreckage, rot and clutter. Remember, although some moments may be better than others, there is no perfect moment to voice
your grievance.

When you're scared, you may want to approach your
partner with something like, "To honor our relationship, I need time to discuss something really important
with you. I'm nervous, a bit scared, and need your help
and attention." However you do it, speak up!

7. **Stay on point.** Hash out only one thing at a time.
Nothing is more maddening, confusing and ultimately

enraging than jumping from point to point, obscuring the problem, making it very difficult, if not impossible, to achieve any kind of resolution. You end up fighting about how you're fighting. A commitment to stay on point is more than just a concern for taking care of the issue. It's a commitment to stay conscious that fighting is serious business. It strengthens and deepens your connection. Give it your best effort. It's lovework.

8. **Don't drag up past complaints.** Since we all have some trouble keeping the emotional slate clean, it's very easy for the small stuff, and even the big stuff, that gets ignored to fester into buried land mines. And then, in the middle of a conflict, you feel desperate and all that old resentment comes flying out with something like, "Do you remember when you . . .?" Unless your spouse is strong enough to remind you that dragging up the past is out of line, suddenly the fight veers out of control and becomes lethal. After a few more do-you-remember-whens, neither of you even knows what you're fighting about. Then you're liable to throw anything into the mess.

9. **Stay out of your individual history.** As a basic rule of thumb, you can assume that anger has to do with what's happening in current time. In contrast, rage is like old, dammed-up water. When it's triggered by something, when your buttons are pushed, the dam bursts and rage rushes forth seeking revenge.

Judith: Early in our relationship we'd made a plan to go to the theater after a picnic dinner in Jim's office. He was working as an investment banker at the time. During the afternoon, I happily poached salmon, steamed asparagus and prepared the picnic basket. Just as I was ready to leave, the phone rang. It was Jim and he explained a new deal had just been signed. Although he was disappointed about our date, he had to stay late at the office preparing for the next day's meeting. I understood. I knew how his business worked. But after I hung up, I began to sob and scream. I blindly stormed around, finally banging into a wall, sliding down in a heap of rage and despair. All this just because of a broken date? Hardly! But if, in my own therapy, I hadn't learned about this kind of rage, I would have certainly turned my wrath on Jim.

Instead, I remembered dinner time all the years I was growing up. My father sold cars for a living. Frequently he couldn't come home for dinner because a potential buyer had just walked onto the lot. Other times, when he was in the middle of closing a deal, he would call and ask us to hold dinner. Thirty minutes later he'd call again telling us to go ahead without him. Although we were all disappointed, neither my mother, brother nor I ever showed our disappointment and hurt. We were "understanding" because we knew how his business worked.

This time, however, in the safety of my loving relationship with Jim, all those years of being stood up for dinner came flooding out with a vengeance, dragging bottled-up rage and impotence in tow.

When the past explodes like that, staying relevant or being reasonable can be very, very difficult. Wounds that have been festering for years demand attention. Unfortunately, no one can undo what has been done.

When you can be conscious that old feelings are flooding into a fight, you can warn your partner, "Don't take this personally, it's old junk and I just need to let it rip." This doesn't mean that suddenly you change emotionally. Not at all. You can be screaming, as you warn your partner. Your rage doesn't have to completely overwhelm and possess you. As we said, *there is more to you in any given moment than just the experience of that moment.* If you try this you will see that you will not lose your intensity and, in fact, you can clear the way to give full vent to what you are experiencing without backing down for fear of doing damage to your partner and your relationship. If your partner can stay separate enough to be a stand-in, she or he can gift you with the chance to vent your rage while she or he is a loving witness to your pain. That reinforces your connection and allows your past hurt to be recognized, validated and healed.

Rules of Fair Fighting

There are several rules that can help keep you both whole and on track. Follow them and you will prevent yourself from becoming lethal.

1. **No dirty fighting.** No character assassination, name calling, mockery, hitting below the belt—using your partner's weaknesses against him or her. When you attack your partner, rather than challenge his or her argument, you're off point.

2. **Use "I" statements.** One way to stay on point and express yourself is to speak your complaint by using

"I" statements. "I feel betrayed when you don't call when you're going to be late." "I'm scared you'll leave me for someone else." When you use "you" statements—"You're so insensitive, you never consider me." "You're always doing that"—your partner will feel judged and will react defensively.

3. **Listen with curiosity and concern.** Listen to your partner's objections and needs so you can understand them. The whole point of the fight is to achieve a mutually satisfactory resolution. To do that you need to fully grasp both sides of the situation.

4. **Stand your ground.** Make certain your partner understands your position. You may have to repeat yourself many times in many different ways. In order to freely and fully participate in discovering the resolution, you both have to feel understood.

5. **Respect your partner's integrity.** Although it can be difficult to keep in mind when passions are flaring, don't use shouting or tears or other weapons just to overpower your partner. That's control, manipulation and dominance. Manipulation means you will do whatever you have to do to undermine your partner's position. In a fair fight, you need the truth your partner brings to the conflict in order for both of you to be ultimately satisfied.

6. **Protect yourself from abuse.** Do not take or give any physical abuse. Protect yourself from verbal abuse as well. As a rule, abuse is anything that is willfully intended to hurt the other, anything that breaks the caring connection. And don't accuse your partner of

abuse just to gain advantage. That's abuse. Keep in mind that your partner's point of view is as important to her or him as yours is to you. Remembering that will give you the basis for respect that keeps a fight from careening out of control.

7. **Keep open to new possibilities.** Neither one of you can predict exactly the best outcome. Stay open to discover the resolution. That's a matter of creativity that emerges as you feel understood and are willing to explore the deeper issues.

8. **Insist on resolution.** Don't back down just to "get it over with," or to show how "generous" or "understanding" you can be. That's relationship suicide. Don't allow the fight to merely fade without reaching a resolution. Unsettled conflicts just continue to fester in silent darkness, where they grow in strength and malice.

Remember, relationships are cocreated and so are fights. If you deny responsibility when fighting erupts, you create your own powerlessness. If you deny your participation, you are totally dependent. If you refuse to see the mutuality of your conflicts, you have withdrawn from the relationship.

However, when you accept responsibility for your participation, you open the door to your creative power, you acknowledge your interdependence with your partner, and you stand courageously in the fierce intimacy of claiming a larger existence together. That's love and that's lovework!

*You can only hope to find a
lasting solution to a conflict if you have
learned to see the other objectively, but,
at the same time, to experience their
difficulties subjectively.*

—Dag Hammarskjöld

An Invitation to Deeper Intimacy

As we've said, a conflict, especially a fight, takes place in an area of your being together that hasn't yet been worked out. But as Einstein understood, you cannot solve a problem with the same consciousness that created it. To reach a real resolution, you must go into the mystery together and face the unknown to learn more about yourselves. To do that you will have to stay emotionally connected. Your connection is the key to a productive, spiritually transformative resolution—two distinct realities working to discover a touching point, a new understanding from which you both can cocreate a more fulfilling future.

Solution Versus Resolution

Finally, there is a serious distinction between "solution" and "resolution." A solution is merely a technique to manage or put up with the difficulty. A solution doesn't produce change, only tolerance and control. A resolution is based on new insight about:

• What was injured and how it happened;

- How your injury can be healed so that forgiveness and release will follow;

- A way of moving into a new future, in which both of you will be different than before you came upon the resolution, so that this kind of injury will be less likely to occur. In short, resolution is an expression of creative change.

Our resolution to the on-the-road problem has evolved over time.

> **Jim:** I've stopped taking out my anger on other drivers. Not just to please Judith, but because I could hear that she was right. What I was doing was sometimes dangerous. I've also learned to keep more distance from the car in front of me, both so I can relax and to give Judith a bit of a comfort zone. And, most importantly, I've learned to be open to the different ways people drive (although not every time) so that I can practice the magic of differences which I know is real and powerful.
>
> **Judith:** I really listened to what Jim said about my scaring him and that my tension and fear are really hurting me. I certainly don't want to scare him. So, I've learned to practice surrendering and trusting Jim's lifelong excellent driving record and his care for both of us. But I still make sure to stay alert.

The touching point leading you to resolution is something new, some way of understanding yourself and one another that didn't exist before. Previous resolutions from your past won't sufficiently address the issue(s) of the current fight, because if they did, the current issue wouldn't be a problem.

The distinction between "solution" and "resolution" is

very important. It means the difference between just coping and real personal development. We will explain how you can tap into the healing power of your most significant differences in chapter 10.

Conflict, correctly understood, is a very powerful invitation to greater intimacy. Through lovework, you and your partner can reach in-depth resolutions that will further open you to a new intimacy with one another. And your new intimacy will resonate throughout the dimensions of your individual identities—through your similarities and differences—and the care you give and receive within your deepening connection.

Chapter 10

SPIRITUAL POWER: THE WISDOM OF DIFFERENCES

A partner will bring up all your patterns.
Don't avoid relationships: they are
the best seminar in town. The truth is that
your partner is your guru.

—Sondra Ray

You begin to see that what is
necessary to the health of your partnership
is identical with what is necessary to your own
spiritual growth, that each of you holds the
pieces that the other is missing.

—Gary Zukav

When you embrace the differences between you and your partner—all of them, not just those you like—you will be challenged in just the ways you need to be. The intimacy you share will reach into more and more areas of your life together, including more trust, more fun, more surprises. Your connection will deepen and you will see that there is a spiritual wisdom in your choice of one another.

When people are truly in love,
they experience far more than just a
mutual need for each other's company and
consolation. In their relation with one
another they become different people....
They are made over into new beings.

—Thomas Merton

The Healing Power of Relationship

The Blessing of Aggravation

Jim: Some years ago, when I was working as an investment banker, I saw an aphorism taped to the wall in a colleague's office. It read, "If you have a job that has no aggravation, you don't have a job." In that moment, I realized that aggravation is part of all jobs. That's just the way they are and that bit of wisdom changed my attitude toward work forever.

Marriage is the same. A marriage without aggravation is a marriage in name only. Just like the sand in an oyster necessary to grow the pearl, aggravation will push you to address the issues each of you needs to heal and grow. To try to live without difficulties and rough spots is a great loss. Yet in a society where people think they are entitled to live discomfort-free lives, this idea has serious competition.

One popular competitor is the romantic notion of a perfect soul-mate somewhere on the planet who will exactly match your list of specifications. When you meet, love will follow immediately. You won't have any conflict—no disturbances or aggravation. You will fit together as if "made for each other." Anyone who expects to meet this perfect match will find the differences and difficulties they encounter in regular, imperfect mortals to be just maddening. Hardly worth the effort, to say nothing of deeply disappointing. Because there cannot be such a person as the perfect, non-aggravating partner. *A real soul-mate will be someone whose differences will challenge you, anger you, and at times, you will almost feel you're with the wrong person. She or he will have the capacity to aggravate you, awaken you, call you out into the healing process of discovering the truth of yourself.*

A passionate and spiritually wise relationship depends on your attitude toward aggravation. You are guaranteed a devastating cycle of despair and dissatisfaction if you try to avoid the aggravation that is part of developing intimacy. But, if you expect and value the inevitable, you will be richly rewarded. You will know that disturbances are opportunities for healing. Instead of backing away, you can open to them. Your relationship will be like a diamond mine. As you do the lovework of clearing away the dirt and rocks, you can find and claim the buried treasure waiting for you.

Toothpick Aggravation

We don't choose each other impulsively—even when it seems that way. Powerful, unconscious forces play a role in determining the person to whom we are attracted. There is a hidden wisdom in our choices, so it behooves us to pay attention.

Judith: When we met, Jim worked in Century City as an investment banker and lived half a block from the ocean in Marina del Rey, one of California's finer beach communities. He drove a vintage Mercedes Benz and read philosophy. I owned my own townhouse condo in Santa Monica with my office just four blocks away. Through my full-time private practice as a clinical psychologist, I earned a solid income and had put away a respectable pension fund. On the surface, we looked just right for each other. Soon enough, however, a major difference got our attention.

Jim: I had the habit of keeping a toothpick in my mouth long after I had need of it. The fact is that I've had dental surgery in all four quadrants of my mouth, and oral hygiene is a high priority. Still, I was unconsciously attached to keeping a toothpick—even to the point of talking with it—in my mouth.

Judith was horrified, repelled and disgusted. She found my habit not only tacky but embarrassing. When we were alone she would snap at me—"Don't you think people notice?"

"I don't care what they think," I would snap back, but I was just covering. She was right and I knew it. Still, every time she would point it out, I felt hurt and angry and invaded. I wasn't about to give in.

Although both of us truly wanted to resolve this struggle, it went on for a couple of years. Before we tell you how it turned out, we want to pose a question: How can relationships heal?

How Can Relationships Heal?

A fever is one of the body's methods of fighting off disease. But it can be profoundly disorienting, even as important healing is taking place. There's no difference when it comes to emotions and the mind. Spiritual healing is often quite disorienting and sometimes can be very painful. However, there is an alchemical power waiting within the struggle and pain, for it is the purpose of each and every challenge to teach you to receive more and more love.

When true love is present, all that has never been loved will surface, because it can, and because it must. This is a fundamental healing principle inherent in any long-term, monogamous relationship. When you and your partner are together over time and you are open to what your relationship has available, the allegiances and masks you brought with you will necessarily be exposed. This is not a mystery. In a long-term relationship it is impossible for you to hide who you really are unless you restrict and suppress yourselves into emotional death.

When you know you are loved and your partner is committed to your well-being, you can risk letting your defenses down and allow what you have hidden to come out into the light. Without the reassurance that you are loved for who you really are, you will have to play-act the idea of loving by keeping both your imperfections and your brilliance in the shadows.

In the presence of love, those shadow parts of you that you have rejected will surface, looking for acceptance. When your partner accepts those "awful" things, and you can re-see yourself through his or her eyes, you can become more consciously whole by learning to accept what you previously disavowed. That is the healing power of love.

Sometimes the healing is quick and uncomplicated. Here are two examples from our lives.

> **Judith:** For one of our early dates, I wasn't ready when Jim arrived. I invited him in and apologized. He said it was okay and sat down with one of my magazines. Although Jim was not at all bothered by my tardiness, for some reason I felt I was doing something wrong by keeping him waiting. In fact, he wasn't even aware that I was anxious. When I told him how concerned I was, he assured me he had no problem and encouraged me to just let it go. It was Jim's ease and acceptance that showed me another way and helped me to relax my own self-judgment that demanded perfection to ensure never annoying anyone.

Jim: My example has to do with staying up late. I can remember summer nights when I was a child lying next to my bedroom window wondering about the stars or listening to a nearby train whistle or just enjoying the wind through the leaves. I needed the time alone and took it after everyone else in the family was asleep. My mother called me a "night owl" in a way that made clear she thought there was something wrong with me.

When Judith and I decided to get married, I knew I had to tell her about my inclination to stay up late. Her only concern was that she looked forward to our going to bed together and snuggling before we fell asleep. I could feel that old judgment. There was something wrong with me. Then she suggested that we could go to bed at the same time and, if I were still awake when she fell asleep, she had no problem if I got up and did whatever I wanted. That was easy enough and the issue has never arisen since.

Sometimes differences are easy to deal with. At other times, however, healing takes determination and in-depth exploration. When complex, deep-seated issues collide, they can seem impenetrable unless you view the clash as a healing opportunity. If you don't see the possibilities for spiritual growth such a clash makes available, it may seem too risky to open yourself. But then you must close yourself off from what is going on between you and your partner and that choice can be very damaging. On the other hand, if you recognize and welcome the clash as an opportunity to face into and resolve whatever it is that has become so aggravating, your love can flourish and your intimacy will grow in safety and tenderness.

In such instances, it is critical that you both begin by

accepting that each of you is who you are now—and cannot be any different yet. It's only on the ground of reality that you can build real change. It is also essential that you both are open to change. Not dominance and submission. Not compromise and resentment. But real healing, personal growth and permanent change. This kind of transformative process will be a spiritual workout of the first order and sometimes disorienting and/or painful.

It's in taking the courageous and loving risk of revealing yourself and at the same time opening your heart and mind to compassionately accept your spouse's previously unloved truth, that you both are healed and made whole. Only then can you embrace yourselves as *imperfectly beautiful.*

Each friend represents a
world in us, a world possibly not born
until they arrive, and it is only by this
meeting that a new world is born.

—Anaïs Nin

Back to the Toothpicks

Jim: The toothpick issue produced one of our most demanding struggles. I despised Judith's insistence on "propriety" and what I thought was her exaggerated concern about other people's opinions. I would not kowtow to other people's definitions of what was proper.

Nevertheless, whenever she saw a toothpick in my mouth, she would try to get my attention. She would step on my foot under the table or she would discreetly point at her mouth. Sometimes it worked, sometimes it didn't. I knew she died a dozen deaths, and I also knew her pain wasn't having much of an impact on me.

Judith: This problem erupted into fair- and not-so-fair fighting. And, since we couldn't arrive at a suitable resolution, it was always simmering on the back burner. We knew this issue was a rich opportunity because we could both see some truth in the other's position. We just didn't know how to go forward more constructively. However, since both of us were committed to a resolution, we used our process of Conscious Creativity as a way to deal with this difficult and painful issue.

Jim: I realized that for me, toothpicks dated back to my teenage days in Detroit. I was a street gang kid. Toothpicks were a sign of being a "tough guy" and were directly linked to my adolescent masculinity. But, when I met Judith, I was deeply attracted to her sense of elegance. It was something I had always wanted. By using toothpicks the way I did I denied myself the elegance I wanted and kept the "macho streets" alive.

Judith: I realized that Jim's toothpicks had powerfully exposed a profound truth about me, one that I had worked very hard to keep hidden. My father had limited education. He dropped out of high school to support his widowed mother. Though he is very intelligent and artistic, he made his living selling cars. I thought of him as a used-car salesman and, as a result, was ashamed of his job and ashamed of my background. I concealed my embarrassment by creating a "Beverly Hills-like" persona. Then I met Jim, a man I deeply loved. With each toothpick, he exposed the truth of my "shameful" background for all to see. I wasn't from Beverly Hills. I was the daughter of a used-car salesman in love with somebody who chewed toothpicks.

Jim: Despite our education, years of therapy, both of our 40-some-odd years on the planet, and everything else that we had been blessed with, we were both cut off from ourselves in certain ways. Jim in self-doubt and me in self-hatred. We both were hiding behind masks when it came to these particular issues. We both needed to change, and we both needed each other to change.

Judith: To accomplish what we both wanted from ourselves and each other, we had to confront each other over and over again and had to be willing to hear each other as well as we could. You can bet sometimes we got very defensive. These issues were old and well-entrenched. We both had built up a lot of stuff around them. But we persisted.

Jim: Judith had to teach me that my allegiance to keeping a tiny sliver of wood in my mouth was undermining the positive impact I was having on other people. She never confronted me in public, never shamed me. But she had to get my attention onto the real problem. She also had to accept that I wouldn't be able to change my behavior easily, much less overnight.

Judith: Jim showed me how my horror with his toothpicks was a measure of my fear of being found out. Even at those times when I thought someone was thinking less of us, of me, I could see that the real danger was in my defining myself by my assumptions about what other people thought was appropriate. Still, my fears of social disapproval and being unacceptable were deeply imbedded, so my ability to change was also slow-going.

Jim: The clash of our "toothpick values" and our willingness to look into the deeper meaning of our resistances, brought us wonderful healing revelations. There was, indeed, profound spiritual wisdom in our choice of each other—as long as we didn't get stuck at the superficial level or succumb to the need to win.

Judith: Toothpicks led us to deep-seated fears and insecurities. Due to our ongoing lovework, I am far more relaxed about social appearances and much more accepting of my previously "embarrassing" family roots. This allows me to appreciate how far I have come in my life and gives me much more self-confidence. Consequently, I am stronger and feel more compassion for and acceptance of others.

Jim: By disconnecting my sense of masculinity from the sliver of wood in my mouth and attaching it to my very real impact in the world, I have grown in my capacity to enjoy my own personal strength and skill as a teacher as well as claiming my own elegance. Through Conscious Creativity, our awareness and commitment to our relationship has not only deepened, we have come to know and understand each other on so many more and different levels. Toothpicks are now a symbol of our special and uniquely helpful interdependence. And that's real romance.

Marriage is a partnership
in which each inspires the other and
brings fruition to both of you.

—Millicent Carey McIntosh

Death and Resurrection

In the crucible of your seriously conflicting differences you have the opportunity to spiritually experience death and a magnificent resurrection. They are yours each time your partner responds with loving understanding and acceptance when you reveal something you are certain is repulsive and shameful. They are yours each time you accept—as the truth about you—your partner's vision of you. As you do, you will "die to the past" that which has shackled you, and you will be "reborn" into a new, more healthy, whole identity.

There will be emotional pain as you risk revealing your shadow stuff. It's like a mini-death, followed by your partner's invitation to go beyond who you have been. But remember, as your partner opens to you, she or he is changed also.

A Plea for Help

In the following letter to Dear Abby's twin sister and fellow advice columnist, Ann Landers, "Trouble in Timbuktu" asks for help with the kind of negative trust that far too many couples create.

> *I have been married for 11 years to a total control freak. From Day One, I have let him have his way about everything. Now I am miserable.*
> *We work in the same building and live an hour's drive from the office because he likes to be "away from the city." I drive the old family wagon while he drives the Porsche.*

I am up at 5 a.m. so he and the children can sleep until 6, have their breakfast and be out of the house by 7. Needless to say, I am exhausted all the time.

I am held accountable for every minute of my day and cannot have a phone conversation without my husband monitoring it and verbally editing my responses.

Our sex life was always lousy because sex was low on his list of priorities—but not low enough, apparently. I discovered a while ago that he was playing around.

I have been neglected, emotionally abused and virtually imprisoned for the last three years. Two weeks ago, I decided I had had enough and told him to get out. Now he says he loves me and wants me to take him back.

The big problem is my family. They think I am not being fair to our children and that I should give him another chance. I tried counseling, which is how I became strong enough to walk away. What do you think?

As sad and empty as this marriage is, there is a profound spiritual wisdom in their choice of one another. On the surface, that might not make sense. You might even argue that he is a gross and cruel jerk, she is an innocent victim, and she should just get rid of him and find a "good man." But that's not how relationships work.

Jane and John

Most people, even marriage counselors, would say this marriage is hopeless. The partners are too far apart in their differences to reach any kind of resolution. But that conclusion is based on the physical model of conflict where differences are incompatible. Since no names were used in the letter, we'll call this couple Jane and John.

What if Jane and John could recognize that their differences offer just the lessons each one desperately needs to learn? Could they develop a relationship in which they feel supported, respected and loved? Let's take a look.

From "Day One" Jane "let him have his way about everything." What kind of allegiances would cause her to act like a servant girl conscripted to please her master? Why does she blame him for her choices and behaviors that leave her feeling victimized?

Notice that Jane feels the "big problem" is her family. She has been living as a virtual prisoner of her husband and yet the problem she seeks advice about is the pressure from her family to "be fair to our children" and "give him another chance." She's seen a counselor and developed the strength to leave John, but what Jane shows us is the enormous power of her allegiance to her family of origin. We can infer it was at home where she learned that a good girl or a good wife concerns herself with everyone but herself. As she wrestles with the "big problem," she remains a very good, very dutiful daughter.

Her family couldn't have just begun treating her this way, because they don't have any qualms about telling her how to live her life now. It's old hat. She grew up with parents who denied, as they continue to deny, her separate and distinct self. They want her to do it their way. She's invisible to them, a thing who is ordered and obeys. No doubt this is what was called "love" right from Day One.

The other major issue dominating Jane's life is the way our culture views women. Notice we said "culture," not "men." Both men and women alike still perceive women as second-class beings. Women's liberation notwithstanding, mothers still teach their daughters that catching a husband is more important than training for a profession or even holding down a job. Females are still admonished, as much by women as men, not to be "too loud," not to be demanding or "bitchy" and not to stand out from the crowd. On the other hand, "being a good girl" is very important: being nice, sweet, compliant and making sure never to hurt anyone's feelings. Between her family and the collective cultural attitude, Jane arrived in her marriage with a heavy psychological load.

John's background is not made explicit by Timbuktu's letter. We know he's controlling, dogmatic, possessive and domineering. He likes to live "away from the city," drive a Porsche and he monitors and edits her telephone calls. He is dissatisfied with their marriage which he expresses by cheating sexually. However, after all that, when he's kicked out, he proclaims his love and wants to be taken back. Even with this limited information, we can still arrive at interpretations that will illuminate the reasons Jane and John are well-suited for one another.

John selected Jane for his bride. We can assume that her passivity was familiar to him from Day One. Because he was indifferent to her during their marriage but wants her back once she finds the courage to leave, it is plausible that Jane's passivity was more familiar than appealing. She was probably similar in character to his mother and perhaps other women in his background. Chances are good he was catered to, teaching him that he not only could get whatever he wanted but was entitled to it. Many mothers treat their sons like princes.

And what does the culture expect from males? Most boys are raised to be aggressive, in charge, sexually accomplished, family providers and protectors of women. In our competitive, warrior-like culture, that's what it means to be a man. However, thick-skinned warriors have a difficult, if not impossible, time being sensitive and tender partners.

When John is aggressive and controlling, when he uses his sexuality to demonstrate his manliness, and when he cheats rather than talk about his dissatisfaction, he's acting like the age-old, stereotypical "real man." The problem for both him and Jane is that he must remain self-centered, emotionally distant and, if he were honest, in many ways not much more than a scared little boy.

So, there we have it. A little girl and a little boy thrust into the adult institution of marriage and family, floundering, unhappy and without a clue.

Jane and John never really got to know each other, except through the roles and allegiances they both acted out. In effect, they never emotionally, psychologically or spiritually married one another. They were little more than robots, possessed by their respective backgrounds, so they could not have assumed conscious responsibility for how they lived together. In fact, it is impressive that Jane expressed enough dissatisfaction to create a crisis.

As we look at their possibilities for growth and recovery, think about your current relationship challenge or one from the past. Take a look at the healing possibilities in each of the serious relationships you've been in.

If Jane and John are willing to learn from their respective programming and personal limitations, they can come to see their choice of each other as a spiritual wake-up call. If not, they will chalk it up to fate or stupidity or to some other excuse. Or they will just remain bewildered, angry and lost.

They have lived an extremely unhealthy life together. He's an oppressive, narcissistic cheat. She's an oppressed, narcissistic martyr. But they complement one another. They chose each other in order to stay in allegiance, to stay in character.

Now, provided they both decide to commit to their relationship as a vehicle for healing and intimacy, it's possible that they could develop a strong and supportive relationship. Remember Yvonne and Sam in chapter 4, who made their way out of gang life and domestic violence? They are a living example of what is possible. Jane and John can also be transformed by the trials of self-discovery and the honest examination of their cocreated failure as marriage partners. In the healing process they would have to take the same steps we took to address our toothpick problem.

Taking Steps Toward the Healing Power of Relationship

Jane and John would have to:

1. Accept that quality marriages are created, not made in heaven.
2. Respect the challenge of maturing together. In the areas that need healing, their self-knowledge is just as limited as their understanding of one another.
3. Be candid and caring in confronting each other's problem issues and behaviors. Let their concern for the well-being of the relationship guide their learning process.

4. Remember that they both bring masks and allegiances to their relationship. Their conflicts, and especially their fights, are flares casting light on what needs to be healed.

5. Stay aware that their previously unconscious allegiances collided to create their problems.

6. Keep in mind that their allegiances are complementary. They are a perfect match of dominance and submission and they have needed each other to play out their roles.

7. Be willing to receive constructive criticism from the other so they can further understand their own half of the issue.

8. Be willing to make the individual and mutual changes necessary to come together as two mature, self-respecting and respectful adults.

This change process isn't always easy. It cannot be accomplished overnight. But without it, Jane and John will surely divorce. Furthermore, because they have not faced their limitations, they will inevitably choose new partners very much like the ones they now have. They won't have any other choice. Their relationship radar won't have changed at all.

We will revisit with Jane and John later in this chapter.

One does not become enlightened by imagining figures of light, but by making the darkness conscious.

—Carl Jung

Love as an Active Force

To benefit fully from the lessons of love, let's look at love, not as an endearment, but as a verb. Mostly, what we've all been led to expect and experience is the *feeling* of love. That can be nothing more than the feeling of lust and/or the feeling of dependent infatuation—usually inspired when one person projects his or her fantasies onto another. That kind of "love" is easy, available for the price of any romance novel or an R-rated movie. Too often, that feeling and nothing else is all that guides a couple to the altar.

Webster's dictionary supplies us with four definitions of love: 1) a strong affection for or attachment or devotion to a person or persons; 2) God's benevolent concern for mankind; 3) man's devout attachment to God; and 4) the feeling of benevolence and brotherhood that people should have for each other. All of these definitions deal with feelings, not with any activity that would demonstrate affection, attachment, devotion or brotherhood.

Webster's definition of marriage doesn't get us any closer to action either: 1) the state of being married; relation between husband and wife; married life; wedlock; matrimony; 2) the act of marrying; wedding; 3) the rite or form used in marrying; 4) any close or intimate union.

What would "intimate" or "close" look like if you were to see them acted out? How do you actively express love? How do you display your loving intentions in action?

Love is not lust and it's not illusion. It's made up of care, respect, value, sexual attraction and a deep desire to be with someone. But, more than that, love is a conscious choice to act lovingly toward and with another person. The activity of love requires continuous, conscious attention to the real-life needs and desires of both you and your partner. *To be actively loving you can't be either self-centered, so that your partner doesn't count, or self-sacrificing, so that you don't count.*

If you don't love yourself, you will judge and punish yourself for every little thing. You'll treat your partner with the same impossible expectations and crippling judgments you burden yourself with. You can't do anything else because you don't know anything else. Then you will indeed "love" your lover as yourself and be shocked when she or he objects.

Confrontation

When your partner objects to something, that can be a real act of love. It can mean that he or she is self-loving and insists on not being being mistreated or made invisible. *Your partner loves you by demanding that you grow in awareness and change to become more respectful, to become a larger, more conscious person. That is the healing action of love.* When you want the best for yourself and for your spouse, you're inspired to risk becoming more emotionally vulnerable, more willing to point out your partner's self-sabotaging behaviors. While love can't protect you from hurting your partner's feelings, it certainly keeps you aware of not wanting to do harm. So, from your love you will avoid condemnation, contempt or ridicule. Instead, you'll point out problem issues, being careful to express compassion and care.

Loving action can always include private nicknames, sweet endearments, special flowers, surprise basketball tickets, whatever your real romantic heart desires. That's the easier part of showing your love. But to invite spiritual healing into your relationship, you'll have to confront each other—not just when you're being mistreated, but also when your partner is mistreating him or herself.

It's difficult to see ourselves in a constructively critical light—which is not the same thing as the horrible, internal pounding many of us live with. We need each other to show us when we're behaving in ways that don't serve us well. So, again, we need our mate to show us how we can grow, in what areas we could become more fully developed.

Compassion and Acceptance

When you allow love to heal you, you open yourself to uncover old wounds. Getting in touch with these wounds will leave you feeling some combination of vulnerable, raw, sad, angry, embarrassed and frightened. When you witness your partner's vulnerability, you can express your love and support because you will know what he or she is going through. You can listen with concern and compassion when your partner exposes the underbelly of old allegiances. You can be patient, because you'll know that the change process takes time, especially when dealing with stuff that's been denied or ignored for a lifetime. Then, when breakthroughs come, you can celebrate together.

Receiving Constructive Criticism

Love is not threatened by helpful criticism. When you know that your partner has your best interests at heart, you can be less defensive when he or she criticizes you and asks you to change. You'll know that you have someone who is on your side, even as they tell you what's wrong.

Love asks you to become more of who you truly are. It demands that you cast off the false self you've hidden behind. Love encourages you to express your highest potential with one another and in the world. That is the profound healing power of love.

There are two ways of spreading light: to be the candle or the mirror that reflects it.

—Edith Wharton

Finding the Wisdom in Your Choice

We'll continue to use Jane and John as examples. Given the depth of their allegiances and behavior patterns, they will no doubt need professional help to get them started. Still, they can provide us with a very vivid illustration of how this process can work.

Better Balance

Even though both Jane and John are emotionally limited, they can definitely learn from one another and become more mature from the experience. By mutual agreement, they can serve as each other's guides in discovering new aspects of themselves.

It's clear that Jane has to develop her own sense of power. She needs to trust herself as her own authority instead of looking to what others think and need. In spite of his insecurity, John can teach her what it's like to be assertive, to push for her own needs and desires.

For his part, John must learn to include the needs and desires of other people, especially Jane's. She's a master at that. She can teach him how she thinks about generosity and what it feels like to identify with others.

What about you and your partner? Do either of you need to:

- Improve your ability to express desire?
- Assert yourself when you feel mistreated?
- Increase your curiosity about your partner?
- Replace contempt with respect for human imperfection?

Changing Perceptions

John no doubt views Jane as weak. From day one she let him have his way so he takes her for granted. But she is quite strong and very competent, even when she's exhausted. To break out of his unconscious mindset, John has to recognize her competence. That will be a major move toward his learning to appreciate others, especially Jane. Her competence can serve as a prod to open him up and dismantle his limited and self-limiting point of view.

Given that she's accustomed to giving him his way, Jane probably sees John as being powerful. He's willful, controlling and needs nothing from her. But he's the one who wants to be taken back. In fact, he's not as powerful as she might have thought. She needs to stop being a little girl, which is what makes her unable to really see John's insecurities. She has to overcome her allegiance to making everyone else important but herself.

It's not unreasonable to assume that John has probably been scared and lonely most of his life. Anyone who needs as much control as he does is not operating from a secure and confident sense of self. The world is too much of a threat and he has to be certain it runs exactly according to his expectations. By wanting to be taken back he's exposed his vulnerability. He'll have to risk stumbling and being awkward in front of her. Quite the opposite of the way he's been with her. They both have to look past their allegiances to see the full complexity of who they are.

Do you and your partner need to:

- Reveal more about what scares you about your partner's beliefs and behaviors?

- Express your fears of asking for what you need from each other?

- Challenge your partner when you see him/her acting super tough, victimized, or any other façade?

- Put forth those qualities you most value about yourself to help your partner perceive you more clearly and fully?

Effective Communication

Jane must learn to express her feelings of dissatisfaction coupled with what she needs. John has to learn to listen to Jane as someone distinct and different from himself.

John must learn to express his emotional needs to Jane, rather than acting them out sexually with another woman. Jane must learn to believe and listen respectfully to John's neediness.

As they express their previously unspeakable dissatisfactions and desires for change, they will surely encounter conflict. Yet, conflict can embolden them to assert their differences, stand strong in their intentions and join together in their desire to find mutually empowering resolutions.

The Three C's, Commitment, Communication and Conflict, play an important role in their ability to transform their relationship. Without commitment, they'll be frightened to take the risks required to transform their marriage. Without facing into their conflicts, they'll never benefit from the magic of differences to help them grow up. And without good communication, they can never know each other beyond the current superficial caricatures they act out.

Do you and your partner need to:

- Speak directly, completely and with a determination to be understood?
- Pledge yourself to open and honest communication as a daily practice of commitment?
- Listen attentively when your spouse speaks to you, or be clear you're not available at the moment and set aside a specific time to talk later?

• Pledge yourself to a daily practice of being more affectionately confrontational in your relationship? While communication—speaking and listening—is certainly not always easy, there is simply no other way to have a lasting, meaningful marriage.

Things You Can Do to Promote Healing

Make a list of the ways you'd like you and your partner to grow stronger, more confident, more successful—individually and together. Now answer the following questions as they apply to the details on your list.

• How would respectfully confronting your partner's limitations or "flaws" help you to develop yourself?

• How could your partner's strengths help you to develop yourself?

• How would respectfully confronting your partner's limitations or flaws help you to negotiate change in your relationship?

• How would your partner's strengths help you to negotiate change in your relationship?

Identify and write down two or three conflicts/fights that keep recurring between you and your partner (or former partner). Now answer the following questions as they apply to the details on this list.

• What parts of your partner's complaints about you are true?

• If you accepted the criticism as a challenge to heal and made the necessary changes, how would it help you to discover more of your diamond brilliance?

• How would it strengthen your relationship if you constructively confronted your partner's deeper issues that contribute to your fights?

• How are you and your partner opposites—neat/sloppy, focused/laid back, playful/serious, etc.? How could both of you come into better balance by learning about each other's ways?

Everything in life that
we really accept undergoes a change.
This is the thing that in the greatest
is a shining light, a pure white fire; and in the
humblest is a constant radiance, a quiet
perpetual gleam. When we stop running away,
when we really accept, that is when even
tragedy succumbs to beauty.

—Katherine Mansfield

Choose Wisely, Choose to Grow

The search for perfection, for absolute security, is an illusion. Spiritual wisdom teaches us that confusion and uncertainty are fundamental aspects of committed love, as they are of life. Problems, which are caused by the differences between you and your partner, are seeds of opportunity which are planted in rich, loamy soil and cultivated in the darkness of conflict, distress and pain before they mature and gain strength to become new life, visible, emergent and holy. Each time you and your partner work your way through the thunderstorms of intimacy, you are reinvigorated, redefined, reborn. Your determination to value yourself and each other, your intention to find mutually empowering resolutions and your willingness to be changed by the process can only leave you stronger and more whole.

We use the metaphor of a thunderstorm. Its power shatters the status quo while its rain waters and nourishes whatever desert of your being is demanding new life. With a committed partner, no problem is too large, no pain too great. You know that the perpetually unfolding mystery of your being together will lead you into ever new expressions of your love. *The deepest spiritual wisdom of your choice is your willingness to be remade over and over again in the extraordinary crucible of your differences.*

Chapter 11

LIFELONG LOVE: THE SACRED GRACE OF DIFFERENCES

When one door closes another opens.
Expect that new door to reveal even greater
wonders and glories and surprises.
Feel yourself grow with every experience.

—Eileen Caddy

That's the thing about love and romance
—no one can predict where it will take you. . . .
Love will fill your heart, break your heart
and then heal the heart that's broken.

—Robert Fulghum

*T*he idea that love is a choice and that lovers need to be conscious participants in the flow of their love is at the heart of creating the new intimacy in your everyday life. With your intention and commitment to promote the lifelong spiritual and psychological development of you both, you become trustworthy guardians for the grace of love's blessings.

> *We need the vision of interbeing—*
> *we belong to each other; we cannot cut*
> *reality into pieces. The well-being of "this" is*
> *the well-being of "that," so that we*
> *have to do things together.*
>
> —Thich Nhat Hanh

The Wonder of Cocreativity

It is said that every morning Pablo Casals, the world-famous cellist, asked his cello, "My dear friend, what shall we discover together today?" Not what they would do separately, but together, communicating with one another, calling on the best both had to offer.

They were an extension of each other, yet neither one disappeared. By joining together yet remaining distinct, they became something that was far more than merely the sum of the parts. They became a single creative voice— more than both and impossible without each of them.

They depended upon one another to transcend their individual limitations in order to create exquisite music. Their music sang of depth and beauty, of the mysterious and the mundane. Sometimes it was bawdy, sometimes angelic, but it was always a lesson to the audience of what was possible from a disciplined, open and loving collaboration.

What if you lived your relationship in the same way? What if, when you wake in the morning, you would say to your partner, "My dear beloved, what shall we discover together today?" What if both of you surrendered to the adventure of your love, going beyond any fear of vanishing in the process? Your relationship would serve as the sacred instrument of your individual and mutual spiritual grace.

I just feel more and more like
I'm coming into myself, owning my life.
Claiming responsibility for everything
that happens. And the more I do that,
the more happiness I get.

—Geena Davis

Commitment Revisited

When you commit to loving intimacy with both your heart and your mind, being with your partner becomes increasingly meaningful and fulfilling. You learn that you can handle, together, whatever comes your way. You begin to look forward to new challenges and responsibilities, because they open you to experience and express your increasing physical, emotional, psychological and spiritual maturity. At the heart of your relationship is your conscious willingness to be changed by love—together. The undeniable fact is that when you love you are changed, and when you are loved you are changed.

Change is the stuff that tells you your relationship is alive and growing. When you are accepting of change you are available for growth, and as you grow your sense of self continues to develop, with increasing openness, self-assurance and creativity. You are exhilarated by what is surfacing from the center of your being together. You become a living, breathing exclamation—YES!—eager to know what you will discover next.

Your relationship then is the cocreated result of two unique individuals with different backgrounds, different intentions, different personal styles, fears, hopes and ambitions and your differences serve as the foundation for your lifelong learning and growing together. As your commitment deepens, the more particular and distinctive your relationship becomes, unfolding the artwork of your life together.

Since the two of you will change at different rates and in different ways, you become interdependent with each other. You become teachers for one another. You help each other understand and appreciate new experiences. Your commitment provides a stable foundation allowing you to change without fear of being rejected or unloved. You can give and take. You can offer and receive. Then your relationship is free to be dynamic and you are free to become all that you can be. You can wake in the morning, welcoming and open to whatever you will discover and share.

Transcendence results in something
novel and emergent... some sort of creative
twist on what has gone before.

—Ken Wilber

Transcendence

Because we are concerned about the practical aspects of how you can experience the new intimacy in your daily life, we have not emphasized the idea of transcendence, although it has been present throughout the book.

Transcendence is often thought to be an other-worldly experience: mystical, metaphysical, ethereal. Yet real transcendence is very definitely available. You won't find it in a dreamy state of "lifting off," high above the difficulties of life on this planet. It is right here as part of your daily living.

Transcendence is a process of both letting go of your allegiances, of no longer identifying with who you've known yourself to be, and of surrendering to the movement of your current life. What used to be at the center of your experience, important and compelling, becomes less significant and less attractive as you grow into a more expansive way of relating to yourself and others. However, you will not experience change as transcendence unless you are conscious of the spiritual beauty and power inherent in growth and personal expansion.

For example, if you move from one home to another, or from one city to another, that is certainly about change. But it's not necessarily about growth. You may both remain exactly who you are, only your address is different. It is also possible that such a move can mean a significant change, one in which you both choose to grow beyond who you have been in order to be effective and fulfilled in your new surroundings.

For instance, if you move from a small town to a large city, or you move from one country to another, you may be required to undergo a pivotal shift in who you know yourself to be. You may have to "dis-identify" from your previous attitudes and values because you experience them as limiting and ineffective in your new environment. Under the influence of new people, new ideas and new ways of being, you may have to let go of beliefs you once thought were certain. You may have to include previously elusive or unavailable beliefs into your sense of self. If you don't, you may not be able to lead a full life in your present circumstances. Your tastes may change. You may alter your priorities. You may even come to a new understanding of yourself, others and life in general. To transcend means to become more than just cosmetically different. Transcendence is a shift in your very experience of being alive.

To visualize this difference, imagine the example of change without growth as a horizontal move. The externals are different, but you remain on the same level of your experience. The second example demonstrates what we mean by transcendence. It is a vertical move, in which you grow beyond your present level of experience. You have to grow and expand to become larger in consciousness, able to create more richness and meaning in your life, able to be more of who you can be. Real-life transcendence is that process by which you develop your awareness so that you can move toward a life that is increasingly inter-connected, mature, conscious and vital.

As you transcend, as your consciousness becomes more powerful and sensitive, able to include more and more experience, the larger and more competent you will become. Through an ever-growing confidence and com-posure you will progressively become the author of your own life. Yet, at the same time, you will be able to com-fortably yield to the wisdom of those powers, forces and graces that are the source of this magnificently vibrant and deeply spiritual universe.

A successful marriage
requires falling in love many times,
always with the same person.

—Mignon McLaughlin

Serial Monogamy with the Same Person

Throughout your relationship, you are guided by your understanding of who you are together, what you want and where you're going. Your commitment provides the vehicle and the fuel for your journey. But some of your best intentions—no matter how inspired, no matter how effective and fruitful—will ultimately exhaust themselves. They inevitably run out of gas. Sometimes because that part of your journey together has been completed. Other times because there is a change in the road. This isn't tragic and it's not dysfunctional. It is quite normal, because nothing lasts forever.

After the initial rush of romance fades, many people believe there is something wrong with their relationship. They have never been taught that the unavoidable fade is simply a signal telling them that a stage in their relationship is coming to an end. Instead of using this time to consider where they have been together, who they are now and what's next for them, they either leave or they collapse into despair. They become prisoners of the question, "Is this all there is?"

In a fully committed, spiritually alive relationship, change and transcendence are foods for the soul that nourish how you live with and treat each other. You know and accept that what you have at any given time can only carry you so far. When change begins, you can remain sensitive to the signals. Rather than panic, you can treat what is happening as an exciting, normal life process. You can let go and open yourselves to whatever is coming. That way, during your life together, you can transcend your relationship, renewing it any number of times. That's a fundamental aspect of the new intimacy, what we call serial monogamy with the same person.

We have had three major transitions in the 10 years we've been together. The first had to do with the development of the business we formed when we first met.

Soon thereafter we both realized that what we had learned about love and intimacy before we met was not enough for who we had become together. We had to let go of a number of beliefs we had depended upon and explore new and more fulfilling ways to live together. The third transition began when we started writing this book. We welcome the changes to come, because they assure us our love is alive, that who we are is evolving and that we are not stagnant or stunted or boring.

We know a couple, both in their seventies, who have been married for 30 years. On the 28th of every month, they set aside time to do what they call "renegotiating our relationship." When they were first together, they used their negotiating time to determine if what they had was still working. Through the years they have expressed appreciation and delight with one another, as well as their complaints and desires for change. Now they continue to use their ritual to celebrate one another and express joy at simply being together.

The idea of serial monogamy with the same person, having a number of different relationships with your spouse, embodies both change and stability. It allows a relationship the room to grow, to peak and subside and transcend, giving way to the freshness of whatever follows.

---

*We discovered in each other
and ourselves worlds, galaxies,
a universe.*

—Anne Rivers Siddons

The Blessing of Continually Created Love

Spiritual relationship is about thoughtful practice. It's about being aware of yourself and your partner. When you base your relationship on continually and consciously re-committing yourselves to love, respect and creativity, your maturity and trust will support you and carry you forward. You will, like Casals and his cello, enjoy a mutually expanding, inspiring and stimulating relationship.

You will know you are both part of the intimacy you are creating while remaining whole within your own separate sense of self. You will be alive in one another's consciousness, not as a limit, but as a permanent loving presence.

Your individual and mutual sense of self will grow deeper and more secure as you become increasingly more conscious—sensitive to and aware of yourselves, one another and the world around you.

You will become larger, more competent and wiser simply from the sheer practice of encountering and integrating the life you are living. You can then more easily accept and participate in the world without needing to dramatize or disown it. With that, you will feel a deep sense of connection. You will come to see the universe as a gigantic community in which we are all immersed—creating a sense of connection that is not sentimental or naive, but a profound experience that we are each part of The All.

Though your relationship will sometimes be difficult, and sometimes even very difficult, it becomes a gateway to more meaningful and richer awareness. You will discover even deeper pools of strength and light as the spiritual purpose of your relationship becomes clearer. Then the mundane becomes sacred. The ordinary becomes alive and blessed. You value day-to-day existence for the miracle that it is. Your resistances decrease and you find transformation in everyday events. Then, change is divine grace, the occasion through which providence enters your life.

Discovering and defining who you are as individuals and who you are together is the goal of your loving adventure. It is magical. Not like sleight of hand—entertaining, but ultimately illusion. It is magical in its beauty, in its realness and meaning. It is the magic of consciousness and surrender, the magic of differences. Your relationship serves as the container and catalyst for your evolution in spiritual understanding, experience, practice and power.

In this way, your relationship is like a brilliant symphony. Your two voices continually expanding their range, perfecting their pitch, your instruments meeting in passionate union, occasionally clashing in B flat, sometimes lingering in minor keys, only to rise again to produce ever new the crescendo of your precious and ecstatic joy. You become bold and beautiful expressions of God's creation as you continually learn to love yourself and your partner more and more every day.

The Magic of Differences™

---⚮---

Creating a New Understanding
Between Women and Men

*J*udith and Jim founded their company, The Magic of Differences, in 1988. They have helped thousands of people realize that it's the differences between two people in relationship that offer the deepest intimacy, the richest passion and the most powerful opportunities for emotional and spiritual growth. Judith and Jim provide lectures, workshops and audiotapes for singles and couples to help them open to the richness of real love.

They provide weekend relationship trainings called "The New Intimacy: How to Create Real Romance in Your Everyday Life," for couples and singles. "The New Intimacy" is approved for 15 hours of MCEP credit by the CPA Accrediting Agency, provider #SHE013.

As consultants and trainers they address the changing gender culture in public and private life, working with professional associations, nonprofit organizations, churches and corporations. Their corporate clients have included Unocal, The Walt Disney Company, The W. K. Kellogg Foundation, Pepperdine University, St. John's Hospital, National Academy of Songwriters and Catholic Charities.

They produce, market and distribute their own lecture and guided-meditation audiotape series entitled "Reclaiming the Self."

Please contact them for information about speaking engagements, workshops, training programs, newsletter and audiotapes or to schedule them for a presentation.

Judith & Jim
The Magic of Differences
12021 Wilshire Blvd., #692
Los Angeles, CA 90025
1-800-287-5696
(310) 829-3353 • FAX (310) 829-4927
jimjude@ix.netcom.com

You can also learn more about Judith and Jim's work and/or order their tapes from their World Wide Web page at:

http://www.magic-of-differences.com

iMALL—What you want from the web!
http://www.imall.com

*We wish you the magic of love and intimacy
in your real, everyday life.*

The New Intimacy Continues ...

We will be editing a book on "The Magic of Differences"—how the differences between two people helped them create the new intimacy, making their relationship richer and their individual lives more complete. We invite you to send us stories about the magic of differences you've experienced. If you have a story (your own or someone else's) that can inspire, educate and/or touch the hearts of our readers, please send it to us. We will make sure that you and the author are given full credit for your contribution. Thank you in advance!

Permissions *(continued from page iv)*

About the Authors

*H*usband and wife, Judith Sherven, Ph.D., and James Sniechowski, Ph.D., are two of the country's most respected, pioneering, and sought-after authorities on relationship dynamics. Through their company, The Magic of Differences, their lectures, workshops and trainings continue to change the lives of both couples and singles, awakening them to a new vision of intimate relationship, and helping them discover the rich spiritual purpose for the challenges of real life love.

They are best known for their work in the study and understanding of differences in relationships and how to turn those differences into exciting catalysts for heightened intimacy in marriage, better communication in dating and greater respect and understanding in any relationship.

Judith is a clinical psychologist, and was the founding director of the Institute for Advanced Training in Experiential Psychotherapy, and has been a psychotherapist in private practice since 1978.

Jim holds a doctorate in Human Behavior and is the founder and director of The Menswork Center in Santa Monica and a cofounder of The Men's Health Network in Washington, D.C. As an international leader and speaker on men's issues, he leads workshops and men's groups, and provides individual consultation.

Judith and Jim are frequently called upon by the media as experts in their field. They have appeared on over 250 television and radio talk shows, including *Oprah, Sonya Live, 48 Hours, The Mo Show, The Les Brown Show, Entertainment Tonight* and *Leeza*.

They have written for or been interviewed by such prestigious publications as the *Los Angeles Times, USA Today, Newsweek, Chicago Tribune, San Francisco Chronicle, London Sunday Times, Wall Street Journal, Redbook, Playboy, Gioia* (Italy), *Manner Vogue* (Germany), *Northcote Leader* (Melbourne, Australia), *Miami Herald* and many others.

More than their extensive professional background, Judith and Jim bring a profound personal knowledge to their work. They have been married for nine years. It's Judith's first and Jim's third. They bring hope from two different perspectives.

THE NEW INTIMACY

Exploring the space between us!

Chicken Soup For The Whole Family

Now the whole family can share the inspirational magic of *Chicken Soup for the Soul!* These beautiful hardcover illustrated storybooks will warm the hearts of children and adults of all ages. A wondrous story unfolds in each captivating book, providing an enduring message of sincere and heartfelt virtue.

The Goodness Gorillas
Code # 505X — $14.95

The Never-Forgotten Doll
Code # 5076 — $14.95

The Best Night Out With Dad
Code # 5084 — $14.95

The Braids Girl
Code # 5548 — $14.95

A Dog of My Own
Code # 5556 — $14.95

Chicken Soup for the Mother's Soul
Code # 4606 — $12.95

New from the *Chicken Soup for the Soul*® Serie

Chicken Soup for the Teenage Soul

Teens welcome *Chicken Soup for the Teenage Soul* like a good friend: one who understands their feelings, is there for them when needed and cheers them up when things are looking down. A wonderful gift for your teenage son, daughter, grandchild, student, friend... #4630—$12.95

Chicken Soup for the Woman's Soul

The #1 *New York Times* bestseller guaranteed to inspire women with wisdom and insights that are uniquely feminine and always from the heart. #4150—$12.95

Chicken Soup for the Christian Soul

Chicken Soup for the Christian Soul is an inspiring reminder that we are never alone or without hope, no matter how challenging or difficult our life may seem. In God we find hope, healing, comfort and love. #5017—$12.95

Chicken Soup for the Soul® Series

Each one of these inspiring *New York Times* bestsellers brings you exceptional stories, tales and verses guaranteed to lift your spirits, soothe your soul and warm your heart! A perfect gift for anyone you love, including yourself!

A 4th Course of Chicken Soup for the Soul, #4592—$12.95
A 3rd Serving of Chicken Soup for the Soul, #3790—$12.95
A 2nd Helping of Chicken Soup for the Soul, #3316—$12.95
Chicken Soup for the Soul, #262X—$12.95

Selected books are also available in hardcover, large print, audiocassette and compact disc.

Available in bookstores everywhere or call **1-800-441-5569** for Visa or MasterCard orders. Prices do not include shipping and handling. Your response code is **BKS**.